THE DEVIL'S GRIP

J. R. ROTHWELL

The Devil's Grip

© J.R. Rothwell 2015

All rights reserved. No part of this publication may be reproduced, stored in a retrieval system, or transmitted in any form or by any means, electronic, mechanical, photocopying, recording or otherwise, without the prior written permission of the author.

National Library of Australia Cataloguing-in-Publication entry (pbk)
Author: Rothwell, J.R., author.
Title: The Devil's Grip / J.R. Rothwell.
ISBN: 9780646940274 (paperback)
Subjects: Criminals—Australia—Biography
                Crime—Australia—True Crime
Dewey Number: 364.1092

Published by J.R. Rothwell and InHouse Publishing

Printed using Envirocare paper.

www.inhousepublishing.com.au

ACKNOWLEDGEMENTS

To my family for withstanding the turmoil that has been my life to date.

To my team of publishing experts that have been critical to the heartbeat of these pages. Jo, Ocean and those who do not wished to be mentioned, thank you for your faith and passion in believing in my story.

GENESIS

I was probably breaking a dozen different laws and couldn't have cared less because the only thing on my mind was getting to where I had to be and doing what I had to do. Driven by fury and vengeance, I pushed the bike hard, savouring the almost empty roads. For most of the way, the engine was at its limit, needles in the red. My helmet muffled everything except the grinding of my teeth and the mechanical action of the gears locking into position as I clicked the shifter against my foot.

It was two in the morning as I rode into Sydney. Streaking past parked cars, I could faintly hear their alarms being set off in my wake. Normally, I would've stuck to the back roads in order to avoid detection but being in the frame of mind I was in, I tore along the main roads towards the city. I eventually reached the narrower streets of the city's nightlife district where I had to lean the bike low enough to kiss the ground in order to make it around the corners in one piece. When I finally got to the club, I left the bike in an alley behind it; retrieved the gun from the compartment under the seat and slipped it into the back of my belt.

The club was the sort you wouldn't want your sister to frequent – the air was hot and rancid, reeking of sweat and alcohol. Lighting was almost non-existent, except for some ultraviolet lights that highlighted white clothing and made one's teeth glow in the dark. The club itself was not large; however, it was packed wall-to-wall with bodies. The walls and furniture looked soiled and the floors were littered with empty water bottles, used paper napkins and other garbage.

As I pushed through the crowd, I felt lightheaded – as if everything was moving in *slow* motion. I made my way down the dark, steep staircase at the back of the club and encountered the proverbial bodyguards at the foot of the stairs. With a quick nod I reassured them. One of them looked at me, long and steady, before responding with a nod and let me pass.

Four men sat playing cards. The room was dark except for the small neon light hanging directly over their table. Alcohol, money, cards and ashtrays covered the green felt. The ashtrays; they were overflowing with cigarette butts – they'd probably been playing for at least six or seven hours. I could smell mould. The occasions when any one person at the table was *not* carrying some sort of weapon were few and far between, and that night was not one of them.

Three of the four men at the table who were facing the door had recognised me and knew what I'd come for. The buzz of conversation which had preceded my entrance, ceased. The only movement in the room was the dry blinking of their eyes; now locked on me.

I saw who I'd come for and as luck was with me, he had his back to the door which made my job much easier. By the time he'd turned his head, I'd removed the Beretta from my belt and grabbed him by what little hair he had and jammed most of the gun into his mouth while taking him to the floor. No one moved or said a word – out of respect – I liked to think it was respect; after all, I was holding a gun and they knew I was going to use it. At the age of nineteen, commanding respect from such men was not an easy task.

THE WONDER YEARS

What was I thinking? I should start at the beginning.

It was the mid-seventies in Boston, Massachusetts. My parents lived in a run-down apartment building that they owned, which also doubled as the local convenience store. My father was a short, angry man and my mother towered over him, making him look like a dwarf. He sported a porno-style moustache and matching porno sideburns, topping it off with a large afro haircut; not at all out of the ordinary for those times.

Even without comparison to the stunted stature of my father, my mother, who had a constant befuddled look about her, was a very tall woman. Come to think of it, everyone was tall back then; at least that is what I remember.

She was only sixteen years old when she fell pregnant and apparently rather naive when it came to matters of the world. For this part, I can only tell the story the way it was told to me later; as it was before my time.

My father had had issues with my mother putting on weight due to the pregnancy and had suggested she take diet pills while she was pregnant with me. Now, I'm no doctor but I'm certain that this was not working in my favour; in addition to this, she was chain-smoking and drinking whisky and soda, which must have been the 'thing to do' in the seventies.

I came home from the hospital in a red Trans Am Firebird with flames on the side and a huge supercharger hanging out of the hood. I was a very unsettled baby, apparently. If I had to guess, I would say it's because I was born with an addiction to the amphetamines in the diet pills and the nicotine in the cigarettes – and was probably in more need of an alcoholic beverage than your average baby.

Not long after my birth, I was returned to hospital for, fortunately short-lived, problems with my heart and lungs. I am told that from then on, I would get ill quite often; which was extremely annoying for my parents.

As far back as I can remember, maybe as early as three years old, it used to bring my father great pleasure to beat and humiliate me. A wide grin would appear across his face as he administered the beatings. I would get a thorough thrashing, two to three times a day with liberal doses of cuffs and kicks in between – and that was on a good day. To this day, my mother still reminisces cheerily about the fact that they could not bring me home quick enough, from wherever we were at the time, to start beating me. But there were times when they could not even wait to get home to start the punishment and being in the company of others wouldn't hinder them; they would just beat me, there and then. Those were probably the worst beatings for me because of the added embarrassment factor.

When I was two, my brother was born and luckily for him, my parents were generous enough with my beatings so he never got touched. For me, the consistent ill-treatment seemed to become more and more brutal yet the strange thing was; my parents were never consistent in anything they did in their lives, except for delighting in inflicting pain and punishment, on me.

There was one particular incident that is hammered into my memory – hammered being the understatement. I was fast asleep and my parents were watching late night TV. My mother decided to inform my father of how I'd misbehaved that day. As you all know, four year olds are bad human beings and must be punished accordingly.

My father diligently took it upon himself to punish me that very second; God knows what other crimes I might commit while asleep. I was woken up by a boot in my back; one of his tan-coloured cowboy boots which were only ever off his feet when he was asleep. As my mother watched, he proceeded to pull me out of the bed by my hair and began delivering a record-breaking array of punches and kicks. Then, out of nowhere, he decided to surprise me by introducing his cowboy belt to the repertoire; you see, what was special about this belt, was the big ass buckle which broke the skin of a four year old with ease. There was blood everywhere – I could see it spray across the room. Eventually, the pain reached such intensity and was so unbearable, that my body became limp and paralysed with the fear that I might actually be killed. He now felt compelled to drag my numb, bleeding body to the toilet, where he could conduct the second stage of the well-deserved punishment. He forced my head into the toilet bowl, closing the lid on my head – nearly choking me and then flushed it. When this sort of horror was going on, I always had hopes that my mother would intervene or a neighbour would hear the screams and save me, but it never happened. To this day, whenever I'm feeling generous, I like to imagine, that living in the basement as we did, the sounds were muffled and this was why no help arrived from the neighbours. More likely, they were a craven bunch, too scared to annoy my father who would evict them at the drop of a hat.

As the years went on, so did the beatings but that was okay because the way I knew it, there was no other way to live. The thing that perplexed me was my mother's conduct; she would applaud him while he pounded me to bits; as if it were a sporting event of sorts. I could never figure out why; maybe she was fearful of my father and was happy to have me be the recipient of his attention rather than herself, who knows?

When I turned six, things really got interesting. They started to use their imagination and came up with more sadistic and entertaining ways to punish me. One of their favourites was 'the heat treatment'. They would lock me in the apartment building's furnace room for hours on end. For those of you who don't know what a furnace room is, it's a small room that can fit three or four people tops in it, used to supply central heating to the building – you'll find one located underneath most Canadian homes. The door was solid and in the centre of the windowless room was a black metal machine with fire roaring inside it. Apart from the fire, the rest of the room was impenetrably dark – there were no little luxuries like light fittings. Whenever I was locked inside, as a form of punishment, the room seemed airtight; all I could see was the fire roaring inside the machine and all I could hear was the sound of my screams and the sharp crackling of the furnace. My fingernails barely made a mark on the inside of the door even though I would claw at it until my fingers bled. There were times when all my fingernails were shredded because I had scratched so hard in the desperate hope of escaping from that hellhole of a room.

Once, I was left in there for over ten hours. When I was finally let out, I was treated to another beating, after which I was made to kneel in the corner of the room facing the wall with my hands on top of my head, and when I fell over from exhaustion, I was whipped with a belt across my back. The blood from my scratched and broken fingernails slowly started to drip down and sting my eyes but I was too petrified to wipe it away. Meanwhile, the rest of the household was watching television; they made the occasional remark about how comical I looked kneeling in the corner. I can't recollect what I'd done that justified such punishment in the first place but what I was put through was seared into my mind, and the memories smoulder on.

X-RATED BABYSITTER

A year or so passed and it appeared that things had started to look up; my parents got one of the local girls in the neighbourhood to babysit during the day while they worked upstairs in the convenience store. I was relieved at first because, for me, this meant I no longer had to spend as much time around my abusive parents. However, being the responsible, concerned, compassionate and loving parents they were, they did not screen this girl in any way before leaving me in her care. I vaguely remember the arrangement being free cigarettes in exchange for her services.

I don't remember the babysitter's name because I was still fairly young at the time; I'm pretty sure it was something like Kimberly or Kelly. Looking back with adult eyes, I have formed the conclusion that she was in her late twenties; a fully developed woman – and even by today's high standards, not very hard to look at.

On the first day, she brought a cassette player with her and placed it on the floor. She then walked around the room and inspected the surroundings – I was curious as to what she was doing. Eventually, she focused on the clothesline that extended between the two walls in the basement and where my mother would hang clothes on when the weather was bad. My babysitter then insisted we should play a game and I cooperated since I was getting a little bored to be honest.

She said we were going to play a game called 'Tents'. She took a blanket from the pile that my mother had left in the corner and put it over the clothesline, forming a perfect triangle. Next, she put her cassette player in the tent and pressed 'play'. The music was very funky and was what I now know as porno movie music; she had an entire soundtrack on that tape. What happened next was truly peculiar for a six year old; she stripped, gyrating to the music, so that she was buck naked and pulled me into the tent and mashed my face into her boobs and then into her bearded clam. Now don't get me wrong, most males would love an opportunity like this. I just don't think it should have been that early in life for me. The experience may have caused some unusual associations in my brain because now, whenever I think of, or see tents; massive vaginas come to mind, which tended to cause some awkwardness whenever I would visit a camping goods store. This is probably nothing that many years of therapy couldn't fix. The irony of all this, was that, when I told my parents what had happened, I got *my* ass kicked for not telling them sooner.

The whole babysitter state of affairs only lasted a little over a week and my parents must have given up on it, as they didn't make further arrangements for a replacement sitter; instead, they resumed their regular regimen of dishing out physical abuse. I suppose, they must have figured, that if you want something done right, you have to do it yourself.

AFTER-SCHOOL SPECIAL

At the age of seven, I turned up for my first day at school and up until lunchtime, had been feeling pretty confident that things were going well. Once I got out into the yard though with the rest of the children; that confidence quickly dissolved. The very first words said to me were, 'Go home Arab and eat a camel!' I was then shoved to the ground and kicked in the face. As if that was not traumatising enough, the rest of the schoolchildren stood around and laughed. Apart from spoiling my day, this whole event mystified me, as it was my first encounter with racial abuse – and I didn't even know what a camel looked like! This routine continued for the next few years, although what they dished out varied occasionally with slightly more creative comments when the linguistically gifted children were the perpetrators. Obviously there was an explanation for this behaviour. My father's treatment of the majority of his customers at the convenience store reflected his ignorance of the concept of client service and many of those with whom he did not get along with, happened to be the parents of the children I went to school with. My father antagonised and abused these individuals in a way that ensured they would seek some form of retribution.

The boy who had pushed me onto the ground on my first day of school had his run-ins with my father on many occasions. The boy's name was Dylan. Dylan lived in the government-subsidised slums with his single mother who was a crack whore and his father could have been anyone she had fucked for beer or drug money. He was about four years older than me which would have made him about ten. Dylan had already started taking drugs and drinking and smoking. One day, he had no cigarettes or money, so he asked my father if he could buy some loose cigarettes on credit, which my father would often allow with some of the other customers. But my father declined Dylan's request. Dylan was not pleased, and told my father to go back to his own country. He commenced swearing at him loudly with extreme and adult proficiency; the entire neighbourhood could hear Dylan's profanities.

My father's response was to take off his boot and throw it at Dylan; he managed to hit him square in the face from at least ten metres away, knocking him to the ground in the process. Dylan picked himself up and snarled, 'Now I have your boot!' My father responded with, 'Then take it home to your mother and let her cook it for your dinner', which was his idea of being humorous. Dylan spat on the boot and dropped it in the gutter, which didn't stop my father from retrieving his beloved cowboy boot once Dylan had run off. The completely logical outcome of this event was an increase in the frequency of the beatings at school. However, it didn't just stop at the physical abuse, thanks to my father's conduct; I was criticised, ridiculed and insulted by the schoolkids, constantly.

My father eventually experienced blowback from the people he had offended. What compounded the problem was the fact that in those days, most people had low tolerance for foreigners. One incident that stands out clearly in my memory was the night the shop was broken into and vandalised while we were out. The vandals, who were disgruntled neighbours, had spattered paint all over the inside of the shop and our apartment as well, destroying almost everything and stealing all of our valuables and personal effects. They also took the time to paint the words 'GO BACK TO YOUR OWN COUNTRY' in large red letters across the front of the building. My father's reaction was to nurture a long-running feud with the neighbours, which in turn escalated my beatings and made them more severe, both at home and at school.

Sometimes the teachers would notice the scars and bruises on my body and enquire as to 'what had happened'. I couldn't tell them the truth. I was given specific instructions on what to say if this situation ever presented itself: that I'd bumped into a door, fallen downstairs or had hurt myself playing sports. My father designed these cover stories and he would have me go over them with him to ensure they sounded sincere. I came close to telling one of my teachers because she pressed me for information; it was almost as though she always knew that something was out of whack with my stories but I denied it no matter how hard she pushed. This teacher eventually took mercy on me and backed off with the questions, although she did randomly give me the occasional tip on how to cope with bothersome situations. She advised me to go to, what I suppose is called these days, 'my happy place' in my head, when life got unbearable. She also suggested that I keep a secret journal and that I document everything that happened in my life which I could not understand; being an English teacher, she had a touching belief in the power of words. Another wild and wonderful idea she had was to stay positive and keep my chin up and it would have worked really well if I could only conjure up one positive idea or predilection while going through such a deluge of emotional distress at the time.

A year or two later, my school hosted an invention competition; it was called the Invention Convention. I remember this *so* clearly, because it was *my* invention that ended up winning the competition; despite being the youngest out of hundreds of contestants.

The item I invented is now sold in stores all over the world. I called it 'The Hand Fan'. It was rudimentary, which means it looked like a piece of crap. Despite the fact that it was, what you might call aesthetically rough, it did what I wanted it to do. I made it from a piece of wood that I cut off from an old hockey stick I used to get beaten with and a little electric motor which drove a fan, cut out from cardboard. I mounted a switch to it and wired it all up to some batteries to power it. I was feeling pretty damn good about myself for that brief moment of glory when I won, which was a foreign feeling for me; sadly it was short-lived.

My father decided to take all of the credit for having invented it; he told anyone who would listen that *he* had designed and made it with his bare hands, even though he didn't know that *I* had made it until I'd won the competition. I started to wish I'd never won; his incessant reciting of the story was starting to give me headaches. The ironic part of all this, was that for a young child to have invented the hand fan was classed as an accomplishment, hence the certificate and award ceremony making a big deal out of it. But for an adult to have invented something that simple, why, they would clearly have to be simply simple!

In time, I became more creative in finding ways to stay away from home in order to try and minimise the beatings. I would take my bicycle and ride as far and as long as I could; staying out as late as possible until the cold and hunger brought me home. This tactic proved inadequate because, while giving me a short break, it would allow the beatings to build up; when I eventually returned home, my father would have even more reasons to beat me.

THE PAPER RUN

Things started to look up once I reached twelve.

First, I got myself a paper run, and second, I'd found an old, run-down dilapidated factory just a short bike ride from home, which manufactured copper rolls or something of that nature, not exactly sure. I'd sneak into the factory at nights through a hole in one of the walls, which was covered by a loose section of asbestos and steal lengths of copper cable from the enormous rolls. It was in my favour that I was still small because I could get in and out undetected. I would hide the wires I had collected, in my room under the bed. When the coast was clear, I would take them out and use a sharp knife to remove the outer plastic and as soon as I had gathered enough, I would sell the clean copper. The local scrap metal yard paid good money for copper in those days and didn't ask any difficult questions about the source.

The nastiest part of the paper run was the actual job itself. It entailed delivering two hundred newspapers to people's front doors. I had to carry the newspapers in a bag over my shoulder and it was excessively heavy and cumbersome; it felt like I had a dead body on my back. My shoulders would ache until the next morning. The run also had to be made at the worst possible time, every day straight after school, which was when all the other kids in the neighbourhood were hanging out and doing stuff that I wanted to be a part of. All of the newspapers had to be delivered on time and it didn't matter if it was rain, hail or shine – or worse still, snow. Delivering newspapers to people's homes when it was snowing, especially when the snow on the ground was over a foot high, made it a particularly challenging feat.

After a few weeks I didn't want to continue with the run because it was a really dreary job but I had no alternative because my father would not let me drop it and he confiscated all of the money I made, telling me he was putting it into a savings account for me. I genuinely could not identify with the logic of saving money that I was never going to be allowed to use, even when I actually needed something. But I didn't really care because I had the covert copper operation; that was my own thing on the side and it made more than three times as much as the paper deliveries.

I used most of the money that I had made from the copper to purchase a home computer at the local flea market. I still remember the model: it was a Texas Instruments T99. The computer itself was surprisingly compact considering the era in which it was released; the casing was made out of aluminium which made it look somewhat futuristic, and it connected directly into a television set.

Back in the eighties, computers were limited in speed and capacity and they did not do much at all but I was fascinated nonetheless. I would spend hours, sometimes even days, glued to the television screen just exploring and trying to learn all I could. The computer came with a basic programming book – I quickly mastered the programs from that and then added to my stash a whole stack of more advanced programming books which I purchased at the flea market. I wrote all of the programs from those too, over and over so many times that I eventually memorised them all.

From there, computer fever kicked in and it became an obsession. If you're a computer enthusiast, you will relate to this. I found myself continually needing to upgrade to each and every latest model; in a never-ending pursuit of more speed, memory, storage and overall processing power. My parents did not take much notice of what I was doing with the computers or with *anything* I did for that matter; however, I do remember one instance when I tried to show them how it all worked. I appeared to have caused them a great deal of mental anguish, judging by their bewildered expressions, just by having them listen to what I was saying. They were not technologically inclined and struggled with using the most basic of electronics. I suppose I was lucky that my parents had no interest at all in becoming involved in my life otherwise they might have become suspicious of how I obtained the money for my shiny new acquisition; as it was, if it kept me out of their sight, so much the better.

GRAND SLAM

Around this time, hanging out in the park playing baseball had become a great way for me to balance my sedentary computer-geek lifestyle. For me it wasn't so much about the game itself but more about another way of staying away from home for as long as I possibly could. Most kids would head home, eat and come back out, but not me. I would delay until every kid in the neighbourhood had left for the day; I wouldn't leave until I absolutely had to. The beatings that awaited me on my return home were still the one thing in my life that were a constant – I could set my clock by them – they were regular, ruthless and for the most part, repetitive.

I started to attract some attention when I played baseball because when I hit the ball, I gave it all I had. I released the anger churning inside me and it was as if I needed to beat the hell out of that ball in retaliation for all the hurt inflicted on me. If it connected, it was either going to be a homerun or a baseball bat that had cracked in half and flown out of my hands – most of the time hitting anyone standing unwarily close.

I was oblivious to the fact that the crowd that hung around the park had started to grow to some extent, until one of the other guys playing pointed it out and told me they were coming to witness my freak-like batting. Word got around. In the small group of fans that had gathered, I noticed a girl who was there every day for a few weeks. She would always sit in the same place and just lean up against the fence, chew gum and watch the game. One night, when the game had finished and the park was almost deserted, she stayed behind. I called out, 'You should go home now because everyone else has'. Back then, that was my idea of *smooth*.

She started laughing and the sound of her laugh was unique and completely free of malice. I was curious so I went over to see what was so amusing and upon closer examination, I saw that she was mighty cute – a strawberry blonde with long curly hair and huge eyes intensified by her delicate facial features. At that point she had my attention; I hadn't noticed her before because she dressed like a boy and wore a baseball cap that concealed a lot of her face.

As I approached, she asked me, 'What is the deal with hitting the ball like that? Something must be making you mad'. I was astounded at how observant she was for her age. Even though I was the same age, I just thought it was weird for someone else to have that sort of insight. I didn't answer her question; however, I did offer to walk her home.

She told me her name was Vicky and that her house was a good half-hour walk from the park we were in. I didn't mind because the later I was out the better it was for me and besides, I wanted to learn more about Vicky. We talked the whole way back to her home – no awkward teenage pauses for us. Some of the time I felt the conversation we were having was profound, touching on all the important issues. Other times I found myself trying to make her laugh because I liked the way it sounded – it was contagious – like when someone yawns in your face.

Before I knew it, we were the best of friends and I was spending the bulk of my spare time hanging out with her in an old garage that had been transformed into a lounge room at the back of her house. It was where her father did his drinking and smoking, late at night, I was told. The garage walls were covered head to foot with numberplates from cars. Vicky told me that her uncle pressed numberplates; he had apparently learned this trade in prison. There were two pinball machines in the garage which we played sometimes, though we spent most of our time just talking and, for my part, listening to Vicky laugh. But however close we became, I could not bring myself to burden her with the knowledge of the abuse at home. I was too embarrassed and humiliated and I hated the thought that it could taint our relationship.

I began to wonder whether I had turned the corner towards a future that did not appear so hopeless. The whole concept of having a normal life or experiencing any sort of contentment was a novel one for me. I did wonder, albeit for a nanosecond, if there was 'someone' or 'some being' out there who had decided to lessen my burden. I had no choice but to get used to whatever road life had decided for me.

HOSTILE TERRITORY

One night, when I got home after being at Vicky's house, there was no beating for me. The place was in chaos; everyone was busy packing stuff into suitcases. My parents ordered me to pack my things too because we were moving to Lebanon to live there permanently, leaving the very next day! The news hit me like a ton of bricks; I felt bewildered and agitated – my anus immediately tightened up a few notches from the stress.

The worst thing about all of this was that there was no opportunity to say goodbye to anyone, especially Vicky. I felt betrayed; I was having my life taken away from me when it was finally becoming almost tolerable. I hadn't seen it coming. All the time I'd spent living my 'real' life in the ball park and hanging out in that girl's garage, had come back to bite me on the ass. It must have blinded me to any hints I could have picked up at home that everything was about to change so radically. I tried to pack everything I owned into the one small suitcase that had been allocated to me but it wouldn't fit; so a lot of hard choices had to be made about what to leave behind. How do you fit your whole life into a suitcase? The next thing I knew, we were in Lebanon.

Driving to the city where my parents had decided we would live, we were repeatedly stopped at military checkpoints along the road by soldiers with machine guns; the only time I had seen a gun prior to this was on television. At one of the checkpoints, we were forced to open all of our suitcases and show the soldiers the contents. Each of them helped themselves to a few of our belongings and we couldn't do a thing about it. It was then that I realised I was fucked.

My grandparents' house was more like a hotel. Everyone was there – all the cousins, uncles and people from all over, and I didn't know a single one of them. They seemed to have come for only one reason. The minute we opened the suitcases to find a change of clothes, they started looting our shit.

All my personal belongings were taken out of the suitcase, passed down a line of kids and adults until they eventually disappeared into the distance. There was zilch I could do or say about it. When I attempted to notify my father that they were taking all my things, he punched me in the face, gave me a nosebleed, loosened one of my teeth and told me, 'Let them have it, they are my family!' So there I was, in a war-torn country and my life, as I had known it, may as well have been a million miles away. I had nothing left to remind me of home.

After a few days, we moved into our new house, which my father had been surreptitiously building for years. I could not *believe* that I had no prior knowledge of any of this; my parents had orchestrated the conspiracy faultlessly. The first time I saw the house I was astonished; it was enormous. To this day, I have not seen anything as large. It must have easily been the biggest house in the entire country. Every room had its own ornate balcony or terrace and sweeping staircases led to the various floors. The landscaping of the gardens could be favourably compared to a botanical garden; large fountains, ponds and swimming pools cooled each of the sizeable courtyards. There was a brick wall around the house and gardens that extended further than the eye could see. The wall was liberally punctuated with concrete pillars which had some sort of artwork carved into them and each one had a large light on top. The main gate, which led onto the property from the road, was colossal; I can't remember exactly but I would say it was at least ten metres high and opened by remote control when approached. Back then, that sort of thing was 'cutting edge'.

Once I had a chance to start looking around, it became obvious that this entire scenario must have been premeditated many years in advance. The garages were already full of brand new European luxury motor vehicles and the house was virtually fully furnished. But it had a cold sterile feel to it and gave me the creeps; in certain rooms the area was so vast that voices echoed. My mother's high heels clacking on the marble floors could be heard several rooms away. But as grand and as extravagant as this house was, it never felt like a home to me.

That country certainly sorted out the haves from the have-nots; every evening around seven o'clock, there would be a blackout in the city and everything went out, including streetlights. We were located high above the city so we could see it all go dark when this took place. The house had its own power source, which was a generator in a room on the top level. It would start up as soon as the power failed and our house would be the only source of light in the whole city – it stood out like a bright, glaring beacon because of the lights on the wall surrounding us. I remember feeling like an asshole because we were watching television and using all our luxury electrical appliances while everyone else in the city was stumbling around in the dark looking for candles.

A GOOD SOLDIER

For me, life in Lebanon soon became an experience that made getting beaten on a regular basis shy away in comparison; however, what struck me as odd was the fact that my brother did not seem fazed by the move at all, maybe it was because he was too young at the time to really understand what was going on.

The only school in our area that would accommodate English-speaking students happened to be a military training facility. The school compound was large, with the sterile, concrete-walled buildings scattered sparsely over the terrain. The area was dotted with simulated bunkers and there were pieces of military equipment lying all over the place. In contrast, the classrooms were pretty standard and run-of-the-mill boring, except that the entire facility reeked of burnt gunpowder. To me, the whole place felt morbid and gloomy. It was almost as though the sun refused to shine there, even though you could see it hanging in the sky above the school; the light from it seemed to be filtered through several layers of grey-tinted glass.

The principal of this school was an army general or something along those lines; his teachers were all soldiers who were armed and always in uniform. I compared them to my English teacher; the one who had suggested I keep a journal. The contrast in the schools would have been fascinating to record; I did think about it.

I was interviewed by the general to see whether or not I would be 'accepted' into the school. My parents were in the room and two soldiers were posted at the door as if to prevent me from escaping. The interview itself was unconventional in nature; the general handed me a textbook written in English and ordered me to stand in front of his desk and read it to him. I must have read three entire chapters before he told me to stop and I was standing the whole time. While I was reading, it was hard not to be preoccupied with the weirdness of having soldiers at the door and walking around the school yard, added to which I was getting tired from standing there and reading that stupid book.

The general knew damn well that I wouldn't understand a book on how to clean and assemble machine guns! He snapped a command to me to summarise what I'd just read for him. I had no choice but to tell him the truth – that I could not remember a thing; the model numbers of machine guns was not something I would have memorised. He did not react as I was expecting him to; I was thinking that perhaps he would like to demonstrate to my parents how understanding and patient he could be with pupils but instead he grabbed the book out of my hand and shouted obscenities at me. He then turned to my parents and told them, 'He is not very intelligent at all. I will teach him some much needed discipline and by the time I finish with him, you won't even recognise him'. I remember thinking, *What the fuck does that mean?*

My parents were obviously excited, thrilled and delighted by this news. The looks on their faces were almost indescribable but I'll give it a try: imagine eating a hot fudge sundae, while being on the receiving end of a sexual favour from a very attractive model and simultaneously taking a phone call which informs you that you have just won the million dollar lottery. Now imagine how happy you would look. Well, they looked even happier than that. Me, I went into a state of panic repeatedly playing the general's words over in my head.

A week later, on my dreaded first day at the new school, I attended the morning class and just my luck – first, the class was one of the few conducted in Arabic and second, I was asked a question about Lebanese history; sure enough I did not know the answer. I could barely even understand what they were saying because at that stage, my spoken vocabulary consisted of ten Arabic words and I couldn't read or write a single word. I was called to the front of the classroom by the soldier teaching the class and was ordered to put my hands out in front of me. Out of nowhere, the soldier produced a rough piece of wood with tiny rusted nails in it and whacked my hands with all his strength. My hands started bleeding immediately. He then told me to put my hands out again. Probably due to the fact that I was conditioned to taking beatings, I put my hands out two more times. I spent the rest of the day with stinging, throbbing hands wrapped in wet paper towels that I had found in the hole in the ground they called the 'toilet'.

When I got home, I was dealt a subsequent beating for making a nuisance of myself on the first day at my new school; my father deduced that I must have done something unsavoury because of the missing skin on my hands. That day I decided to dedicate all of my spare time to educating myself in how to read, write and speak formal Arabic. Most parents would have made sure that they had prepared their child for a move to a country where another language was spoken but my parents seemed to take the 'sink or swim' approach and didn't much care in my case which was the outcome. It only took me roughly two weeks of study without much time for sleeping to become fluent, although I did have adequate motivation – if it had taken any longer, my hands would have been worn down to nubs. This newfound knowledge stopped my hands being shredded for that particular reason; however, the soldiers still managed to find any excuse to draw blood from me. I started to wonder if my parents might have instructed the school to give me a little extra education because I was getting pulled up and tortured more frequently than anyone else and for the most part, without any good reason.

During the period that I was at that school, I learned a lot about defending myself, both through hand-to-hand combat and with various weapons. I was being taught important lessons of how not to trust anybody and how all humans had ugliness in them. That was the curriculum, in a nutshell. The sports classes were interesting. I was taught to throw a hand grenade, which I saw as an act of lunacy; I failed to understand how they could think giving young children live hand grenades would be a good plan. This type of sporting activity was always foreign to me because even though I was raised by savages, I was still accustomed to living in a civilised country.

The remainder of the sports classes was mostly about running, climbing and building stamina; we would be pushed a little harder and further every day. They also tried to instil these incongruous philosophies into the students. One of them was: it is not how *hard* you can get hit, it is how *fast* you can get up and keep going after the enemy once you have been hit, no matter how severe the injury. The teachers made getting your ass kicked sound like an achievement, and if that were the case, I would have been the world champion ten times over. I was starting to suspect that this school wasn't about education at all; it looked like they were attempting to produce mindless puppet soldiers for their wars.

At the end of each school day, I would be delivered home in a military vehicle. I would then spend most of my time studying, in order to avoid pain. When finished, I would brush up on my shooting. It was easy to learn a lot about weapons because in Lebanon there was an abundance of them. My father had an assortment of handguns and shotguns in a special cabinet in his bedroom; he also had enough bullets to last a very long time. It was easy to access the weapons because the cabinet was left unlocked. When my father was not around, I would take out a weapon and practise with it until I became proficient in pulling it apart and putting it back together if it was a handgun or learning the effects that the different shells had when they hit a target if it was a shotgun. Believe it or not, in those days, it was not uncommon for a thirteen year old to be wielding an assault rifle in Lebanon; it was actually fairly normal practice.

THE HERMIT

It became a habit for me to go into the forest with my dog and stay there for hours on end. I had first come across the stray dog there but when I took him home, my parents gave him instead, to my brother. I knew I could just play a waiting game and sure enough, my brother soon lost interest and my parents reluctantly allowed me to take the dog back under my wing. Walking the dog was a good excuse to remove myself from the vicinity of my parents. No one else was remotely interested in the dog, which worked for me, as it meant I could safely hide my journal in his basket under the blanket. Yes, I had decided to take up the advice of my English teacher.

The forest consisted of dense thickets of evergreen trees and shrubs and with no defined walking paths; it was difficult to navigate through it. It smelt of pine, which oddly soothed me to some degree. There were some particular areas that I had come across while exploring the forest that were truly amazing; they were beautiful natural tropical gardens which were untouched by man and this sort of made it like God's private design.

It was an easy walk from my home to the forest; most days I would just hang out there and practise shooting. It got to the stage where I could shoot down a bird mid-flight with a shotgun and hit standing targets using the handgun at any distance within reason, without wasting a single bullet. That got too easy and monotony crept in. Consequently I started experimenting with explosives, even making my own. The forest started to look like a war zone; the irony was that this forest was one of the only peaceful places left in Lebanon.

Most of my time was spent alone with the dog in the forest and it quickly became another hideout for me; I basically replaced the park where I used to play baseball with the forest. There was something very serene about being in the middle of nowhere just surrounded by nature; then blowing it all to pieces with as many bullets as you can carry; priceless.

One person, who remains crystal clear in my mind from those days, was a morbid, ancient and decrepit man whom my father had discovered in the forest. He was a hermit; apparently having lived alone since a child. I remember thinking it was so sad that he had lived that way. His home was in the depths of a location not shown on any maps, in a minuscule hut made from scraps of straw, wood and a few old rusted car parts. He grew or hunted his own food, which must have been a struggle for a man in his mid-nineties. His fingernails were so long that they curled at the ends and were encrusted with dirt. And, he was the hairiest man I had ever seen; it was as if he had never had a haircut or shaved in his entire life. He smelt like death warmed up; it was an evil stench I can tell you. There was some funky green shit leaking out of his ears, which exacerbated his stink and stuck to his facial hair. It looked like he had performed a frontal lobotomy on himself because large portions of the skin from his face were gone. But what stood out most to me was his missing eyeball. Yellow pus-like substance oozed out of it, and it did not occur to this recluse to cover it up. The saddest part of all this was his clothes; they were made from old potato sacks, as was his sleeping area.

Even in retrospect, I still cannot fathom how it was possible for a man to have lived in those conditions for such a long period of time, without reaching out to anyone for help or even companionship.

What happened between this apology for a man and my father, before I myself met the hermit, is even more remarkable. When my father had stumbled across the ragged recluse during one of his infrequent forays into the forest, it seemed that he had become fascinated with him because from then on, he would take a trip into the woods every day and bring the old man some home-cooked food. I did wonder whether it might have been a unique act of compassion but with my father being who he was, I doubted it. I had heard the stories about the hermit; however, I had yet to meet him.

The first time my father took me along with him to visit this old man, I immediately took a dislike to the dirty recluse; there was something about him that definitely seemed off, and it was not just his appearance and rank odour. I did not know it then but that was my introduction to the true nature of evil as it really is. I could see straight through this guy as if he was made out of glass and what was lurking inside was vulgar and wrong. I took a little too long to introduce myself, as I was so busy taking in what I was seeing; the state of the hermit and the squalor he lived in was a lot to take on board. I must have affronted the old man because he turned to my father and said, 'Who is that, and why isn't he saying anything? He should have at least greeted me'. Before I had a chance to explain, my father pushed me to the ground and kicked me in the ribs a few times.

About a week later on Easter Sunday, my father went to visit the old man with some food and a basket of coloured eggs, which is what Christian people typically did on Easter Day in those parts. Being the naturally inquisitive soul that I was, I dug around in books until I found out that in ancient Egypt and Persia *people* exchanged decorated *eggs* at the start of spring. It was something to do with fertility though I'm pretty sure my father didn't know that because he sure would have been wasting his time with the ancient and extremely repellent hermit. Anyway, I was instructed to come along but was reluctant after the beating at the previous meeting. I had to face it though, I did not have many alternatives – it was either go or get my head kicked in right there and then; I chose the former.

When we arrived, my father presented the old-timer with the basket of eggs. The dirty hermit, pointing at me, told my father, 'He must choose one of the eggs'. My father said, 'You heard the man, take one!' I reached in and took a random egg. The old man cried out, 'I knew it, he is evil – he chose the orange egg!' He then informed my father dramatically, 'That child will be the cause of much of the trouble in your life!'

I had the distinct feeling that my father wanted to please the old man for some reason and decided that he would resolve the quandary of my allegedly being evil right there and then which resulted in the most brutal, malicious and merciless bashing I can remember. He picked up a piece of timber that was lying on the ground and proceeded to beat me as hard as he could all over, breaking the skin and drawing blood on every part of my body. I begged him to stop as it felt as if he were killing me but he didn't even slow down – not until he ran out of breath. During my beating I managed to catch a glimpse of the old man; he was just sitting there, contentedly eating his eggs. He even ate the evil orange ones.

Looking back, I suppose that my father felt that this old man knew best; this freak of nature who had never been married nor had any children – apart from my father, he didn't even have any friends and had obviously received no education as he was illiterate. The issue that concerned me was the fact that, for some reason known only to himself, my father regarded him as an authority on manners and parenting and, even more bewildering, was convinced that he had a gift as a fortune teller as well.

We later found out from some elderly people in nearby villages that the old man did have some brief contact with people who passed through the woods while they were hunting. Everyone who knew of or who had encountered this man, verified that he was suffering from senility, paranoia and delusions. We were also told that he believed everyone he met was 'evil'. In spite of the new information that had come to light, my father still insisted on giving me beatings on the old man's recommendations, *just to be on the safe side.*

My father began to rely on the hermit's fortune-telling abilities – any decisions he had to make he would postpone until he could consult with the hermit. To make matters even worse, he ultimately decided to invite this foul sociopath into our home. My mother didn't care and hardly seemed to notice, even when my father insisted on feeding him at our table. As an additional benefit, I had to sit next to this creature at dinner on most nights, and for dessert, I would be served a smack in the face or get pushed off my chair while I was eating, thanks to that old prick's suggestions.

PUTTING ON THE RITZ

I spent just a year in Lebanon and it felt like the longest, damn year of my life. Summer had arrived, which meant the school year had finally ended. Every night of that year, my father would host an extravagant event in the main courtyard in order to entertain a group of high profile people and primarily to rub their noses in his success. Somehow, all his entrepreneurial wheeling and dealing always worked wildly well. The amount of money that was spent on catering, alcohol and entertainers was obscene. The parties were the epitome of decadence and were tailor-made for a crowd of individuals who were pretentious, pompous and arrogant. Having said that, the cars that the guests would arrive in were truly amazing; it was like being at a car show and seeing the latest, most luxurious exotic sports cars and sedans that money could buy, all parked in front of our house. I remember hearing people boasting about their Rolls Royce, 'which was the last of its kind' and a Lamborghini that was 'custom-made' and so on.

I had devised a simple strategy in order to avoid any physical and verbal abuse but moreover, any humiliation in front of the guests. I would quietly disappear into the forest and sit there alone; waiting it out. Ironically, I felt safer being alone at night, in a forest inhabited by wolves and snakes rather than being in the company of my own family. I had spent the better part of the summer hiding in the forest. As it turned out, the most notable thing about that summer in Lebanon was that it would be the last time I would be beaten by my father, ever again.

It was near the end of summer on a Saturday morning and I was sitting on the balcony that was connected to my bedroom, minding my own business and listening to a Walkman. I had managed to smuggle back some of the tapes that were pillaged when we had initially arrived in Lebanon. I had a 'Cool and the Gang' tape playing while I sprawled out on a cane chair and was tapping my foot on the railing of the balcony, oblivious to my tapping as I read a magazine. My father suddenly stormed up behind me and, out of nowhere, punched me in the back of the head; the headphones flew off my ears and I dropped the Walkman, which caused it to break into pieces. He shouted at me, 'You look so stupid tapping your foot, you're an embarrassment!' He kicked the crap out of me for a while and then forced me into the wardrobe which was already full of clothes and could barely fit me inside as well, and locked the door on me.

The wardrobe was claustrophobic and I felt I was going to asphyxiate if I did not escape. I began to have painful flashbacks of the furnace in Boston and almost instinctively, I gave the door a kick, with what must have been everything I could muster and then some because the door didn't just break open, it flew off its hinges. Before I had a chance take a breath of air in relief, I realised that my father had been standing only a metre or two from the door and it had flown off with such force it had knocked him to the ground. Immediately I thought to myself, *What the hell have I done? I'm a dead man now*. I braced myself for what I thought would be the beating that would end all beatings. He did nothing. He stood up, dusted himself off and walked away. I was mystified as to what had caused this to transpire. As I panted and gradually recovered my breath, I thought about it for a while. Perhaps he was no different to any other bully and that once confronted, he did not have the balls to keep fighting; however, I did not want to test my theory, as I was still *very* much afraid of him.

MURDER

Later that day my father dropped me and my brother off at our grandfather's house where we spent the afternoon bored out of our minds. The rule in that house was that children were to be seen and not heard and the being seen bit was with some reluctance too. I was under the assumption that we had been *quarantined* there because my father was having a quarrel with my mother; which was not at all rare in our household. My father picked us up in the evening. He was in a foul mood and as usual, drove like a maniac back home. When we arrived, I got on with my normal evening activities, trying to ignore the fraught atmosphere that pervaded the house. I fed my dog and threw him the ball for a while, then went upstairs and played some video games, watched a little television and went off to bed at approximately nine o'clock. I was soon sound asleep.

About an hour later I was awoken abruptly by very loud screams – I'd never heard screams as loud, fierce and frantic as these, even from myself during my worst beatings. By the time I realised that it was my mother who was screaming and it was coming from the courtyard downstairs, my brother was also awake. I told him not to move an inch, and ran down the stairs and into the courtyard.

I came pelting around the corner and then froze on the spot at the sight of my father lying on his back on a sofa with his head split almost into two halves. My mother was standing over him, still screaming her head off. It looked as though he had been bludgeoned with an axe. There was blood everywhere; it was a truly gruesome sight. I couldn't make it past the courtyard wall and I had to hold onto it because my head was spinning. I remember feeling numb and cold right down to my core; I was afraid I was going to be sick. Trying to process what I was seeing was not possible, although I did not have a chance to attempt it for long.

Almost immediately, people started to show up from all corners, most likely because they had heard the screams; within minutes, there were people everywhere. Without warning, a large man, who was one of my father's hunting friends, literally carried me off the scene by force, ignoring my kicks and protests. This made me very angry because I had no chance to find out what had just happened and why. I had so many questions and I believed the answers to be right there, where I had been standing.

I had to spend the night alone with strangers who claimed to be neighbours. They lived in a small, very dirty house, which added to my discomfort and I was kept in their unused bedroom. By the time I started to think clearly, I realised that I had no idea where I was because I had been too stressed to be able to recall much about being taken there in the first place. And where was my brother? Why had we been separated?

Several days spent in isolation and bewilderment passed before I was permitted to return home and for the duration of this hostage-like situation, I was incapable of eating or resting. By the time I was allowed to leave, the funeral had already taken place. It troubled me that I was not given the opportunity to be present at my own father's funeral! According to my mother's rationale, it was an excellent idea to leave me alone in the care of complete strangers, for days on end, with nothing but the mental images of what I had witnessed, which were constantly haunting me. They still do.

Once I arrived home, there was no chance to get answers to any of my questions or find out anything more about what had happened, as there was a massive upheaval underway in the house. It seemed that my mother was going to be taken away by the Syrian military; she was going to be interrogated, which inevitably meant tortured, then put in prison for her crimes. The Syrian military, who happened to be the local law enforcement at that time, believed that my mother had murdered my father and they allegedly had enough evidence to corroborate their claims.

However, just at the last moment my mother, who, come to think of it, had seemed strangely unperturbed by her imminent incarceration, managed to elude the military and thwarted their efforts to investigate further; they did not even get a chance to speak to her in person. From my perspective, this all started to look like a conspiracy and the more I tried to learn what had happened, the less I would find out. Sadly, my brother was no help; he was too young to understand what had happened so I couldn't glean any facts from him either.

THE BARBARIAN

The man responsible for getting my mother 'off the hook', started making regular appearances at our home. He was supposedly a friend of my father's or so I was told. He had attended a few of my father's parties with his Australian wife who was frail, blonde and ghost-like. Even though I had caught sight of him at the parties on one or two occasions – when sneaking off to the forest – I was surprised as to why he would dedicate so much of his own time to our cause. My mother claimed that the friendship between my father and him was the main reason for his support. He had connections inside the corrupt Syrian military – presumably liberally greased with his seemingly endless bankroll – and was able to bring the entire investigation to a grinding halt. I was at a loss as to what the fuck was going on. On the one hand, my mother was out of harm's way but on the other, there was no way to find out *who* had killed my father and *why*. The strangest part of all this, was that it seemed that I was the only one who cared.

The alleged saviour was tall with a heavy build and appeared to have spent a large part of his time training and lifting heavyweights; he was almost bald with a thin comb-over and had large warts all over the top of his head. He always wore a smart black suit but still looked like a barbarian; something about him was very unsettling. Due to this man's barbaric appearance and sheer size, I began to think of him as Conan, as in *Conan the Barbarian*. It seemed that I was not the only one as it wasn't long before he became known as, Conan.

My uncles from my father's side had caught wind of the fact that the investigation had ended. Abandoning the investigation with no results was not acceptable to them; they started talking to people themselves and throwing their money around which made waves. Conan had no choice but to make it appear as if he had engineered the reopening of the investigation into my father's murder.

It got to the point where Conan would be at our home every single night, apparently 'investigating'. My mother would cook for him and serve him as if he were a king; she would laugh at everything he said and hang off his every word like a schoolgirl in love. I found this behaviour somewhat odd and disconcerting.

Conan began to exert a strong influence on our household. My mother instructed me to be very polite and careful about what I said in his presence. I was not about to disobey her with Conan constantly strutting around the place sporting a machine gun or some other weapon but I began to feel as though I was a detainee in my own home. I also started to feel restless and what I now know to be depression, came over me in such a way that it felt as if I were drowning. I attempted to self-medicate by drinking; I would take a few bottles of whatever alcoholic beverage I could get my hands on and head to the roof of the house where I would consume them. It didn't take long for me to become immune to the alcohol's numbing effect. I could still feel the pain. In order to make things a little more exciting I started to play a moronic game. I would sit right on the edge of the roof looking down at the three-storey drop; I would then knock back as much alcohol as it took to render myself unconscious. By some freak chance, whenever I regained consciousness I would miraculously still be on the roof and not on the ground, fifteen metres below. I seemed to have cheated death and fallen in the wrong direction every single time. Let's put it this way, if something or someone had in fact been watching over me, by that stage, whatever or whoever, would have been well and truly regretful for taking on the assignment.

The excessive drinking and lack of rest was starting to make me unwell. I eventually finished the entire reserves of alcohol that were available to me and was unable to purchase any more because of my age. My mother's finely honed maternal instinct had not primed her to notice my drunkenness. Also, she seemed to be unaware of the fact that the copious alcohol supplies had dwindled drastically. Maybe she assumed that Conan, who by now had the unrestricted run of the entire place, had helped himself. Once I had dried out, the boredom and desperation returned tenfold. I inevitably occupied my time with trying to find the answers to what had happened to my father and why. I approached my mother in an effort to obtain some information. She responded by shrieking at the top of her lungs, 'It's not any of your business!' which I thought was a highly unusual notion presented in a rather overdramatic way. How could the murder of my father not be any of my business?

THE INVESTIGATION

This brush-off by my mother did not sit well with me at all. I began covertly investigating in and around the house of my own accord. I discovered a bag containing the items my father had had on his person when he was murdered; it had been concealed at the back of his wardrobe under a large suitcase. The item that caught my eye was his ostentatious Rolex watch – the smashed glass face had bloodstains all over it. I removed it from the bag and rinsed it off under the tap; now I could see that the hands of the watch had jammed at close to ten o'clock. That was around the time my mother had started screaming when she discovered my father's body. I realised this watch would implicate my mother and bring her a world of trouble if it fell into the wrong hands. I took the watch to her but before I could speak she belted out another, 'This is none of your business!' She was like a broken record. She followed it up with, 'And never go into my room again!' snatched the watch out of my hands and that was the last I ever saw of it.

This situation was obviously fucked but it spurred me on to search for the truth; however, my efforts to find even one more shred of evidence were proving to be an act of futility and frustration. And then I realised that I had been going about it all wrong. Instead of looking for still existing tangible clues, I commenced searching for things that were no longer around that should have been. Lo and behold, I could not find the axe that was normally in the shed with the rest of my father's tools. My father had used it around the house on a regular basis as it was a multipurpose tool with an axe on one side and a hammer on the other. I spent two whole days searching for it but no luck.

I was flabbergasted. Because of the layout of our house, this meant, that whoever had come to kill my father – if they had in fact used that particular tool – would have had to know exactly where to find the axe, which had been kept in one of the many outhouses. They would have had to walk right past my father in order to get to it, before returning to carry out the murder. This seemed very unlikely because my father, who habitually watched television in that room following dinner until he went to bed, would have seen whoever it was, pass by him and would certainly have been alerted if it was someone who should *not* have been there at the time. This gave me a new theory; I now believed that whoever my father was with that night was the killer.

Even though I knew I would probably be wasting my time, I approached my mother in order to discuss my latest hypothesis. You would not believe what she said next; or maybe you would. She turned red and cried out at the top of her voice, 'It's none of your business!' This was starting to become a generic answer for any questions I may have had. It was becoming abundantly clear that I was getting nowhere with the investigation because I was regarded as a child which meant, in her book, that I had no right to question anything.

In my mother's defence, she was preoccupied at the time. She was very busy collecting all of my father's worldly possessions and packing them into boxes. She was meticulous and methodical about it; each box was carefully packed and painstakingly labelled. As it turned out, she was doing this in preparation for transporting the boxes to her parents. I was somewhat disgusted because my father's body was barely cold before she started clearing the house of any sign of him.

The incongruity of this was the fact that my father had by no means consented to his in-laws, my grandparents, ever setting foot in our home. According to him, they were scavengers and always had their hands out for money. This had been the source of countless feuds between my parents. My mother insisted that it was not true; she constantly tried to reassure my father that her family did not want anything from him at all.

As is probably obvious by now, I am, by nature, inquisitive; plus I could not accept the reality that I simply did not know what had happened to alter my life so dramatically. The murder of my father had left me feeling even more insecure than ever. From that point on, I no longer had a father to put a roof over my head and food on the table, even though those essentials came packaged with the beatings. At the end of the day, he *was* my father and nothing anyone could say or do would change that fact. I had always sought his approval and had been hopeful that one day I could accomplish something that would have made him proud of me; I now felt that I had been robbed of that chance. Is he up there looking down on all this mess? Does he know how much I want to please him?

My father's worst fears were realised; I witnessed it with my own eyes. The lowest blow I can remember my mother serving my recently deceased father was a direct defiance of an often-stated wish. My father had a secret recipe for pizza sauce. He made it extremely clear that he did not *ever* want anyone else to know his secret recipe and would 'take it to the grave with him'. Ironically, one of my mother's earliest actions following the funeral was to mass-produce the recipe using a photocopier. The first people who had the privilege of getting a copy of the recipe were her parents, even though they didn't care much for pizza. I can recall the day she gave it to them; it is clear as crystal in my memory. When we walked into their home, they had the boxes containing my father's possessions all over the floor and they were celebrating as they shared in the spoils of what they had received for a zero dollar net effective cost.

The larceny seemed to have no end; my grandparents took my father's clothes in addition to his jewellery, cars and money; my mother even gave them most of our furniture. As a result, we barely had anything left. My mother seemed ecstatic, more so than I had ever seen before; I suppose it was primarily because she was going against my father's wishes. I still do not know whether my mother had bothered to stop for a moment at some stage and actually consider what she was doing, as she had effectively given away everything, including all of my father's savings! I was by no means an expert on finance, however, I was able to predict that life might become difficult moving forward; bearing in mind we no longer had any funds. My father's parents had no idea of what was going on because, since my father's death, she had refused any of his family entry to the house – perhaps as some form of payback.

I regarded the entire situation as disappointing. Although my father had been sadistic and violent, it did not seem right to go against a dead man's wishes; I figured he was still a human being and deserved to die with some dignity. To me, what my mother was doing was excessively vindictive and spiteful. I'm not sure why she acted that way; however, if I had to make a presumption, I would put it down to the fact that she had married at a very young age and had not sufficiently considered her decision. Therefore, once she had become aware of the reality in which she lived, she began to manifest feelings of resentment, regret and maybe even rebellion.

Meanwhile I sure as fuck needed to find some answers and by now it was obvious that I wasn't going to get them by asking questions. I started to hide in storage spaces around the house and wait for hours on end, hoping to overhear something that would be of help in my investigations but on one particular occasion, I really wished I hadn't been eavesdropping because I managed to catch wind of some truly disquieting information.

I overheard a dialogue between my mother and her younger brother. The discussion I heard caused the already mediocre level of respect I had for her to drop even further. My mother was, in a roundabout way, confessing to her brother that she had had a curious relationship with one of my father's friends, and she expressed great gratification about the fact that my father had never detected it. My uncle could not have been any less concerned about what my mother had been telling him; instead kept asking her, 'Do you still have any of your husband's valuables? I sure could use the money'. My mother told him about some rings she had found and handed these over, which further added to my disgust and dismay.

TROPICAL PARADISE

A few days later I found myself eavesdropping again; I obviously had not learned my lesson. I was slightly perturbed when I overheard a conversation between my mother and Conan; they were discussing their plans for the future. Unfortunately, the location I had chosen to hide in that day was not the best situated – the words were not coming through as clearly as I would have liked. I could vaguely hear something about my mother going to a new country with Conan; from what I could make out it sounded like he was saying something like, 'I will take you away from this place, to a beautiful tropical paradise'. My mother responded with excessive excitement to Conan's declaration. It suddenly went quiet after her outburst of joy and happiness. At that point I decided I did not want to hear any more, so I snuck out of my hiding place and left without being noticed.

The following day when I woke up, I found my mother busy preparing an elaborate feast; I was assuming that she would be entertaining a large number of valued guests as it was an impressive and sizable banquet. I thought I would help myself to something from one of the many trays of food because I was starving. My mother swiftly stopped me with a rap on the knuckles from a wooden spoon and said, 'Don't touch that – it is not for you. I have been working all night on that!' I became curious as to who was coming to eat the mountain of food that was now at the stage of being almost ready to serve. I hurried to the front balcony, waited and watched. Before long, I saw Conan's car coming up the hill. Seconds later my mother ran downstairs so hastily she all but fell over but she made it to the outer gates in time to be waiting to greet him. *What the fuck was going on?* The barbarian appeared to be the only guest who would be attending my mother's feast. When Conan came upstairs into the house, he went straight to the dining room, sat at the head of the table where my father used to sit and commenced eating on his own. I came to watch, concealing myself near the doorway.

I knew it was rude to stare; however, I was finding it hard to look away. Conan was the only person at the table – my mother was apparently holding a party for one. I struggled to make sense of an utterly nonsensical situation and to make matters even more confusing, my mother waited on him hand and foot, acting as if it was a privilege to serve him. Out of nowhere Conan abruptly stopped eating and stood up. He walked over to the wall which had a large, framed, memorial photograph of my father hanging on it; he paused and looked at the photograph for a brief moment and then proceeded to take it off the wall and lay it face down on the floor. He belched and picked at his teeth and announced, 'I don't want him looking at me while I eat; just the sight of him bothers me'. Conan then returned to the table and recommenced stuffing an assortment of foods into his large head.

I was unable to see his removing my father's photograph as being anything other than a sign of immense disrespect; I could not just sit there while someone was basically shitting on the memory of a man who was no longer around to defend himself, in his own home. How could anyone be expected to feel in that type of situation? I entered the room, went over to the photograph and picked it up; as I did so, I heard a metal click directly behind my head – the sound sent a chill down my spine and I came pretty damn close to crapping myself. Because of my activities in the forest, I knew that sound all too well. I slowly turned around only to confirm my fears; Conan had a gun aimed at my face and with a deadly serious look ordered, 'Put the picture down'. Given the situation, I had no choice but to comply with his demand. I was petrified because I was quite convinced that he would shoot an unarmed child in the face without thinking twice about it – he would probably even have continued eating after he had killed me. What kind of sick fuck would do something like that in the first place? I was equally shocked by my mother's response or I should say lack of one – she did not open her mouth or show any sign of concern for my wellbeing whatsoever; I could have sworn that in a strange sort of way she actually seemed pleased with what was happening. If I had had even the smallest scrap of respect for her at that stage, it was just about totally gone after that.

Not surprisingly, I had difficulty sleeping that night which helped in a way because, while I was lying in my bed awake, I managed to concoct a brilliant plan, or so I thought. The next day I looked in the garage for the very small and ineffective motorcycle that was only used within the boundaries of our property. The bike was never maintained, serviced or even cleaned because it was never intended for on-road use. My plan was to take a few supplies and whatever cash I could get my hands on and hit the open road, as opposed to being taken to, fuck knows where, with my mother and Conan.

DESPERATE TIMES

Almost immediately, I encountered an obstacle in the preliminary stages of my plan; the bike would not kick over. I wasn't surprised as it had built up a bad reputation for itself with a history of breaking down repeatedly. It was in no way suitable for my escape plan as it had a very small engine and was not built for long trips but I was not exactly spoilt for choice. I figured that if I push-started the motorcycle the battery would eventually charge and I would be on my way to freedom; however, my feet only just touched the ground, which made it practically impossible to get enough momentum. I decided to acquire some assistance from a mechanic in a local workshop, which happened to be within walking distance from our house. I had always been banned from any contact with this man, which annoyed me as he had access to some of the tools which I would have loved to have used in many of my inventions that I still tinkered with. Still, in those days of turmoil in the household, who was likely to notice if I spoke with the mechanic? What no one had bothered to tell me was that the man was rumoured to be a pedophile.

The mechanic seemed more than happy to be of service, which was great, because my plan was back on track. I sat on the bike and the mechanic took hold of the grab rail behind the seat and started to push the motorcycle along the road, telling me to wait for his signal before I released the clutch while he built up speed. All of a sudden, he grabbed hold of my neck and pushed me off the bike onto the road face first – at that stage he was already running as fast as he could. He did not stop pushing even after I had hit the ground. This naturally resulted in painful injuries to my face. The skin was sliced by the broken remnants of glass bottles tossed negligently onto the road from the workshop and was grazed all over from being dragged along the road. Small pieces of gravel and glass lodged into the cuts.

When I finally picked myself up from the road, I could see that the motorcycle was badly damaged which put an immediate end to my plan because I had no means to repair it. The mechanic seemed to be pleased with what he had done; as he walked back to his workshop he called out to a few of his fellow employees in order to boast about his achievements – he was actually proud of himself. They just stood there and laughed liked maniacs. I failed to see what the fuck could have possibly been so funny about that situation.

I later came to learn that my father had been responsible for what had occurred; it seemed that, even from the grave, he could manage to inflict pain towards me. I found out he had argued vehemently with the mechanic over religious issues. The mechanic was a radical Muslim Syrian and my father was a devout Catholic, which meant they could not see eye-to-eye on many issues. Later on, when someone finally enlightened me to the fact that he was a possible pedophile, it made sense as to why I was not permitted to have any contact with the mechanic. But from where I stood, he was also a vindictive sadist, taking his revenge on a defenseless child. I wish I could say that he got his just desserts – not only for his ill-treatment of me but for any unfortunate child he had abused – but I never heard any more about him after that day. Hopefully fate caught up with him at some stage.

I dragged the motorcycle home and threw it in a back corner of the garage; I couldn't bear to look at it any more as it just reminded me of my failed escape attempt. I went upstairs in order to tend to my wounds. My mother failed to notice what had happened to my face; she may have been preoccupied with Conan and the notion of living with him in a tropical paradise.

Desperation started to kick in. I needed a way out and I just couldn't find one, no matter how hard I tried. I decided to end it all, there and then. I broke a window in my room, picked up a large shard of glass from the floor, which was conveniently shaped like a knife and jabbed it through my wrist until the pointed end of the glass came through the other side. This was no mere cry for attention, as I made sure to aim it in the direction of the vein, making it difficult to repair if discovered too early. I figured that it would be over quickly and I would finally be free. Gritting my teeth, I tugged the glass from my wrist, the blood started to spray all over the place and I became faint;

I assumed that the end must have been near. My mother happened to walk past at this point and saw the mess that the blood had created. Sighing in exasperation, she casually handed me a sock from the basket of washing she was carrying and gave it to me to wrap around my wrist so that I would stop getting blood over everything, although by that stage the blood seemed to have almost stopped flowing of its own accord. I was evidently having a bad day as far as planning went. The wound slowly seeped blood for days and eventually became infected due to the lack of medical attention. It took many weeks for the wound to heal completely. I still bear the scar on my wrist to this day.

WAR ZONE

This may all be getting a little too sensational to accept as true, hell, sometimes I struggle to believe it myself. This next segment will only add to your skepticism.

The Syrian army invaded our home; we were the only house in the entire city which was targeted, due to our atrocious luck at being so well-positioned strategically to overlook the city. The military knocked down a large part of the wall around our house and positioned a fleet of army tanks in the courtyard. It did not appear to me that Conan had used his influence in any way to dissuade the military from commandeering our grounds; instead, it seemed as though he was coordinating the soldiers as if he were a general, or perhaps a bum licker who yearned for their approval. But he may have been instrumental in preventing them from taking over the house in addition to the grounds as, mercifully, we were not bothered by the soldiers as long as we remained inside.

For the initial two weeks, the soldiers spent their time establishing what appeared to be, a base camp. I spent hours on the balcony monitoring their activities; I was very careful to remain as inconspicuous as possible. The way I saw it, there was no telling what they would have done to me if I had been caught spying on them.

The Syrian armed forces appeared to be a tremendously crude and uneducated group of individuals. I was unfortunate enough to witness one of the soldiers' eating rituals. They would forcibly take chickens from a nearby neighbor's chicken hutch, and then proceed to shove their hands inside the chickens where they would search for eggs. In the event of the soldiers finding an egg, they would pull it out completely destroying the chicken in the process, use their teeth to crack it open and swallow the contents raw. The fact that their hands and the eggs themselves were covered in chicken blood and guts did not seem to bother them in the slightest. Next, they collected random shrubs from the ground and consumed them. The soldiers all seemed very satisfied with this serving of food, which led me to believe that this dish must have been a delicacy in Syria. I remember it taking an immense effort to remain silent, as watching the soldiers conduct themselves in such a fashion just about caused me to heave every single time.

Another of the soldiers' traits, which I found to be particularly repulsive, was the fact that they would defecate in the vicinity near where their meals were prepared. The smell of the faecal build-up was rank; however, it appeared to have no effect on the militias' appetites. We could quite clearly smell the disgusting odour from inside the house and because they were in such close proximity, on a hot day, the stench would become overpowering and insufferable.

I was worried that the soldiers were going to hurt my dog, as he had become a nuisance to the army men, continuously wandering around what was, after all, his territory, while they were setting up their equipment. As it turned out, my concerns were justified. The time came when the soldiers had had enough of the dog. The leader of the men grabbed hold of my dog by its head, and removed a large knife from his belt. Even though I was defenceless, I still had to try to do something for my poor dog; I yelled down to the soldier from the balcony and pleaded with him to stop. The soldier looked at me and smiled while he hacked the head clean off my dog; then he summoned another soldier whom he ordered to skin the dog and prepare it for dinner. I was devastated. What made this situation totally fucked was the fact that it was entirely unnecessary. There were shops within close walking distance which had an ample supply of food and amenities, including toilets. In those weeks I learned more about military culture than I ever cared to know.

I don't know how I managed to fall asleep the night my dog was butchered but at three o'clock in the morning I was jolted awake by an earth-shattering explosion; my bed slid across the room and I fell out of it. Before I had a chance to figure out what was happening, there was a second explosion which had such force that just the sheer volume of sound was the breaking windows. I picked myself up and ran to the shattered window in order to see what was happening outside. The sky was lit up with what appeared to be large projectiles which were approaching fast. When I looked down into the courtyard, I realised that the explosions which I had heard were rockets being launched from our house. I did not procrastinate for very long before I started moving. I took my brother and, for some strange reason my pillow, and ran out of the house into the street. I remember exactly what the sky looked like while we hurried down the street; it was filled with green and white stripes, which were made by the rockets and bullets flying overhead.

We had no choice but to take refuge at my grandfather's house where we reunited with my mother who had been escorted there by Conan. We stayed up for the rest of the night and listened to everything exploding around us. I could not find anyone who was able to provide any coherent explanation to me about the war – who started it, what did they want, who was killing who? My mother's father did try but he too seemed bewildered by the complications of allies who became enemies, borders that seemed to expand and contract daily and the huge numbers of casualties being reported.

I kept my fingers firmly crossed in the hope that none of the missiles landed on my grandparents' home, killing us all. When the barrage finally ceased around dawn, my fingers-crossed plan had proved its worth, because we had survived the night. The next day my grandfather managed to find a taxi driver crazy enough to drive us out of the country in spite of the war zone around us. All the roads to any civilised countries were completely blocked because of the war. That meant we had to get out through Syria, in order to leave the Middle East, via Damascus airport.

THE ROAD TO PERDITION

I certainly was not looking forward to going to Syria, especially after having witnessed firsthand what they were all about and we were headed in a straight line for their motherland. Luckily we were only scheduled to be in Syria for a few days, however, for the duration of our visit I did not eat a single thing except for a bit of boiled rice, as their cuisine did not agree with me – maybe the chicken-eating spectacle I had witnessed had left its culinary mark on me.

From Damascus we flew to Boston, where I assumed we were going to live. Well, you know what they say about assumptions. We moved in with my mother's cousin Michael; he was single, young and lived like a party animal. There were pizza boxes, beer bottles and women's underwear all over the place even though he claimed to have done a major clean-up before we arrived. We had to sleep on the floor of Michael's cramped one-bedroom apartment for three weeks. Just as I was starting to settle in and become somewhat comfortable, glad to be in a country that had nuts and bolts I was familiar with, we had to pack our bags and we were off to the airport again.

I was overcome with terror when I learned that the final destination was Sydney, Australia. As a result of my eavesdropping capers back in Lebanon, I could put two and two together and come up with the sixty-four thousand dollar answer: Sydney was the tropical island paradise promised by Conan and I knew he would be joining us there.

In the taxi from Sydney airport, I finally prised the plan, for the immediate future, out of my mother. A bunch of people my parents had known in Boston had made their way to Sydney. We were to move, gypsy-like, from one friend or acquaintance of my mother's to another, only staying a few days with each because apparently, while she would be very welcome wherever she went, my brother and especially I would not. Along the 'way', she would be seeking a place for us to make a new home.

From the airport we travelled to the first of our temporary homes in a far western suburb of the city. I remember looking out the window and seeing hundreds of Asian people; I had only ever seen that many Asian people before in Bruce Lee movies. It seemed as though we had inadvertently gone to Vietnam.

When our taxi arrived at the house, where the first of my mother's friends resided, not a single person came outside to meet us or even help carry the bags; I could see one of them gawking at us through the window and it was eerie. I must say they were not welcoming at all and did not appear to be overly enthusiastic to see us standing on their doorstep. My mother's friend opened the door. She startled me because she looked and sounded like a witch; she had a leathery, greyish-brown complexion and an unusually large and bare forehead towering over diminutive, beady, black eyes, which were cold and glazed over. She looked like one of those people who would not summon up a smile for a warm loaf of bread, even if they were starving. She had a grim expression on her face whenever she looked at me, giving me the distinct impression that I was an inconceivably heavy burden on her.

By the time we settled down I was so hungry I could have eaten a small- to medium-sized donkey. Between the war, Syria and the party-animal's place in Boston, I was by then semi-starved, as at no time had the food presented to me been adequate for the needs of a growing boy. More recently, all I had eaten was a bag of peanuts on the aeroplane! Dolores did not so much as offer us a glass of water when we arrived at her abode. I was too uncomfortable to ask for anything, as I was nervous about how the unwelcoming, dry-faced, witch-like woman would react.

The first words that came out of Dolores's scaly mouth to me were, 'Your father was a very bad man'. I did not appreciate her comment, yet I could not reply. I was lost for words. I could not conceive of what could possibly have provoked her to say that to me, as she knew that my father had only recently passed away. What really heightened the tension caused by her faux pas was the silence that followed. That crusty bitch must have stood there for at least two minutes just eyeballing me, waiting for a response, which she did not get.

Later that night, Dolores finally decided to get off her ass and cook something. She, my mother and two other adults sat around the table and seemed to take pleasure in what they were eating. The aroma of the food made my stomach grumble loudly. I saw my brother sitting in a corner looking very unhappy; he was suffering from the same hunger pains as I was, as he too had encountered problems trying to get food over the past few days. I approached my mother and asked to have a word with her in private. I intended to inform her that I felt as though my brother and I were going to starve if we did not eventually get something to eat but did not get a chance as she turned me away, and told me to not be rude. As it turned out, the dinner that had been prepared was exclusively for the adults. I was evidently interrupting her while she was enjoying her meal. I felt an overwhelming surge of anger come over me; as the one person who was supposed to have her children's interests at heart, she had chosen to serve herself and leave us hungry.

They appeared to be having a ball while they ate; everyone at the table was reminiscing about old times but the conversation gradually took a turn for the worse. They commenced a trash-talking session about my father and everyone in his family. Dolores spitefully pointed out how greatly disappointed she was to see that I looked like my father. Her comments were made out of pure malice as I in fact did not resemble my father in any way, shape or form. By then my hands were starting to shake and my blood was just about to boil. I felt hungry and betrayed. I so badly wanted to let her know that I thought she was unequivocally the most disgraceful low-life I had ever met. However, I bit my lip and kept my mouth shut.

It was a wise choice to keep quiet because eventually, my brother and I got to eat something. The children had a distinctive menu that comprised toasted bread with brown skid marks on it. They told me it was Vegemite. The brown paste completely caught me off-guard, as I had never heard of it before; it looked, smelled and tasted like something that was used to lubricate car parts. Although I was on the verge of collapsing from hunger, I could not bring myself to eat the soiled toast, as the brown stains on them looked too suspect for my liking. I decided to hold off until the next day. I then snuck into someone's bedroom and quietly helped myself to some loose change, which took a while since I was not familiar with the new currency. I remember picking out the fifty cent coins because they were the biggest and the odd shape stood out.

I was up at dawn. I felt lucky and with my newfound funds in hand, I quietly left the house and walked for what seemed like miles until I found a store that sold take-away food. The text on the signs and food labels was entirely in Vietnamese. An elderly Vietnamese man, with three very long hairs on his chin was tending to the shop. I attempted to communicate with him but to no avail. The old man just nodded in agreement to whatever I said. I eventually figured out that I needed to point to what I intended to purchase. I selected a bread roll that was stuffed with different coloured pieces of god knows what; it appeared to be the safest bet, as I couldn't even describe the other selections. On closer examination, the roll looked very crude; it had very old carrots, which were so dry that they looked like wood shavings, and some sort of meat that I had never seen the likes of before – it could have been sewer rat for all I knew. I was incredibly hungry and had no alternative but to eat it; I either ate or starved. It smelt like mould and tasted like cardboard; a real treat! I returned to the old man every day at the same time and ordered the exact same thing, as I had at least survived the first encounter and I was keen to avoid taking any more chances than were necessary. However, on the meagre rations that were handed out by Dolores, I didn't really have a choice. I eventually managed to persuade my brother to eat a bit of the strange concoction as well, to stave off starvation.

As we moved our temporary abode from one of my mother's acquaintances to the next, we met with varying levels of hospitality but it was more than hard to shift that first harsh impression. And I still can't eat Vegemite.

HOME IS WHERE THE HEART IS

Two weeks of living with one or other of my mother's friends had gone by when she announced that she had found a rental property, in oh-so-lovely Cabramatta, and that we would be moving into it without delay. What my mother had failed to mention was that another one of her vast reserve of cousins would be moving in with us. When he turned up, I realised that yet another detail that my mother had omitted was the fact that her cousin was black. I was speechless as I was certain that I would have remembered having any black relatives – I mean, that sort of thing would have stood out. On closer examination, it became apparent that he was, in fact, more of a dark mahogany brown. This was on account of his being a sun worshipper. In the weeks that followed he spent many an afternoon spread-eagled in a most unattractive, not to mention disturbing manner on our small patch of grass in the backyard. This was my first encounter with a representative of the large cohort of leather-skinned Australians who seemed to think looking like a burnt kipper was beguiling. His name was Tommy and he was quite the charmer. He would cut his toenails at the table while we ate. On one particular occasion, a piece of toenail flew off and ended up square in the middle of my plate. I was trying to have my dinner at the time; I decided not to bother to complain as no one would have listened anyhow. Tommy was a tremendously hefty man, with toes like bananas; they were the largest toes I had ever seen even to this day. He had to wear sandals as a conventional shoe could not house his freakishly large toes. Needless to say, the size of the toenails and the bits flying round the dinner table were record-breaking too.

Tommy the Toe aside, it proved to be an arduous task adapting to the meagre living conditions. I was living in squalor; the undersized townhouse resembled the sort of movie set used as a crack house or indeed any house that was meant to suggest poverty and crime. Every soiled wall was a different, out of the ordinary colour, the carpet was sticky and had cigarette burns and blood stains all over it, none of the doors or door handles worked and the pipes creaked in the walls, constantly making a tiresome commotion. With unerring instinct, my mother had managed to unearth the cheapest furniture available from soiled, waterlogged and torn sofas to pre-owned tarnished cutlery. She even managed to obtain a black and white television with a coat hanger for an antenna, which was rare in the late eighties.

I was frightened to go outside, as there were regular Vietnamese gang fights directly in front of the house. What concerned me most were the used needles that littered the ground around my home. I attempted to remain indoors as much as possible. After a few months of having survived this shit-hole, Mr Banana Toes decided to move out. As a result, my mother could no longer meet the expense of renting this magnificent resort. The only thing left to do was to move, yet again.

We relocated to a reasonably sanitary environment, although due to limited funds we had to move into a much smaller apartment. It was so small that it could fit no more than three people at once; it felt like I was living in someone's bathroom. Once we established ourselves in the new place, my mother went all out and prepared a very large meal. This turned out to be an attempt to reprise the last feast she had created in Lebanon. I assumed it was to be a feast to celebrate her newly achieved independence. My mother cooked up a storm which worried me a little because I realised, that this one meal would exhaust the bulk of her remaining money. She even set up the coffee tables in a sad attempt to convert them into a dining table, as we did not have one. Once again, as a haunting echo of the previous feast, when I attempted to reach for a piece from the tempting piles of food, she told me to stop. At that very instant there was a knock at the door. When my mother opened the door, Conan was standing there. I should have expected it but the shocking reality still caught me off guard. I remember feeling an overwhelming sense of despair and thinking, *This cannot be fucking happening.* Conan entered the room and went straight to the food, all the while disregarding me – treating me with his usual, unmitigated contempt.

My mother and Conan began enjoying their quixotic candlelit dinner. I was appalled beyond words; I left and went into the other room – the apartment only had two rooms. One of the downsides of being in such a small place was the fact that I could hear everything that happened in the other room. The shrill tone of her frantic uncontrollable laughter was horrendous. What added to my dismay was the fact that I could clearly hear Conan's chews and grunts as he ate, while I was starving. I ended up falling asleep, hungry once again on a mattress on the floor which was the sleeping arrangement.

At first light, I was woken up sharply by the sound of moving furniture. When I asked my mother what was going on, she grunted, 'Pack your things, we're moving'. I packed what little I had left; by that stage, I struggled to fill a shoebox. My mother refused to say where we were going. However, it was not rocket science; even though I chose not to believe it, I knew precisely where we were headed. When we reached the end of our journey, Conan and his family were waiting at the door to meet us. That was one welcome party I could have done without.

ALONE IN THE DARK

My life had become a sequence of déjà-vu events. History tended to repeat itself over and over and over again like an old-fashioned record stuck in a groove and there seemed to be nothing I could do to break the cycle.

The one small piece of luck was that Conan's house was large – large enough for me to avoid him and his sad-faced, timid wife for the most part. I later discovered that the ostentatious house had been purchased from the proceeds of his heroin dealing and activities as a pimp, which constituted what passed for a job in his case. My mother and Conan's wife were overly polite to each other. Both of them seemed keen to avoid causing Conan any annoyance; wise behaviour given the barbarian's hair-trigger temper. Meanwhile Conan strutted around like a peacock among its hens.

At the time that this strange living arrangement commenced, I had just started at a new school. It was within close proximity to the small apartment, which made it convenient. After we moved in with Conan, commuting to school suddenly became an ordeal; it was a journey which entailed two buses and a train, and the total trip took several hours each way.

Once I was at school, I mostly kept to myself. The school itself could only be described as a jungle, as it was common practice for the vast majority of students to act like animals who had to validate their existence by beating each other senseless; this ritual would determine who was the biggest thug. The victor would then strut around the schoolyard as if he were a hero. This being the case, I was mindful to seclude myself; I avoided interaction with just about everyone but it became increasingly difficult to go unnoticed. I had Conan to thank for that, because every day when I arrived home from school, Conan would smack me around for 'sport', until he got bored. Apparently, my mother was attracted to the kind of man who enjoyed this kind of activity. In my secret journal, I ran a tally of the beatings and measured Conan's up against my father's in a weird sort of league table. However, there was no doubt that the fact that the barbarian, being a virtual stranger to me and therefore having even less right to lay a hand on me than my father, added salt to the mental wounds I was receiving in addition to the physical.

When I arrived at school with cuts and bruises on my face, the students must have drawn the conclusion that I appeared to be an easy target as someone had already done half the job for them and that resulted in the beatings once again occurring on a daily basis, at home and at school. The larger students would always coordinate the incidents in such a way as to ensure as many students as possible would witness them pounding me into the pavement with their fists and feet. I believe their intention was to yield the maximum amount of embarrassment and exposure thus rendering them heroes in their own minds. It began to dawn on me that there was a predominance of students attending the school, who were in fact, mentally impaired in some way. I could find no other motivation for such deeds. Had I been sent to a 'special' school?

After a few months of having attended the school, I grew accustomed to the beatings, until one day when I was in the schoolyard, doing my best to mind my own business; I was confronted by an abnormally large student. He insisted on beating the crap out of me for no perceptible reason. For that noteworthy occurrence, the thug didn't even have spectators to gratify. My lip split open and I bled on my school uniform. In order to avoid more humiliation, I left school ahead of schedule and did not tell anyone what had happened. Come to think of it; I did not actually have anyone to tell. I sat in a park not far from the school and when the school day ended, I returned home. Conan was anticipating my arrival, as my mother had been notified by the school that I had absented myself from the afternoon session, and she had deemed it necessary to involve the barbarian.

Upon my walking into the house, the barbarian grabbed me and began to beat me unmercifully. Sure, I had taken a lot of beatings in my life but it was different this time; he showed no restraint at all; it was almost as if he wanted to finish me off. Conan hit me in the head so many times that I could hardly even feel the blows any more. He must have prepared earlier, because out of nowhere he grabbed a chain and wrapped it around his fist. I felt like he was smashing every bone in my body when he introduced the chain. Conan eventually got tired of wielding the chain and started to lose his breath; however, he did not let that stand in his way. He commenced kicking me with his steel-toed boots as a substitute.

That was the most I had ever bled during a beating in my entire life. He had no right whatsoever to lay a finger on me, he simply took it upon himself to serve out what he and my mother believed to be justice. The image of my mother standing there and cheering him on, with a euphoric look on her face, was truly haunting. One might think that I would have expected her to act that way by that stage or perhaps I may even have become accustomed to it, but I would have to say that it did not get any easier witnessing it. The punishment went on for over an hour; my blood splattered across the walls of the room and my clothes were drenched in even more blood and sweat. After a while, Conan began running out of ways to injure me, so he picked up my desk lamp and smashed it into my head, the long fluorescent tube inside exploded and the little pieces of glass cut up my entire face. He then picked me up by my neck and pinned me to the wall and shouted, 'I'll make sure you die an ugly death, just like your father did!' and I believed him. When he left the room to search for another weapon, followed by my mother who was eager to help, I used the opportunity to climb out of the window in my room and escape.

Once I was free, I ran as fast as my legs would take me until I reached the public phone booth two streets away. I figured I could call the police and they would help me. I told the police officer who answered the phone, 'I can't go back home because there's a man there who is trying to kill me!' The officer replied calmly, 'Stay where you are, a car will be at your location shortly'. There were two police officers in the car that arrived; one of them got out of the car, looked at the sorry state I was in and asked where I lived and who was trying to kill me. I provided the information; he climbed back into the car and after a short, whispered discussion with his fellow officer, opened the back door for me. Once in the car, they turned it around and headed back towards the house. I called out to the officers in the front seat, 'What happens now? If you take me home and leave, the man I escaped from is going to finish the job and kill me!' They ignored me completely.

We reached the house and they knocked on the door. I cowered behind them, as I was too afraid to face Conan, even in the presence of the police. Conan came to the door and saw the law enforcement standing there; oddly enough he appeared to be pleased, addressed both officers by their names and shook their hands. He then invited them in for a beverage. By some freak fluke it just so happened that the cops who came to take me back home were corrupt; not only that, but it looked like their particular brand of corruption took the form of being in business with the barbarian. I didn't like where this was going at all. I mean, out of all the fucked up things that could have happened. Conveniently, while still standing behind the crooked cops, the whole situation became crystal clear. I turned around and sprinted off into the darkness; one of the cops was about to run after me when I heard Conan call out, 'Don't worry about him – he won't get far; I'll deal with him later'.

With that dire prediction of my future in mind, I must have pelted along for an hour until I eventually ran out of breath. I stopped at a miniature park, which was situated between two houses. I searched the park for a suitable space in which to hide from view but I ended up choosing the lone park bench, as there was nothing better on offer. I was still bleeding and feeling so cold as it was getting late. I was inappropriately dressed for winter, which did not help matters either. I took cover under the bench for the entire night, trembling uncontrollably due to the cold but moreover the fear.

THE TURNING

While under the park bench, something happened to me. The memories of an eternity of abuse came flooding back to me in one big broiling pile and they had some adverse effects.

My heart grew colder and darker than the night itself. I stopped shaking as a deadly calm spread through my body and I understood with a piercing clarity what I had to become in order to survive what humankind had in store for me. As my body ceased to shake, my eyes became bleak and unforgiving; at that instant, I was in a position where no man or thing could ever hurt me again, because there was nothing left to take. From then on, I was devoid of emotion apart from the overpowering feelings of rage and fury. That night was the turning point for me. I was reborn as hell on earth, in the form of a man. I turned my back on the world and everything in it; my new philosophy was; if I wanted it, I took it, if I felt like it, I did it – and fuck the consequences. It was as if a huge weight had been lifted off my back and shoulders yet at the same time something felt off; putrid. It was as if an evil force had taken control of me and would not let go.

In the morning, I walked back to the house, relishing the luxury of walking slowly, almost sauntering because I no longer had to move for anyone except myself. The sensation of freedom was powerful. I waited until everyone had left the house then kicked the door open, as I had never been given a key. I collected what I thought would be essential for my survival living in the streets and packed it into my school bag. In an effort to rinse the blood, sweat and dirt off I had a shower and then patched up my injuries as best as I could in the little time I had. I realised I needed money and turned the place upside down searching, although it was not a very lucrative exercise. I left home with twenty-three dollars in my pocket, my school uniform, and one other change of clothes.

I arrived at school a little late that day but managed to sneak in and got to class as usual. At lunchtime, the standard harassment commenced. A burly student walked towards me determinedly and judging from the expression on his face he had only one intention – to beat the crap out of me. Without wavering or even thinking, I clocked that motherfucker square in the face, breaking his nose in the process. I dragged him by his hair into the toilets and repeatedly smashed his mouth onto the edge of a toilet bowl until I broke almost every one of his teeth. While he was lying on the floor bleeding, I removed a compass I had stowed in my pocket earlier in the day, and jammed the pointy end into his nose and used the needle to pull him to his feet, also to ensure I had his full attention. I looked him in the eye and told him, 'If you so much as look at me the wrong way ever again, I will kill you, but only after I've followed you home and massacred your entire family. You have my word on that!' He started crying like a little bitch; I slapped him in the face and ordered him to get out of my sight.

I calmly washed his blood off my hands. I felt serene, as if nothing at all untoward had happened; my heart rate did not even increase slightly. Most people would have regarded that incident as a psychotic frenzy; however, I did not. I saw it as a moment of clarity, and it was truly cathartic. As an additional benefit, my foe had made the necessary arrangements to ensure his friends would bear witness to the entire event. What made it even sweeter was the fact that they had run off to call others to the show, rather than helping him. They were too late; as I had concluded my business by the time the would-be spectators had started to arrive.

For the first time in forever, I was privileged to experience the entirely unfamiliar feeling of 'dignity'. I deemed respect by all and fear by many. The positive outcome to that event was that I was finally left alone and free from abuse. That being as it was, I still had another issue to contend with, as when school had finished for the day, I was officially homeless. I was not sure what to do so I walked the streets for hours. I ended up back at a park, which was not far from the school and made camp there; I unavoidably ended up sleeping on the park bench.

As time went on, hiding the fact that I was residing on the streets from the teachers and fellow students started to become an issue as I was losing weight due to malnourishment and I was beginning to smell. After a few days, I stopped worrying that my mother would come looking for me or contact the school. I should have known that I would be the last thing on her mind; all she cared about was her suspect relationship with Conan. No doubt she was happy that I was not there to mess it up.

Around this time I struck up a friendship with another loner in my class, a student named Richard, who I found somewhat fascinating. From what I could tell, he was living the ideal life where everything he needed or wanted was provided by his parents. It wasn't so much his apparently perfect existence, it was more his loving family life I envied; it was something that I had always wanted and, frustratingly, he did not recognise the value of what he had. Richard was continually glum and discontented and constantly sought out criminal activity, as some kind of rebellion I suppose. Ironically, I would never have set a foot wrong if I were in his position, as I would have given anything to have a family that offered that level of care and support. Their largesse, however, did not extend beyond their beloved son. They were tight arses and made it very clear that I would only be tolerated in their abode for a couple of hours at a time. I was certainly not permitted to take such liberties as eating a snack or taking a shower; even though it must have been glaringly obvious that I was desperately in need of both.

Richard's house was near the park in which I was living. I hung out with him in order to pass the time. We spent most evenings at the local billiards room; it was called 'Joe's'. The place was a total shithole – dirty as hell, the air smelled like cat urine, the floorboards were so dusty it was impossible to tell what colour they were under the dirt, and the toilets looked like they had never been cleaned. But it did have the essentials: pool tables, lots of arcade machines and a jukebox which had an outstanding assortment of music. The worthy member of society who ran the place had no scruples about allowing two, obviously underage boys, the run of the place. Richard would typically go home after a few hours; however, I stayed behind and played pool with the locals until they all left. I would then play video games until the place closed, as it gave me shelter from the cold. I became adept at appearing to be a normal boy whilst in social situations, but the reality was that I was still extremely undernourished and homeless.

It became a habit for me to make a beeline for Joe's after school, but one time, Richard stopped me and insisted that I accompany him to the local cemetery. When we arrived, two other people I had never seen before were waiting. One of the guys offered me a cigarette, 'Sure why not?' I said and took one. That was my first ever smoke and not a day has gone by since then without at least one packet of cigarettes going into my lungs. Richard then started to prepare some weed in order to smoke it. He asked me, 'Do you want to smoke with us?' I told Richard, 'As much as I would like to, I don't have the money to chip in for it'. Richard replied, 'No problem, I'll take care of it'. They rolled eight joints and gave me two of them; I smoked both of them but I did not feel affected in any way. Richard assured me, 'Don't worry; you never feel anything the first time'. I was puzzled as to why he would have wasted his weed on me knowing that it would have no effect, but as it turned out, he was only just getting into it himself and was on the lookout for a smoking buddy. As they smoked and got progressively more stoned, they became talkative and inadvertently divulged a great deal of information about the drug trade in my school. They gave up the names of every single student who attended the school who smoked pot or had ever taken any other drug; I was surprised to learn that there were so many. I was totally engrossed in what was being said; I sat back and listened, all the while committing every single word to memory.

A NEW DEALER IN TOWN

Suddenly I knew what had to be done and precisely how I was going to do it. Later that night I returned to Joe's, where I remembered seeing a busted Wonder Boy in Monster Land tabletop arcade machine. I sat next to the machine and covered the damaged coin slot with my school bag. Fortuitously, Joe was in the back room, where he tended to his illegal gambling racket most evenings. I slid the coins out of the machine little by little into the bag, the whole time being careful not to draw any attention to myself. The first part of my plan had gone off without a hitch, and I walked away with a little over one hundred dollars in my bag.

As soon as I got to school the next day I sought out a student who, after the revelations in the cemetery, I now knew to be a recognised dealer. He sold me a quarter of an ounce of weed, which was all I could afford at the time. I found an unoccupied classroom and broke up the weed into approximately one-gram deals, using the torn-out pages of a schoolbook to package them. Within an hour I had doubled my money, thanks to the list of potential clients which Richard and his friends had unwittingly provided me.

As soon as I had offloaded the last package, I went straight back to my supplier and purchased twice as much, which doubled my money yet again. Over the next few days, I repeated the process several times and ended up walking away with over fifteen hundred bucks and some leftover gear, otherwise known by the authorities as cannabis. I came up with a menu of exotic and enticing sounding names for the weed, such as Scandinavian Red, Botswana Blast and Peruvian Gold, which went down very well with the clientele. It didn't take me long to figure out that I would make more profit by attaining higher volumes. It was all about buying power; the more you buy, the cheaper it gets; as simple as that. As my venture expanded, the money problem rapidly started to dissipate.

I no longer slept hungry on the park bench at night; I checked myself into a motel and ordered some real food as an alternative to starving outside in the cold, which had begun to lose its attraction somewhat. I tell you, I ate like a king the first night I came in from the cold; a Domino's pizza had never tasted so good! I had a long, hot shower, watched some television and finally got some much-needed rest. I had not slept much while in the park; my mind had always been preoccupied with the question of where I was going to find food and better shelter.

I took my start-up dealership very seriously and threw my heart and soul into it because there was no conceivable way on earth I was ever going back to living on the streets. I couldn't help but expand the business rapidly as the trade was continually gaining momentum on its own. I modified my buying pattern to better accommodate a much larger clientele. This involved bypassing my original supplier but as my new supplier happened to be his father, he was unable to complain or make my life difficult in any way. It must have been my winning charm because I took over the entire trade in the school. I started to branch off into other schools through client referrals, which was surprising since I had only been in business for a week!

Four months later, by the time the Christmas holiday season came around, the business was doing exceptionally well and I bought my brother an exceedingly costly and elaborate gift for Christmas. I snuck in and gave it to him when Conan and the others were out of the house. He must have shown my mother because she suddenly wanted to reach out and talk to me, which struck me as anomalous, as she had never shown any concern about my welfare before! When she caught wind of what I was doing and the fact that large sums of cash were involved, she immediately decided that it would be such a good idea if we all moved back in with each other. I figured it must have been because Conan's wife was sick and tired of my mother freeloading off her husband.

This worked out favourably because I already had a location in mind and was just about to make the necessary arrangements to move into the two-storey rental property on my own – I had discovered that flashing bundles of banknotes around, miraculously removed any niggling doubts a real estate agent might have about renting to a minor. The place I selected was intentionally located between the supplier from whom I purchased my gear and the school. Before we even had a chance to settle in, my mother started with the leeching; she was extracting money from me as if I were an automated teller machine. She persistently needed money for provisions to apparently feed a small- to medium-sized army, despite the fact that I always ate out. I had the bills and rent covered in addition to any other expenditure that may have occurred. I endeavoured to comprehend what she could possibly have needed so much money for, as she was always dressed like a vagabond and never attended any events, socially or otherwise that would have required that level of funding. She had a full-time job as a shop assistant. I did not mind handing over the cash, as I had more than enough to go around. That being as it may, my mother eventually felt that the money I was giving her was insufficient, and rather than asking for additional funds, she simply helped herself. She must have spent a very long time searching, as she managed to discover the extremely well concealed location where the cash and the gear were stashed.

My mother was conscious of what I was doing; however, as long as the cash kept coming in, she didn't care. When it came to my attention that I was being robbed, I made the mistake of confronting my mother. As usual she became defensive and started shouting at me, then picked up the telephone and reported me to the police. I disposed of everything that had been on the premises just in the nick of time because the police arrived at record speed. I hid everything underneath the neighbour's house, because I figured the police wouldn't search neighbouring houses without sufficient cause. Fortunately my theory was correct, as the search ended up being a comprehensive waste of their very valuable time. Even though I eluded the police on that occasion, I could not ignore the fact that they now knew about me and where I operated from. Due to my mother's vindictive and spiteful nature, I no longer had the luxury of having my clients come to me because shortly after she ratted me out, I was placed under police surveillance.

But as I had a business to run, I wasn't about to let a minor detail like police surveillance hinder my progress. If I could not have my clients come to me, I would go to them. The problem with my plan was that my client base had expanded to such an extent, that I could not possibly have serviced all of them using conventional modes of transportation.

New Wheels

I made my way to a local prestige motorcycle dealership. Upon entering the showroom, I was not approached by a single salesperson; in fact, I found it difficult to get anyone's attention – it was almost as if they were intentionally ignoring me. I assumed that it must have had something to do with my age and appearance as I was rather young and had not shaved or had a haircut for a while; both of these items being somewhat low on my list of priorities at that time. I wanted some assistance, so I decided to attract attention to myself; I walked over and started manhandling the most expensive sports bike they had in the showroom. It worked because the staff finally sent a trainee salesperson over to assist me. I pointed to the bike that I had been fondling and asked, 'Do you have anything better than this?'

He looked at me with a blank, glazed-over expression and replied, 'I'll have to go and check sir'. He came back with a brochure, handed it to me and said, 'All the information you need is in this.

I answered, 'Look man, I want the highest-performance machine you have got and I'm not really bothered about the price. Is this bike it?' I pointed to the bike in question again.

'Hang on', he answered and went back to consult with one of the senior salespersons yet again, who, this time around, started to laugh out loud; I could hear it clearly from where I stood.

When the trainee returned he told me, 'That is the best motorcycle available on the market but it is very expensive; maybe I can show you something else?'

I said, 'I only have two more questions for you; firstly, do you have one I can take now? And my second question is, do you accept cash?' I took the bag off my shoulder and removed a few rolls of banknotes from it. The salesperson who had been laughing, now looked like he was going to fall over; he ran across the showroom like a fool and with a fawning tone to his voice exclaimed, 'I overheard you asking about that bike, let me show you'.

I stopped him abruptly and said, 'Can you do me a favour and get the fuck out of my face? Now you want to talk to me, you mutt!' I gave the original salesperson the money and I tipped him a hundred for trying his utmost to help me out. I rode the bike out of the showroom doors and roared away along the highway.

I was worried that just having the highest-performing standard motorcycle was not going to give me a large enough advantage over the heavily modified and powerful police vehicles. I wanted enough power to make escaping a walk in the park. I took the bike to a performance workshop and had them make a few modifications. Even though the modifications cost as much as the bike itself, I felt that the money spent was justified. I also had the workshop fit the motorcycle with a sophisticated remote starting system, which was perfect for a quick getaway. The system also featured a small pager that was built into the remote, which could detect and inform me if someone attempted to mess with the bike.

Having taken delivery of the fully enhanced bike, I paid a visit to the school janitor at his home. He was an elderly Italian who always did his best to carry out his job without getting in anybody's way. The students who attended the school made his job difficult as they constantly ridiculed him because of the clothes he wore; being the halfwits that they were. They assumed that he was a peasant just because of the way he dressed. I found that behaviour to be acutely distasteful, as I knew precisely what having nothing entailed.

Contrary to popular practice, I spent a lot of time conversing with the janitor and getting to know him. In time, I came to learn that he was a genius with electronics, in addition to being a qualified engineer. When I arrived at the janitor's home, I was blown away because he appeared to be living an extravagant lifestyle in a luxurious mansion! Later, when he had attained total trust in me, he confided that he had been an engineer in Germany and had spent many years working for BMW – apparently a very lucrative gig. He instructed me to ride the bike into his workspace, then he poured me a scotch, handed me a cigarette and said, 'Watch some television while I do this for you, because I can't focus if you are watching me work'. He installed several hidden compartments on the motorcycle as well as a system that swiftly rotated the number plate.

Of course it was prohibited for students to ride a motorcycle to school, which ultimately resulted in the purchase of a car. I didn't allow minor issues such as being under driving age spoil my plans to acquire suitable wheels. I knew that the sensible thing to do was to stay low and fly under the radar but I could not help myself. I went out and purchased a showstopper of a car. It was a '69 Mustang Fastback which was powered by a Jet 428 ram air V8 from the sixties, which caused a commotion and consumed ridiculous amounts of fuel whenever it moved. To make matters worse, it was bright orange, fixed with hydraulics and looked like a race car that had been modified for street use. I may as well have painted *DRUG DEALER INSIDE* across the doors. The car and the bike started to attract a lot of unwelcome attention.

GREEN-EYED MONSTERS

The school I attended was private. I was often called into the principal's office querying as to when my mother would settle the school fees of which she had absolutely no intention. Ultimately, I ended up having to offload a stash of my money to the principal to keep him happy. It worked.

The school was great for business because the majority of the students had parents who were cashed up to the teeth – although at times having to pay attention to those spoiled brats was torturous. The situation worsened when I began driving to school because I was challenged to a race by just about everyone. They wanted to race me either in their families' station wagons or in overly expensive sports cars that their mothers had bought them for their birthdays – with the safety factor being foremost in their minds. I did not see the point in accepting any of the challenges as the car I owned was designed to win races and the cars they were driving were designed to pick up groceries. But there was one time where I agreed to one particularly persistent and annoying challenger's request to race. If I had known that there was a massive ritual involved, I probably would have turned the challenger down on the spot. I had instructions to meet up with the other driver in an industrial area out west. When I arrived, I was a little surprised and very confused as he had arranged a large crowd to watch the event. It was a shame because he did not get his money's worth; the race itself only lasted a few seconds. We lined up the cars and raced the quarter mile. When I crossed the finish line, the other driver was less than halfway down the stretch. I did not stop when I crossed the finish line – I kept on going and went straight home.

Trying to muster up any form of respect for my fellow students was an ordeal as most of them were ill-mannered, arrogant, selfish and so full of shit that they needed to hang a cup on their ass just to catch overflow. I had – and still have – very little time or patience for people who are crap talkers. It bothered me in ways that are almost, too multi-faceted to comprehend but one reason I felt the way I did, was because not one single person in that school, understood the concept of truly doing it tough, while they spoke as if they could write a book on the subject. None of them had ever had to put their life on the line just to put food on the table; the largest concern they had was what colour car they were going to have their mummy buy them. Paradoxically I was overwhelmed at times and made the mistake of confiding in the occasional student and sharing something about my life. In most cases, it resulted in my words being twisted and turned into lies. The new version of what I had allegedly said, would then be used to insult and belittle me for the purpose of making the person I trusted in the first place, feel better about their pitiable, monotonous, bug-like, sad excuse for a life.

Something that confirmed my presumption about Richard being a mindless sheep without any form of identity, personality or imagination, was the fact that, only days after I had purchased my motorcycle, Richard made his mother go out and buy him the exact same model. Even though he was an outright pansy for letting his mother purchase his motorcycle, he still managed to walk around with his head held high. I overlooked the lack of testicles and rode with him nonetheless. I just wanted to hone my riding skills and who I did it with was irrelevant.

Richard ramped up the amount of drugs he was using, as did I. We also started experimenting by mixing different drugs together, just to see what the effects were. All the while, we spent every free moment riding all over the country, crossing into neighbouring states and pushing our boundaries a little more each day.

Richard and a few other junkies from the neighbourhood became permanent fixtures in my house. They were there for the free ride as I provided limitless free drugs and food. In hindsight, I realise this was a very one-sided arrangement as I was prohibited from entering any of their homes by both my hangers-on and their parents, let alone eating and taking drugs which they had paid for. At first, I ignored the fact that I was clearly being used by the group as they continued to come to my home every single day; trashing the place in the process. There would leave an enormous mess that I would have to tend to when they eventually left; they typically stayed until way past midnight and sometimes until dawn. I began to feel as though I was paying too high a price to have friends.

FELLOW MOBSTERS

As time went on the money kept systematically rolling in and consequently, I caught the attention of a fellow drug dealer who attended the same school as I did; his name was Sam. He was a hardcore junkie and at first glance appeared to be criminally insane. He gained a huge amount of pleasure, almost to the level of ecstasy, out of constantly plotting new felonies. Like Richard, Sam had scored a decent family who would have done anything for him. This bewildered me; it did not make any sense at all that someone would throw away a normal life in order to pursue one of corruption and crime by choice. I found his actions to be particularly perplexing because, although he did not have any motivation or probable cause; he was both compelled and fully committed to the felonies he executed. On the other hand, Sam's networking skills were impressive as he was affiliated with a good number of the heavyweights in the industry, and he was diligent and focused when it came to making new connections.

When Sam initially approached me, his pitch went something like this, 'I think that if we combined our efforts, we can take what we do to a whole new level'. I was dubious about his proposal as I knew that if something sounded 'too good to be true', it usually was. Nevertheless, when business began to plateau somewhat, I started to consider it, and providing I proceeded with caution, Sam may have something of value to offer. As it turned out, I was mistaken to have hesitated, because the impact of dealing with Sam was instantaneous. It actually worked out just the way Sam had said it would; not only did we take the business to a whole new level, we monopolised the entire market, adding suburb after suburb to our domain, and destroying our competition – who never saw us coming – in the process. Within weeks, we had transformed what we had from a small business, into a smooth running organisation.

I took the time to meet the majority of Sam's contacts – which opened the door to a world of new opportunities – the more people I met the easier it was to make money. The realisation hit home that everyone always had something to sell and, at the same time, everyone was looking to buy.

The rules of the game had become unmistakable: I recognised that fear equalled respect, money equalled power, and the cardinal rule was, 'do not trust anyone – under any circumstances'. That rule was, for me, the hardest to follow, because the way I perceived it, if the world had reached a stage where no one could be trusted, I would have had to give up on humanity altogether. Unfortunately, the truth of the matter was that the world was already at that stage and, in order to survive, I could not afford to be any other way.

I met with Sam on a regular basis in order to discuss our strategies and plans for future developments within the business, although I was constantly distracted during our meetings because Sam would consume his drugs in a suicidal fashion. I would watch him smoke himself to oblivion; he would then throw a fistful of pills into his mouth and wash them all down with alcohol. Oddly, Sam appeared to be completely impervious to everything he ingested, as his behaviour was not affected in any way whatsoever. Richard would frequently come along to the meetings with me and we too would get high, although in our case, it was more of a recreational exercise.

Before long, Sam's attitude and temperament started to become of concern as, in addition to developing delusions of invincibility and grandeur, he became increasingly self-conceited. Even though I understood the astronomical risk involved in Sam's eccentric schemes, I still proceeded with them. However, we rarely agreed on the planning as Sam preferred to do the jobs spontaneously without any forethought as opposed to my approach of meticulously planning things out to perfection. I managed to talk him into seeing things my way every time, which probably saved his life on more occasions than I can even count. In no time flat, Sam, Richard and I were dedicated to a life of full-time crime.

STEPPING STONES

Our criminal professions started at the very bottom; we took any work that came our way in order to earn some recognition in the world of organised crime. In the early stages, we mainly specialised in motor vehicle insurance jobs. It did not take long to develop a good standing in that particular market; this was obvious from the number of requests to undertake insurance jobs, which increased drastically over a very short period. At first, we were considerably innovative and enthusiastic when it came to the demolition of the cars. In due course, we discovered that far less effort was involved in just dumping the cars in the local river and letting them sink to the bottom. However, the jobs had built up to such a degree that on one instance, when we took a car to the river in order to dispose of it, it failed to sink, as the river was full of previously-dumped cars! As a result, because the car was already submerged, we had to destroy the other half by setting fire to it.

As luck would have it, notwithstanding our strenuous efforts, the event that caused us to become notorious was entirely unintentional. I was at home smoking weed and playing video games with Richard one night – we were obsessed with Mortal Kombat – when we heard a disturbance in the street in front of the house; someone had pulled up in a loud car and was sounding the horn repeatedly. I immediately surmised that it was Sam 'on a high' – and probably in a stolen car – and ran outside, as I did not want to draw any unnecessary attention to the house. Richard followed close on my heels. When I got outside Sam was still beeping the horn. I requested that he 'shut the fuck up', as he was highlighting the fact that he was in a stolen vehicle and advertising my location at the same time. Sam acquiesced but I could see that he was revved up as he said, 'I have a big job lined up; do you want in?'

I replied, 'Sure, why not, I've got nothing better to do tonight anyway'. Richard was keen to join in the fun so we both jumped into the car. Once we had driven away, Sam confirmed that the car we were in was in fact stolen and that there were two additional cars that needed to be collected. I was impressed that he had managed to organise three jobs for the one night. We determined that it would be astute, and most interesting, to have a destruction derby in order to demolish all three cars simultaneously. It was entertaining while it lasted, although it did not last for very long. In fact, it was mental. We raced around in the car park of an industrial estate and, when we'd built up enough momentum, smashed the cars into each other, no holds barred. We kept doing it until there was only one car left standing. We all got into the surviving car, which was Sam's, and made our way towards the river where we were going to put it to rest. It was tricky to drive because the front wheels were slightly bent. We thought we would boost another car on the way as a contingency plan, just in case Sam's car broke down as it had taken a lot of damage. We had acquired a set of master keys from like-minded friends in the business that had been modified to open a large number of cars. As soon as we located a car that was compatible with the keys we had, Richard stuck the master key out of the window and attempted to put it in the keyhole. Immediately, a police siren chirped behind us, and the much-dreaded red and blue lights started flashing. We later established that it was just excruciating luck that the police had been on the spot. Fortunately, they had not noticed us earlier or witnessed the carnage at the industrial site.

We were obviously in agreement on what had to transpire next because we all hollered out, 'Drive the fucking car!' simultaneously. The chase was on; the police must have pursued us for close to an hour; calling on additional reinforcements. The only word I can use to describe Sam's driving that night is 'unrelenting'. Being apprehended was not an alternative as far as we were concerned. Regardless of the countless times we were surrounded; Sam somehow managed to elude the police, while performing miracles nursing the car. Surprisingly, the car held together at its top speed of 160 for the duration of the chase, which was remarkable; it had been on the verge of falling apart before the chase had even commenced. Law enforcement had to earn their pay that night, because we were making them work very hard. The more we resisted, the more cars the police would despatch; it was bordering on ridiculous. At one stage, we had seven vehicles in pursuit of us concurrently.

Richard jumped out of the car while it was still in motion, in an effort to escape on foot. I attempted to do the same, although the rear doors were jammed shut because the exterior of the car was badly damaged. I was swinging around in the back of the car, when Sam eventually turned into a dead-end street. Sam also fled the car before it had come to a stop, which did not work in my favour at all, as I was in the back of a moving car, minus a driver. I attempted to climb into the driver's seat in order to get hold of the steering wheel, but I did not make it in time, as I had run out of road and the car had collided with two large metal posts, causing me a few minor cuts and bruises. I opened the door closest to the curb and while trying to sneak out, heard a voice behind me shout in a movie-like tone, 'Freeze!' The police officer sounded as though he was extraordinarily pleased with himself.

Two more officers rushed past me while I was being handcuffed to the car door, then the one who had been dealing with me left me unattended in order to assist the other two officers. For cops they were not what I would call lateral thinkers, because I was left alone with access to tools that were in the car. I used them to rapidly disassemble the car door and break free; however, I did not get very far. Just as I made a run for it, a police car came out of nowhere and stopped an inch away from me. Two officers leapt out of the car and one snarled, 'Get down on the ground now!' They handcuffed my hands behind my back, picked me up by the handcuffs and threw me into the back of the paddy wagon with excessive force.

I would not accept the fact that I had been captured, so I proceeded to look for a way to break out, although my efforts proved to be in vain. They left me waiting in the back of the paddy wagon for the better part of an hour; a police officer eventually opened the door and declared, 'We found your black friend!' to which I replied, 'You are obviously gifted, and deserve a medal for it', but I was thinking to myself that it was odd, as no one in the car with me had been black. Another police officer arrived with Sam in tow and threw him in with me. Sam's face was covered in dirt and scratches and was black as though it had been pounded into the ground. A few minutes went by when the door opened yet again and they threw Richard in with us. They had apparently located him while he was attempting to hail a taxi. For the duration of our journey to the station we did not say a single word to each other. However, there was an air of disillusionment in the paddy wagon that night, as we felt defeated. I don't think any of us had actually considered the fact that we could be arrested.

At the police station we were fingerprinted and our paperwork was processed. Once the formalities were over, we were escorted to separate interview rooms. Prior to the interrogation, a detective walked into the room, presented me with a pen and notepad, and instructed me to write a statement; meanwhile, he prepared an antique-like recording apparatus; probably a polygraph. The detective then proceeded to ask me a series of questions to which I did not respond; neither did I pick up the pen. I maintained my silence for the duration of the interrogation because I had no intention of cooperating. They were persistent. In time, they resorted to deception and coercion, although they clearly did not have any sort of set strategy. They endeavoured to persuade me to believe that Sam and Richard were in the next rooms alleging that I was the mastermind who had prearranged everything that had happened that night. I knew that there was not even a remote prospect that they would have ever contemplated such an act. I knew this to be true, because Sam's ambition would not allow it and Richard did not have the balls to face us if we were ever to find out. Besides, we were working our rings off in a mammoth effort to build our reputations in order to move up the ladder of organised crime. If they had ratted me out that early in the game, it would have been over before it had even begun, which was a risk none of us were prepared to take.

I eventually wore out their patience because they hauled me out of the interrogation room and hurled me into a holding cell. Then one of the cops noticed the motif on the back of my sweat-shirt which read, *FUCK THE POLICE* in large, red letters. It was the title of a popular NWA song. I was a fan of them at the time. Apparently, the police were not fans of that particular group because they did not appreciate the slogan at all. The cop asked, 'What is this supposed to be?' I replied, 'Look man, I did not make the shirt, I bought it like this'. He must have taken it personally, as he called out to some of his colleagues to come into the cell, in order to ask their opinions about the shirt. What happened next was unexpected; they threw me to the ground and kicked the crap out of me, being mindful not to hit me in the face or anywhere visible so they would not leave any marks that they would have to explain later. They focused their attacks predominantly on my back, the back of my head and my ribs; it was an outstanding example of police brutality at its finest.

We were remanded to appear in court only a week later, and we did. We were charged as adults even though we were juvenile offenders; below the age limit to be tried by such means. I made the crucial mistake of allowing legal aid to represent me, as I was inexperienced at the time and did not recognise the value of a good lawyer. However, Sam and Richard's parents hired them the best lawyers they could afford, which helped their cases substantially. My so-called legal representation clearly demonstrated by his demeanour that he believed I was guilty, and requested that the sentence be delivered promptly, almost as though he had somewhere more important to be. The judge doled out my sentence as though he was handing out chocolates; I was convicted and as a result, ended up with a permanent criminal record, two years of probation and was ordered by the court to no longer have any contact with Sam or Richard.

A few days after the court cases were finalised, I overheard some banter between a few of the students in the schoolyard; they were recounting an alternate version of the events that had purportedly occurred on the night that we were arrested. I approached the students who were telling the tale and pressed them to enlighten me as to who was the source of their 'misinformation'. They informed me that Sam had told them the fable and that they were not the only ones who had heard it. Sam had apparently told the story to just about anyone who would pay attention to him. In Sam's version of the events, he was a self-proclaimed superhero of sorts and in his fantasy, Richard and myself were a hindrance to him and the reason he ultimately got pinched. The fact that Sam had told these stories was a real eye-opener; however, I did not confront him about what he had been saying, as we were making too much money together and I wanted business to proceed as usual. As for the court's ruling about staying away from Sam, my response was, screw the court – they weren't going to put food on the table. I decided that rocking the boat at that point would have been pointless and a detriment to my trade. My philosophy was the exact opposite to that of Sam's; my priority was to remain below the radar and I tried to be invisible to everyone outside of the industry because I knew my survival absolutely depended on it. On the other hand, Sam was on a mission to become famous; he would stop at nothing to achieve celebrity status, which made me very nervous.

THE NEXT LEVEL

Bearing Sam's actions in mind, it did not take me long to re-evaluate my business and concluded that it would be an entrepreneurially savvy idea to upgrade what I was doing, to cater for a more respectable and mature clientele. However, therein lay the conundrum – I did not have the funding that was required to break into that market, because the product cost an absolute fortune. The idea of dealing with more reputable clients was very appealing to me as my experiences of dealing with deadbeats and time wasters were starting to become rather tiresome.

A solution presented itself one night when we were at Sam's house doing our typical thing. The usual suspects – the regulars who we did business with, drug dealers, car thieves, large people who specialised in personal security, basically an assortment of criminals – sat in the backyard at a hefty table near the swimming pool and smoked weed while everyone discussed money-making concepts and schemes. Suddenly, the mother of all ideas popped into my head. I believed what I had come up with was a stroke of pure brilliance; the key that would give me the funding I required to upgrade my business post-haste. I announced my idea to the group; without any hesitation I said, 'We are going to rob a bank'. As expected, Sam and Richard laughed at me and Sam said, 'You should slow down on the drugs, because they are rotting your brain'. However, once I had explained the concept, everyone went dead quiet – to such an extent that I could almost hear them blink. Sam quickly changed his tune and told me, with admiration in his voice, 'What happens inside your mind is truly scary; you're an evil man'.

My idea was sure to be a successful one for the reason that it was not a bank robbery, per se. Bank robberies evoke images of men wearing the proverbial balaclavas, clutching guns and yelling, 'Fill the bag!' The way I saw it, that idea had been thoroughly thrashed and having to deal with the security and all the bullshit would have been too much of a hassle. I figured, that rather than going into the bank itself, we would emphatically target selected business owners when they took their takings to the bank at the end of the week. It took a lot of surveillance and a relatively large crew but I knew the ends would justify the means.

The operations, in their entirety, were always planned to perfection and with great precision, right down to the most infinitesimal detail. Most of the useful input to the plans was down to me – it was my area of expertise. We used three independent cars; two of which were stolen and 'prepared' beforehand. Each vehicle was inspected meticulously for mechanical defects by our own specialty mechanic – who also happened to be one of our drivers – his name was Hammer. If Hammer did not give the vehicle his approval, we would acquire another one instead, because the cars needed to be in the best possible condition in the event of a police pursuit – we had certainly learnt our lesson on that one, the brutal way. Hammer was always the driver of the first car, as his driving skills were the most impressive I had ever come across. It took a notable effort to just try and describe what Hammer could make a car do.

The foremost reason that Hammer was the nominated driver for the first car was due to the fact that it was the vehicle used for the initial part of the heist, which made having a skilled driver paramount for our escape. The basic plan itself was not overly complex; we would keep cover and wait until the mark arrived with the money. Once the perfect opportunity presented itself, we would send our fastest runner to snatch the bag or briefcase and bring it back to the car. Hammer would then drive the car to a predetermined location, which he was briefed on only moments before the job started. Meanwhile, two of us would clandestinely follow them from a distance in an above-board vehicle; we would monitor Hammer and the runner as a precautionary measure, just in case they had any sudden notions of keeping the money for themselves. Once Hammer had arrived at the location, a second stolen car would be waiting for him; the second car would typically not have to travel a long distance before reaching its final destination, which was a safe house that only Sam, Richard and I knew of. The first car would be soaked in fuel and destroyed once the money had already started its journey in the second car with Sam, Richard or I as the driver. We would meet at the safe house and allocate the money immediately after the job. We all agreed that it was the only way to do it, as it did not leave any room for finger pointing or conflict at a later stage. Having said that, there was always more than enough to go around, and we were very generous when it came to paying the runners, the drivers or any supplementary staff we may have recruited.

Everything was beautiful that summer and I felt like a giant, I mean I was living proof that crime does pay, and I couldn't imagine doing things any other way. I hadn't opened my journal in a long while and had the urge to write and record all that was happening; it felt good. We were all making more money than we had ever seen, and we did not even break a sweat doing it. We'd make reservations at the most expensive restaurants for the core group and a few key players from the heist and go there in order to celebrate our triumphs over a large meal and drinks. This became a ritual and we eventually become so confident in our abilities to pull off the jobs that we started to book the restaurant before we had arranged for the heist itself! However, the entire operation inevitably ended.

It all collapsed, largely, due to Sam's idiocy. Despite my numerous attempts to advise Sam against bringing new people in on the operation, he maintained that it would be the best course of action. His reasoning was that we would no longer have to misuse our time managing each job ourselves, and as a result, we would be able to direct our time and resources into other bigger and better projects. I, on the other hand, did not regard what we were doing as a waste of time, because it was securing some major cash. Sadly, it all turned out just as I had predicted. The whole operation turned to shit and it was truly a shemozzle; people were getting caught everywhere. It was not long before the police honed in on how the entire process worked and it was over. Sam, Richard and I got out of it and terminated all of our connections with everyone who was involved, just in time.

In a way, it was comical to watch the little punks and street gang members whom Sam had recruited, actually take the credit for all the bank hits and go to prison for it. They were sent away for a very long time, even when they had only done a few jobs. The group that Sam had hand-picked clearly must have had the mental capacity of rocks. They were more than happy to be arrested merely to get noticed by their fellow imbeciles; they were trying to live out the lyrics of a rap song, or some sort of fantasy, which existed exclusively in their minds.

The only one of the core group that the police could link anything back to was Sam. He'd left himself open when he had recruited his crack team of intellectually- challenged thugs. I stayed completely off the radar, as I had insisted on not meeting with any of them in person. Richard was also safe, because at that stage he had drifted away from the action somewhat and was starting to settle down; he had become more interested in the drugs and mind-reduction pills, and had no interest in the money as he didn't really need it. I urged Sam to get out of town for a while; at least until the investigation had subsided. In the end, we all headed up the coast, where we stayed for a few weeks.

Ecstasy was already becoming a prominent portion of Sam's business by the time we departed for the coast, and, once again, Sam's overwhelming desire to be a celebrity took over. He brought a very large bag of pills with him and immediately began distributing them to the local girls where we were staying, free of charge.

It was like déjà vu all over again as Sam started to attract unwanted attention. The resort where we were staying rapidly filled up with girls from all over the Central Coast; there were bikinis everywhere, and I mean everywhere – I even had bikinis turn up in my bar fridge. Now don't get me wrong – it was the place to be and I must confess it was like being in paradise but I had an idea in my mind and I needed to act on it without more ado. I got up at the ass crack of dawn, while I was as high as a kite, and rode back to Sydney.

I took advantage of the opportunity afforded by Sam's absence and concentrated on my strategy. Because of the success of all the bank jobs we had carried out, I now had the necessary funding required to accomplish my goal. I overhauled my entire business from the ground up. I needed somewhere impressive to set up my base of operations. I settled on the Sheraton on the Park as the hotel rooms were pretty pimped out, especially the executive suites, which has almost every facility you can think of and if there was something it didn't have, the concierge could get it for you. It overlooked Hyde Park but all that luxury came at a price; they charged like a wounded bull.

I checked in under the name of one of my clients; he was happy to let me use his name in exchange for some weed. It didn't take me long to set up the business and build a client base of lawyers, doctors and nurses mostly. However, in order to break into that particular market, it was a prerequisite that I upgraded the products that I sold, which meant stocking the white powders. In my case, they were meth amphetamines and cocaine. The transition performed instant wonders for my income; I immediately started securing more money than I had ever dreamt was possible. Along the way I had also made some new, valuable and serious connections; I found myself dealing with older men and women, who appeared to have been in the industry for their entire lives. That was exactly where I wanted to be at that point in time.

DICK-MEASURING CONTEST

At least a month had passed when I realised that I hadn't heard from Sam – nor had the rest of the crew for that matter. I tried calling him but his phone was switched off or was out of range. I decided to ride back up to the Central Coast and check on him personally, as I was concerned. I didn't want to spend a lot of time away from my new business but figured that I could spare just enough time to allay my fears about Sam's unusual silence. I rode up late at night in order to avoid traffic and law enforcement as I rode like a menace. When I arrived, I could not believe what I was seeing – Sam had occupied the entire resort; he had invited the majority of our associates to join him, in addition to a large number of people I had not met before. Each one of them was staying in a different room, mostly at Sam's expense; the local girls were walking in and out of the rooms in herds, looking the worse for wear – undomesticated and haggard. I sat down with Sam, and while we had a drink and caught up, I told him what I had been up to back in the city, which gave him an avaricious gleam in his eye and prompted him to pack up and return to Sydney with me the following night. I did not reveal my sources to him, as I had identified a beneficial opportunity: I supplied Sam with the new products, which increased my bulk purchase volumes and thus pushed my buy price down even further. The money just kept piling up.

Alas, the summer holidays ended and it was back-to-school time. Upon my return, I found myself in demand a great deal more, as I had become the 'go to' man for just about anything that anyone needed at the school in the field of recreational substances. As far as business was concerned, I was in direct competition with Sam; strangely, we were allies at the same time, if that makes any sense at all; friendly rivals, perhaps.

In order to get an edge and increase my market share, I diversified my business in the schoolyard. For a reasonable fee, I offered protection to students who were constantly being bullied. I would pass on a small portion of the takings to the bullies themselves, in exchange for their cooperation. I had not forgotten the bleak horror of my earlier schooldays when, as a victim, I had lurched from one bullying session to the next, and in some dark and private backstreet of my mind, I allowed myself to feel some pride in preventing the same damage being inflicted on others. Besides, the vast majority of the students I was protecting could more than afford to pay and the entrepreneur in me saw it as creating some goodwill, in that these same students would be more inclined to turn to me for their recreational supplies.

Apart from Sam, I was the only student in the entire school who owned a Skypager, which was the forerunner of a mobile telephone in those days. It was a tad inconvenient, as I would have to seek out a public telephone in order to respond to the messages but having one of those devices back then went hand-in-hand with being a drug dealer, it was iconic. I loved the sound of the electronic beeps that the pager would make, because the more it beeped, the more money I made.

Meanwhile, Sam's aspiration to be number one started rapidly shifting from rivalry to petulance. I remember once arriving at Sam's house and a few of the drug addicts who used to leech drugs and money off Sam, heard my motorcycle approaching and rushed outside. They could not wait to inform me that Sam had been popping pills all night long and one of them added, 'Your ears must be burning because you were the only topic of conversation all night'. According to the junkies, Sam was criticising how I ran my business and attacking me on a personal level to boot. Well aware of how these deadheads operated, I knew their only motive in telling me was simply to betray Sam, as they clearly did not think very highly of him, which was sad, as he had chosen those people to be his own private entourage. In my opinion, his actions did nothing more than highlight his lack of common sense, as he had confided in a pack of parasites, which had effectively jeopardised our relationship, while I was, to all intents and purposes, controlling more than half of his income.

I walked straight in and confronted Sam, demanding, 'What's this about you talking shit behind my back?' Sam didn't answer and strategically changed the subject. He told me how pleased he was with some performance modification he had evidently made to his car. I was feeling rather vindictive due to his unwarranted criticism of my business tactics, which influenced my decision to push his buttons a smidgen.

I bragged, 'The GT would tear the charger to pieces on the quarter mile; your car is a child's toy'. I didn't have to be a fortune teller to predict what would happen next. At first Sam recoiled and then he leapt to his feet and announced, 'Why don't you put your money where your mouth is!'

I retaliated with, 'Fuck it, why not. Five grand says I beat you down the quarter mile.' I honestly couldn't have cared less whether I won or lost; Sam on the other hand, was on some sort of mission to prove that he was the greatest.

Sam insisted that we raced on a busy road at dusk. I was not overly impressed with this idea, as the road on which he wanted to race had a substantial amount of traffic in the evenings, mainly featuring cars that were extremely bulky and heavy. With so much horsepower behind the vehicles with which we would be sharing the road, I had a lingering suspicion that it was all going to end badly. In hindsight, that was without a doubt, one of the more imprudent activities I have participated in, as it put the wellbeing of innocent people at risk.

Once the cars were in position, we started the race. The roar of the engines was deafeningly loud; the reek of burning tyres and fuel filled the car when I took off. The cars were evenly matched and we were neck and neck under full throttle, until we hit the halfway mark when a car came out of nowhere. Sam headed straight for it and had no alternative but to swerve in order to avoid it as the road barely had enough room for our two cars in the first place. Sam's tyres must have hit the curb, which caused his car to capsize. I quickly spun my car around and rushed over to assist Sam. I dragged him out of the car and as luck would have it, he was not seriously injured – he made it away with a few minor cuts and scratches. On the other hand, his car was totalled; he was devastated as it was a collectable and way beyond repair.

THE DRIVER

Not long after Sam's car accident, Richard and I took up rally driving as a hobby in order to alleviate the boredom we were experiencing in the classroom. We ditched school and set forth to a stretch of road we had discovered in the mountains, which we referred to as 'the race track'. The track had extensive, winding dirt roads and overlooked oodles of high cliffs; the lack of fencing or barriers on the sides of the road made speeding along it an interesting experience. It was a great way to pass the time, although we did encounter a few tribulations only a few days into our new sport. On the day in question, we took two cars to the track, as a few of our school friends had tagged along. Richard and I shared one of the cars and alternated between being driver and passenger. Every time we swapped over, the driving gradually became increasingly aggressive. As with everything new that I tried and originally found thrilling, the novelty soon wore off unless I upped the ante. I was driving as though possessed; for the duration of my laps around the mountain, a good portion of the car would hang over the cliff on the corners. At first, the buzz had been amazing; it seemed the only way to maintain the thrill was to push the car harder and become even more reckless.

After I had finished one of my jaunts, I got out of the car and swapped over with Richard. Richard, like Sam, was competitive, as he always had to top my achievements, although he was a lot more subtle and shrewd about how he went about it. I did not mind the contention as much when it came to Richard because in some ways it motivated me to strive for a better result and demand more of

myself and, unlike Sam, Richard did not take it seriously enough to take away the fun. When Richard took the wheel and started to drive, he punished the car; he was trying his utmost to exceed what I had pulled off before him, which caused him to make several momentous mistakes. He was putting the poor car through hell, to such an extent that he was damaging it. Rather than using the brakes, our practice was to put the car in a lower gear in order to drift around the corners. We were approaching the tightest corner on the track, which also happened to be smack bang in the middle of the highest cliff, when I recognised that Richard had failed to gear down. By the time I realised what was happening and made an effort to say something it was too late, although I did manage to announce, 'That is it, we are fucked!' The car flew off the side of the cliff and flipped over in mid air, so that the wheels were facing up towards the sky. I had a fair idea how high that particular cliff was and I was a little surprised when we landed as quickly as we did. On impact, the roof crumpled which caused the windows to shatter instantly and glass flew everywhere. Apart from a few
cuts and tiny pieces of glass lodged in our hands, we were in relatively good shape considering.

    We had landed in a very large tree when an enormous branch had caught the car on its way down. I forced the car door open and climbed out of the mangled wreck without paying much attention. As a result, I fell out of the tree and plummeted to the ground, landing with a sickening thump which rattled every bone in my body. There was no chance to warn Richard that we were a long way from the ground and he climbed out and fell directly on top of me, smacking me even further into the solid ground. The other car had stopped at the top of the cliff and our school friends were looking down at us from the edge as though they had seen a pair of ghosts; they could not believe we were still alive. I suppose I was lucky to sustain only some bruising from the combined effects of the fall and providing Richard with a soft landing. We climbed back up to the road and made our way to the nearest pay phone where we called the police and reported the car stolen. The car belonged to Richard's mother and there was no conceivable way he was going to admit to losing her car in a tree during school hours. Richard was really spooked by what had happened, which brought the whole rally driving fad to an end.

I took a few days off school in order to tend to my wounds even though they were moderately superficial; the truth was I didn't need much of an excuse to take time off and stay away from school.

Once back at school, I had several of the regular smokers hound me incessantly for some weed. Though I did not have any at hand, I obligingly contacted a few of the common suppliers and it turned out that there was a drought. There had been a massive bust and the police had seized a big haul coming in from overseas. Rumour had it that it was being sequestered in the evidence lock-up before the police sold it; however, I did not believe for a minute that our police officers were capable of being that entrepreneurial. I called Sam; he told me that he was in possession of a small quantity, which he proposed that I acquire from him at nearly double the street value. I told him what he could do with his suggestion and hung up.

Never before had I experienced the consequences of being out of stock as there had always been an abundance of gear. I had therefore not deemed it necessary to overstock my drugs, since it would have effectively exposed me to an avoidable high-risk situation. However, I now had a critical situation on my hands, as the weed was, in spite of everything, still a fat fraction of my trade, which meant, unless I came up with a resolution, I was going to be in serious trouble. Not coming up with the goods during a famine would have made me look like a lightweight in the eyes of my clients and would have caused them to look elsewhere for future purchases. Bearing that in mind, I set forth on a mission, in order to attain the much-needed pot.

THE FAMINE

Time passed and I wasn't having any joy in finding a resolution to the drug drought. Then I suddenly remembered having heard a passing comment from Jethro; one of the junkies who lived in the neighbourhood. He had told me that he knew the whereabouts of an enormous plantation which belonged to his brother. He was talking about ripping it off. At the time, I feigned polite interest but in reality, paid no mind to his story, as he was mentally challenged and the fact that he was a drug abuser only exacerbated his whole demeanour. In spite of my uneasiness about doing any sort of business with Jethro, I called him. The way I saw it was, if you have lemons, you make lemonade. I was in no position to be choosy as I had exhausted almost every alternative and still did not have a solution to my problem. When I called Jethro, he appeared to be overjoyed to hear from me.

I asked, 'Can you come by tonight? I need to talk to you about something,' to which he replied, 'I was just going to call you because we're having a huge feast at my house, and I'd like you to come over tonight and join us.'

I accepted. However, after I had hung up the phone, I wondered why the hell he would invite me to come and eat at his house, out of the blue, when he had never issued me with an invitation like that before in his entire life.

When I got to Jethro's house, the first thing I noticed was the foul odour in the air; it smelled like a decomposing corpse that had been left out in the sun to rot. It was – apparently – the cuisine that his family had prepared. I was tempted to ask him if they were baking a turd but figured it would be best not to say anything at all. Jethro had a large family, including nine other siblings, one of whom was his twin brother, Toby. They all had boggle eyes, which I assumed was a result of inbreeding. The boys were bizarre-looking enough but the girls had apparently not read the instruction manuals that came with their make-up because it was in all the wrong places, almost as though they were in a frantic rush to conceal their hastily-stitched-together heads.

The entire family and more sat at the table to eat. They served a lot of meat products. I have no problem with meat, as I am a carnivore; however, none of the meat that they had arranged had been cooked. Come to think of it; nothing on the table was cooked.

I did not eat a single thing, which was awkward because they were pressuring me to eat. I kept telling them that I wasn't in great health; I just sat and observed as they ingested the bleeding meat, whole raw onions and cloves of raw garlic. They ate the onions as though they were eating apples. Just watching them made my eyes water; they, however, were not fazed by the fumes or the stink in any way whatsoever.

Jethro and Toby were not identical twins; they actually could not have been more dissimilar. Jethro was tall and lanky and his eyes looked in both directions simultaneously, whereas Toby was short, fat and did not have a neck. Toby's teeth were orange with green blemishes on them; he obviously had never used a toothbrush; I believe he may have had gangrene on his teeth if that is at all possible. Moreover, Toby's eyes looked as though they were trying to have sex with each other. If it was not bad enough that I was getting into business with someone from this group, what added to my uneasiness was the notion that Jethro wanted to cheat his own big brother, Jim. I was not at all shocked as I had encountered many individuals like Jethro in my line of work. What did surprise me was how common that type of conduct had become, and how easy it was for people like this to screw their own families without any compunction or remorse.

Once they had completed their 'meal', I was extremely relieved. Watching them eat had been truly horrific and I felt quite nauseous. Jethro asked me to join him outside to discuss his 'plan'. Once outside, I realised that Jethro had taken my earlier, polite interest in his plan seriously – which saved me having to negotiate a role for myself – as he said, 'We've got to get the crop tonight because my brother's going to harvest it tomorrow.' Jethro's strategy didn't impress me, as it was rather impulsive but I already knew that I didn't have much of an alternative, therefore I said, 'I'm leaving now, I'll be back to pick you up at one o'clock in the morning. Make sure you're ready'. I picked up the car and took it to Hammer. I asked him to give it a quick once-over, to make sure it was up to the task, then headed back home and packed the car's boot with sleeping bags and empty tent bags. By the time I'd made the necessary arrangements, it was already midnight.

When I arrived back at Jethro's house, he was already in the street. When he climbed into the car, I queried him as to where we were going. He answered, 'Don't worry about where we are going, I'll tell you how to get there'. I was a little irritated, as I couldn't see the point in him not being forthright about the location of the crop. But Jethro remained resolute in his decision to direct me to the final destination on a turn-by-turn basis, which was aggravating. I believe he was apprehensive because he may have assumed that I was going to throw him out of the car and go get the crop on my own. This bothered me somewhat because I had learned early on in life that if someone can't trust you, you sure as hell can't trust them.

We made our way towards the plantation; I didn't know what to expect because I didn't trust Jethro. It took us two and a half hours just to get to the area to where the crop was located. However, the car could only take us so far; we had to walk an additional hour through the woods to get to it.

By the time we had pulled out the plants and cleaned them up, another three hours had passed. By this stage the sun was about to come up, so we had to get out of there as swiftly as possible. We loaded ourselves up with as much weed as we could carry and made our way back to the car. In addition to packing the interior of the doors and the spare tyre, I stuffed the camping gear and sleeping bags full of the weed and shoved them in the boot in an effort to conceal as much as possible. In spite of our efforts, we still had a full garbage bag sitting on the back seat in plain sight, as there were no more hiding places left. We began our drive back along the highway at dawn.

Exhausted after the two-hour drive back, I suggested to Jethro that we should get some much-needed rest before splitting it all up. I informed him that I would drop him off at his home and meet with him later. My suggestion did not sit well with Jethro. The truth of the matter was he was a greedy cocksucker who insisted we split it there and then.

I eventually agreed as he was giving me a headache. Once we had divided everything I dropped him off; however, I deliberately didn't go very far as I wanted to see where he would hide his, as I was unable to rid myself of the rotten feeling I had about him.

As I headed back home, I was mindful to ensure I wasn't being watched. I stashed the gear at my house and then took the car to a local car wash and had it detailed in order to remove all of the evidence. From there I went to the Truck Stop Café and met with Sam for breakfast. The Truck Stop was where we would typically go after a long night of drug abuse. When I arrived, Sam was already there. We had breakfast and Sam saw that I was a mess. He eventually asked, 'You look like hell, what have you been doing?' Noncommittally I answered, 'I had a long night'. Sam took mercy on me and gave me a few lines of speed to get me through the day. As it turned out, my timing was impeccable, as Sam was in the middle of arranging a trip up the coast to look for some weed and it just so happened that I had some. I managed to get rid of a few pounds over breakfast. I didn't want to give him too much because of the drought but I wanted to help him out just to keep the wheels greased and to make sure everything kept running smoothly.

Once I returned to school, I discovered that the news had somehow already preceded me. Word had gotten out and travelled at light speed to all interested parties that I was in possession of a substantial stockpile of some high quality weed. I played the situation to my advantage and leaked the bogus information that I had just procured a shipment of some highly exotic marijuana from a foreign country, thus enabling me to charge an overly exorbitant rate for my product. I went one step further and created a unique name for it – 'Genetically Modified Skunk'. The smoker drones lined up in droves and had to make an appointment just to talk to me. I ducked out of school for a few hours and called on the help of a few of the local smokers to assist me in bagging up several hundred deals. When I returned I was stocked to the teeth. I didn't waste any time; I moved all that I had. I collected so much money it was literally hard to fold. In less than a week I cleared the whole lot; the rate at which I had managed to move it all was phenomenal.

Feeling triumphant and overly confident, I had some grand notion that I would be spending my summer living large like a hog in the fat house. Just when I thought I was in the clear, Jethro called me and verbalised that his brother had figured out who took the gear and wanted it back. I thought to myself, 'Bull fucking shit!' – Jethro had told him. I didn't respond to Jethro, in fact, I didn't utter a single word. I knew I had to be very careful as I had a serious combination of difficult circumstances on my hands. I immediately made tracks to see Jethro's brother in order to explain myself, as Jim was not the kind of guy you played games with. He was notorious for being excessively violent, mentally unstable and rumoured to be a homicidal psychopath.

When I arrived at Jim's place, Jethro was sitting next to him with a smug look on his face, obviously exceedingly pleased with himself. Jim, on the other hand, looked as though he was high on heroin or some sort of fish paralyser, and to make matters worse, he was cleaning his gun in plain sight, right outside the front of his house. As I approached Jim, he shook my hand and said, 'Let's go talk out back'. I thought to myself, 'That's it, I'm fucked. This guy is going to kill me for sure'.

The three of us walked along the side of the house towards the back gate. Jim stopped suddenly, then walked over to the sewer grate and removed it. It was heavy and traditionally needed four to six men with special tools just to slide it across the road. Not only did Jim remove it, he lived up to his reputation for having freak-like strength and single-handedly hurled it across the street on his own. I looked inside the drain and saw a little orange bottle of prescription pills; he asked me if I could get down and retrieve them for him, so I did. Upon closer inspection, I realised they were Rohypnol, otherwise known as the date rape drug. Once I gave Jim the bottle he opened it, poured himself a handful and then proceeded to stuff them into his mouth. This guy was using date rape drugs on himself – which explained why he looked the way he did. We proceeded into the back yard where we sat down on an old, used sofa which he had outside. Gently placing the gun on a coffee table, he asked me if I would like a drink. I declined but he gave me one anyway and ordered me to drink it. I placed my drink on the table next to the gun and waited for whatever was going to come next.

Jethro looked anxious, as though he couldn't wait to jump up and yell, 'My brother already knows that you have the weed!' Jim said nothing; he just stared at me with dead eyes and I stared back. I took the initiative and said, 'I did have the weed but I sold it all, every last leaf'. At that point, the strangest thing happened;

Jim looked quite impressed. 'You already sold everything?' I replied, modestly, 'It wasn't that much'.

Jim mused, 'Not bad; not bad at all'.

By this stage, Jethro was starting to become cantankerous – he had obviously been expecting a different outcome – and asked, 'Where is the money then?' in a high-pitched, voice; he was really trying to turn this entire situation on to me.

I told him I had the money. Turning to Jim, I pulled out twenty-five thousand dollars in cash and handed it to him. Jim's jaw dropped; he could not believe what he was hearing and seeing. I stood up, said to Jim, 'Sorry for the misunderstanding,' and walked off. When I reached the gate, I turned and shouted out to Jim, 'The rest of the gear is in your garage; Jethro can show you where it is!'

Jim looked furious and Jethro turned grey.

GETTING CONNECTED

I believed I'd made a good play that day; I might have made an enemy but I had also made a very strong and useful ally. Besides, I still had ten grand left over which wasn't at all a bad effort.

I'd just got home and stashed the rest of the money in a safe place where my mother couldn't find it, when my pager went off; it was Toby. I had to go back because Jim wanted to see me again. I didn't want it to seem like I was a puppet so I made a strategic phone call to Jim directly and told him I had shit to do and I would catch up with him later, even though I actually had nothing urgent to do.

I wasted a few hours playing video games and smoking weed before going back to Jim's place. When I got there, Jim offered me another drink; this time round I accepted the scotch he was waving in my direction because I had learned that saying no to him was pointless. He took me into his office followed by Jethro. Jim told him to 'fuck off' and go for a walk; at that point I could see the potential for Jethro becoming a big problem. Jim asked me to have a seat. I was thinking, *What now?* This guy is probably going to get me to do some sort of grunt work for him where I end up in jail, or worse. However, Jim surprised me with what he said next; he told me he wanted to open a new bar with pool tables and various other modes of entertainment. He had initially planned that Jethro and Toby would look after it for him but added, 'Jethro's an idiot, not to mention unreliable and Toby's too dim and feeble to make key decisions'. He then asked if I would be interested in the job. I swiftly replied, 'Done. However, I would like Toby to come in with me to help me out'.

The very next day, Toby took me to the seediest part of town where even the lowest form of scum would have felt uncomfortable. We stopped in front of a dilapidated, miserable, rundown building and as we stood in front of it, Toby announced, 'This is the place!' I used the key that Jim had given me and proceeded up a long flight of stairs. I was amazed, as the place was a palace inside; red felt pool tables, large television screens, video games, a bar – I even had my own office. The venue was truly awe-inspiring. The club was conveniently pre-stocked with alcohol and office supplies. I went into the office and started setting myself up. I had to bring in my own laptop but other than that, the office was fully furnished and equipped with a safe, an expensive desk and a super, comfortable leather chair. That office was where I conducted the majority of my work. It did not take me long to get established and commence with the day-to-day operations.

Jim rebranded the venue as 'Club 505' and from the minute we opened the doors, the place had a lot of traffic; there were people coming in from far and wide. The pool tables seemed to be the main attraction, as there was always a line of people waiting to play. Toby ordered the stock and did a lot of the housekeeping, which kept everything in order, leaving me free to do my thing.

One night, shortly after we started up, I overheard one of the regular customers trying to offload a stolen car stereo to a complete stranger. I called him over and said, 'Not in here; let's talk in my office'. I then advised him, 'I can't have you blatantly selling stolen goods in my club. However, I'll buy this item from you now and whatever else you bring in; just come and see me when you have anything you need to move and I'll take care of it'.

The arrangement eventually became somewhat lucrative as I was exchanging weed, which cost me next to nothing, for the stolen goods; I would then flip the stolen merchandise for near retail value.

The irony of it all was that most people thought they were getting a bargain if they bought something that was 'allegedly stolen'.

Before long, the storeroom became jam-packed with stolen property and bags of weed, which was ideal as I was making a small fortune from both. I did have to kick fifty percent of everything we did on the side up to Jim, which was fair as he kept the cops off our backs and paid all of the bills. It was almost too good to be true – I was practically living in the club and the money was pouring in. I was hustling around the clock, which didn't give me many opportunities to leave the club. At one stage, I was there for so long without leaving that my clothes started to smell, my hair became tangled and grew almost down to my belt and my goatee was so long, that I began to resemble a wild animal. My eyes were constantly bloodshot because I was high most of the time. The amphetamines made it so I could not feel the effects of weed or alcohol, which in turn resulted in my drinking and smoking at least ten times more than usual.

School was the loser in this arrangement. Club 505 started up during the holidays but I was too busy looking after the business to spend much time at school once the holidays were over. It seemed irrelevant to me at the time – I was learning and earning far more at the club than I ever did at school.

Like all good things, the fun and games inevitably ended when the local residents petitioned the council to close us down, and just like that, it was over. Jim was not as upset as I thought he would be, in fact his exact words were, 'I never thought you would last this long'. We were only in business for a few months but according to Jim, I had made more money for him in that short period of time than anyone he had ever worked with before.

During the time we were running the club, Sam was overseas. His parents had sent him there to dry out because they suspected he was on drugs; if they had only known the extent of it. When he returned, I filled him in on what had transpired in his absence and he didn't hide the fact that he was envious. I'd never seen him so upset.

He was mainly distressed because I'd made such strong connections to which he didn't have access.

I'd met some of the legends; survivors of several decades of crime, which in that industry was close to a miracle and definite proof of their major prowess. I believed I could learn from their experience and had plans to eventually have access to their resources as well.

EDUCATION IS KEY

It was back to school for one last year and I was feeling rather confident as I had successfully established myself in the world of organised crime and also managed to earn the respect and recognition of a few formidable and influential gangsters.

Thinking back, I can't say for sure if it was just me or a side effect of the constant drug abuse but I began to think and feel that I was indestructible. This was hazardous because I put my theory to the test relentlessly. Upon waking each morning, I would start off by doing one hundred push-ups, followed by snorting a few lines of whatever I had on hand which was typically speed; this would then be followed by a few cigarettes and a drink of some totally undiluted red cordial to wash it all down. For me, the red drink was the cornerstone of every nutritious breakfast. By the time I walked out of the door, my body was completely charged and my heart would be pumping as though I had just run a marathon; thanks to the amphetamines and the sugar coursing through my veins.

Studying suddenly became the top priority for the vast majority of my clients at school, as the final exams were approaching quickly and the entire student body was pursuing prestigious careers, which was an idea that had been drummed into their heads by their arrogant, self-righteous, wealthy parents. The sudden interest in studying was bad for business because nobody wanted to smoke weed as it was a downer that would effectively make them want to eat snacks and go to sleep; what they needed was to be as alert as possible in order to cram for their exams. Where most people might have simply accepted defeat, I saw yet another opportunity. I knew that if I wanted to survive in this rapidly changing market, I too had to change. As it turned out, I accidentally discovered during my ongoing experimentation with drugs of all sorts, that speed somehow increased learning capacity in some strange way, as if it were supercharging the brain and aided in exams as well – at least it did for me. Once I began using the stuff, I started acing every exam and, oddly enough, I didn't even have to study for them.

In no time at all, taking speed as a study aid quickly became the new craze at the school; hardly surprising as I marketed it as a tool for thinking and reacting faster and a great way to cream exams. Soon everyone was wired and the teachers were suspicious. For some reason, I was called to the principal's office at least twice a day in order to be interrogated and to have my bag searched. I felt that the actions the faculty was taking were an infringement on my constitutional rights; I was not sure exactly what that meant, but I felt that way nonetheless. When I arrived at the principal's office, he would have me sit opposite him and he would gawk at me silently for at least five minutes. I was somewhat bemused by his behaviour as he looked like he was getting ready to either hit me or molest me – he had an unnerving look about him. The fact that I was getting called in so frequently led me to believe that there was probably a rat in my circle of so-called friends and clients.

Even though the constant interrogations and bag searches were as annoying as hell, I was not too concerned since I had a strategy in place to cover my tracks. I never kept anything on me physically that could get me into trouble. Conveniently, my good relationship with the janitor helped, as he showed me some great hiding spots around the school. I would stash everything when nobody was around and retrieve it when needed.

My reputation around the school was rapidly becoming tainted by bum-licker students who were gossiping and spreading rumours. To make matters worse, a nearby school had just expelled a dozen retards. They somehow all ended up at our school and an amazingly upright bunch of citizens they were; expelled for a mixed bag of offences: suspected drug dealing, offensive behaviour, lewd conduct and generally being stupid. They arrived with the preconceived notion that they would take over the drug trade; one of them actually had the audacity to tell me, 'Now that we're here, we are going to take over'. They were sadly mistaken as it turned out. I ended up selling them large volumes, which they in turn took back to their own neighbourhood, which was a good result, as I did not want them dealing in my school or surrounding area because they were so loud and stupid they would have gotten everyone in the business pinched.

I made a killing off those guys; they went from 'taking over' to becoming mules; admittedly, outsmarting them was not much of a challenge and when they showed up, they were unwittingly rather helpful, as they took most of the unsolicited and unnecessary attention away from me.

The end of the school year came about. When Sam left school, he was privileged enough to be taken into his family business. Sam's uncle owned a successful electrical contracting company which guaranteed Sam an easy job. Even though Sam was snugly established in what appeared to be a great career, he didn't make any less effort in his criminal profession. Richard's parents, on the other hand, had actually given him full control of their painting company. I don't think Richard understood how easy his life actually was for him; he was well and truly guaranteed a secure position at a young age and no longer had to be concerned about making a living.

I scored surprisingly high marks in my final exams and managed to get better final exam results than Sam and Richard combined, thanks to the drugs. However, due to a lack of guidance and better judgement, I decided to leave furthering my education or pursuing any sort of career out of the picture. I figured I should simply stick to what I knew and sought out a life of organised crime. In hindsight, it would have been so easy and convenient to have had one of those family businesses to which I could have resorted. I believed I had no alternative but to play the hand I was dealt. I could have found a minimum wage job and started at the bottom like a lot of people, although from my perspective at the time, it seemed like a lot of trouble to go through. The fact that I would have had to work my ass off for ten years just get to the position and pay grade that Sam and Richard started on, was certainly unappealing.

Opportunely, Jim set up another business and commissioned me to run it for him; however, the second time around the location was even worse. It was in the most poverty-stricken and crime-ridden neighbourhood. Jim personally showed me the hotel, and was pleased to inform me the bar had a 24-hour liquor licence. That place may as well have been built in hell; I walked in at midday and it was already littered with drunks. The state of the bar itself was atrocious and the regular customers looked very grungy. I remember thinking that the situation was not good as the potential to make money from people of that calibre would prove difficult to say the least. I accepted the challenge nonetheless, as I had nothing else to go to and my habits were consuming the bulk of my money and more.

When I first started, I called Jim and asked him to send Toby in order to assist me in running the business. Jim declined my request and would not give a reason as to why, but I knew it was because he didn't want his brother to get killed in that place. However, he did agree to send his older brother Henry to check in on me from time to time.

THE HOTEL

I set up office in one of the filthy hotel rooms. The first order of business was to hire some security and I managed to find some outsized goons with a tremendously intimidating appearance. They were real tough guys; covered in tattoos from head to toe and looked as though they could eat meat and shit out vegetables. They were Torres Strait Islanders and each one of them would have tipped the scales at over one hundred and fifty kilograms. Having those guys around helped set my mind at ease.

Within the first week of running the place, I decided to make a few refinements in an effort to attract a better quality clientele and to get more people through the doors. The place was lacking anything resembling an atmosphere, so I organised a live jazz band to come and play on most nights, in addition to hiring a few attractive cocktail waitresses.

Once I'd settled in and everything seemed to be going according to plan, I began doing what Jim had put me in there to do but only a few hours after I had begun to hustle, the dramas began. I had to go take a piss and while in the men's room, one of the local alcoholics, who had evidently been watching me, walked up behind me and held a large knife to my neck. He said quietly, 'Give me all the money and the drugs or I will cut your throat'. I found this annoying to say the least but I replied in a soothing voice, 'Okay, fucking relax, I'm just going to slowly reach into my pocket and get them out for you'. He appeared to be high, as his eyes were completely bloodshot and his hands were shaking; he shook so much that he in fact cut my neck a little while he had me at knifepoint.

I pulled my wallet out and gave him the money. As I handed it to him, he loosened his grip on the knife in order to hastily stuff the takings into his pocket. I had made a practice of always keeping a device in my wallet that resembled a credit card, only thicker; it had a razor sharp, thin knife concealed inside it. I held out the device to my assailant and told him, 'The drugs are inside'. As I had anticipated, he hungrily snatched the card out of my hand which worked out well, as I kept hold of the blade handle; he was left holding onto the casing only. Without stopping to think, I quickly drove the blade all the way into his shoulder and I actually felt it hit the bone. He had no choice but to drop his knife, as he had completely lost the use of his arm. I kicked his knife across the floor and hit him in the nose with everything I had, which knocked him down. Once he was on the floor I spent the next five to ten minutes kicking him in the face and ribs; I told anyone who tried to come in and use the facilities during that time to 'fuck off', which they did. I think I would have broken the majority of his ribs and a few other bones in that beating. I took my money back out of his pocket and my blade out of his shoulder, cleaned my knife in the basin and tended to the cut on my neck. When everything was in order, I briefly ducked my head outside and summoned one of the security guards. When he walked into the men's room, I barked at him, 'How the fuck could this have happened? That lowlife nearly killed me! What the fuck am I paying you for?' The guard looked at me with a bamboozled expression as I instructed him, 'From this point onwards your top and only priority is to keep both eyes on me at all times, no matter what'. As I walked out I added, 'I want you to make an example of this clown in front of everyone; drag him out by his hair and throw him in the street but rough him up a little more on the way through so that everyone can see what happens if they want to fuck around in here'.

As I had ordered, the security guard picked up where I had left off; dragging the assailant out of the men's room by the hair and walking him out onto the main floor for everyone to see. Once he had gathered enough attention, he proceeded to smash the lowlife's head against the bar. After five or six hits, I called out to the security guard, 'That's enough; get him out of my face'. The guard took what was left of this guy and threw him on the street, not on the pavement but in the actual road.

After what had started as an overly hectic evening, I finally got the chance to sit down with Sam and Richard whom I had invited for a few drinks and to listen to the band play; I'd have to say the music was superb. I ordered a round of drinks and as we sat at the bar, one of the local women stumbled over to me and offered to suck my cock for another drink. Under normal circumstances – far be it from me to shun that type of arrangement– I would have agreed; however due to her ripe old age and lack of teeth I had to respectfully decline her proposal. I couldn't have her walking around badgering and trying to sexually harass my customers, so I instructed the security guard to discreetly escort her out of the hotel. Sam turned to me and asked, 'What the fuck are you doing here? This place is fucked; if you stay here you're gonna end up dead'. While Sam was talking, Jim's brother, Henry, walked in and attracted a lot of attention. He was wearing a glossy silver suit. His reflective suit made him look like a disco ball but what was worse, was the fact that he was short and wore a pencil-thin rapist style moustache, in addition to oversized serial killer glasses. He walked past the woman who was being escorted out and exclaimed, 'Wow! Look at her she is gorgeous' and then added, 'I would like to land on the Aboriginal woman like za eagle'. My stomach took a turn.

I told Henry to follow me upstairs and once in my office, I gave him what little money I had made for the day. He left the instant the cash was in his hand, which I thought was terrific, as he gave me the creeps. Once he had left, I opened my desk drawer and took out a bag of speed and a bag of coke, threw them to Richard who had wandered in and said, 'Can you get this ready? I just have to go and get something out of the car; I'll be back in a few minutes'.

When I got to the car, already on my guard following the earlier incident, I was a little dubious as I could hear a beeping sound coming from the boot of my car; it was a constant high-pitched beep. I said to myself, 'Fuck me, what now?' The first thought that popped into my head was that a bomb had been planted in the car as some form of retribution for what had happened in the men's room earlier that evening. I went back up to the office to notify Richard and Sam of what I suspected and to advise them to move their cars just in case; however, they were already high and pretty useless.

I went back downstairs and decided, 'Fuck it, I'll open the boot and whatever happens, happens'. Holding my breath, I opened the boot of the car. My anxiety was immediately alleviated when I saw that it was just my pager stuck up against something in the car. One of the buttons was jammed. I felt a little silly, especially as it was the pager I had been coming to collect but the primary emotion was relief.

I locked the car and returned to the office. The day was totally fucked and I needed a few minutes to collect my thoughts and clear my head. I sat at my desk and looked over at Richard who had passed out on the sofa, whilst Sam was out on the balcony, smoking weed. They'd finished every last gram that I'd given them and hadn't even had the consideration to leave me as much as a speck.

I reached into the desk, pulled out another bag and inhaled it all. Not satisfied that the quantity I'd just consumed was going to be sufficient; I was still livid over the proceedings of the dismal day that was almost ended, without thinking, I opened yet another bag and finished it as well. After the second bag, everything started to become a blur; however, I do recall starting on a third bag and at that stage, began to feel cold and numb. I pushed through it, even though everything was becoming obscure. Despite the odd feelings, I persisted and continued to rack up one line after the other. My nose started to bleed heavily. The next thing I knew, I was having sharp pains in my chest and must have blacked out. When I regained consciousness, it was already the following evening and everyone in the room had left some time while I was unconscious.

You would have thought that Sam or Richard would've tried to revive me or at least call an ambulance for me before leaving, considering that I was lying face down at the desk in a puddle of my own blood. Absurdly, I only had myself to blame as they were the calibre of people I had chosen to surround myself with.

Another three months of working at the hotel, my nineteenth birthday went by in the blink of an eye and to be frank, I was astonished that I had survived it. In some societies, people go through their entire lives not knowing what their limits are and not knowing how far they would have to go in order to survive. Not me. My survival depended on my being at full capacity almost all of the time.

On one of the busiest nights of the week, while I was upstairs in the office tending to my drug habit and doing some paperwork, I heard a disturbance downstairs. A riot had broken out; the security guards had fled the building, due to their lack of balls. There appeared to be close to a hundred people rioting in the street in front of the hotel, fuelled by huge quantities of drink and drugs. All I could do was sit on the balcony upstairs and watch. It had quickly escalated way too far past putting a stop to it, and I was by no means going to be a hero. Someone must have called the police, as police cars started turning up one after another until they eventually regained control of the situation several hours later.

A few days went past and I had heard no more about what had happened in front of the hotel; I just assumed that it was over until I got a call from Jim who said, 'The hotel's gonna be closed down'.

Rumour had it that it was because the media had put the blame on our hotel selling alcohol in that particular area and instigating unsafe drinking and disorderly social conduct. The most pitiful thing about that entire saga was the fact that before we arrived, the locals were drinking methylated spirits with lemonade, and sniffing fuel from cans.

PAYBACK'S A BITCH

Once the hotel closed, I went to Jim's place to square everything off and give him the outstanding money I owed him. When I arrived, Jim was drinking as usual and insisted I sit and drink with him. After a few hours of drinking and talking, I discovered that Jim was doing business with Conan. I explained to Jim where I stood as far as Conan was concerned, and as it fortuitously turned out, Jim was having problems with him. The two men appeared to be having some sort of turf war; Jim didn't provide too many details, although what he did tell me sounded serious. The ultimate opportunity had just presented itself; I told Jim, 'Let me set things right for you with Conan free of charge, as it would be my pleasure'. Jim was jubilant about my proposal. I also told him, 'In order to do this I'm going to need a gun'. Jim went into the next room and came back with a gun, which was brand new in the box, in addition to a box of bullets. He handed it to me and said, 'This is yours, you can keep it'.

Jim made all of the arrangements for my reunion with Conan; he told me where he was going to be and how to get to him. I could not believe I was so close to finally settling the score with that prick, as he had caused me so much anguish and had obliterated any prospect I might have had of living a normal life. In addition to Jim's assistance, I also made my own preparations and was diligent about my research because I wanted this particular job to be flawless.

On the night of the job, I was probably breaking a dozen different laws and I couldn't have cared less because the only thing on my mind was getting to where I had to be and doing what I had to do. Driven by fury and vengeance, I pushed the bike hard, savouring the almost empty roads; for most of the way the engine was at its limit, needles in the red. The helmet muffled everything except the grinding of my teeth, and the mechanical action of the gears locking into position, as I clicked the shifter against my foot.

It was two in the morning as I rode into Sydney. Streaking past parked cars, I could faintly hear their alarms being set off in my wake. Normally I would have stuck to the back roads in order to avoid detection but I was not in a level-headed frame of mind to put it mildly, so I was tearing along the main roads for most of my trip into the city, until I reached the narrower streets of the city's nightlife district, where I had to lean the bike low enough to kiss the ground in order to make it around the corners in one piece. When I reached the club, I left the bike in an alley behind it, retrieved the gun from the compartment under the seat and slipped it into the back of my belt.

I walked into the club – the sort you wouldn't want your sister to frequent; the air was hot and rancid, reeking of sweat and alcohol. The lighting was almost non-existent, apart from the ultraviolet lights that made white clothing and teeth glow in the dark. The club itself was not very large; however, it was packed wall-to-wall with people. From what could be made out in the shadowy room, the walls and furniture looked soiled; the floors were littered with empty water bottles, used paper napkins and other garbage. As I pushed through the crowd I felt lightheaded – almost as if everything was moving in slow motion. I made my way down the dark, steep staircase at the back of the club; I encountered the expected bodyguards at the foot of the stairs and I reassured them with a quick nod. One of them looked at me, long and steady, before responding back with a nod and letting me pass. Thanks to Jim's arrangements, they did not put up any resistance whatsoever. A group of four men sat and played cards; the room was dark apart from their table, which was lit by a small neon light hanging overhead. The table was littered with alcohol, money, cards and ashtrays. I distinctly remember the ashtrays; they were overflowing with cigarette butts – I estimated they had been playing for at least six or seven hours. The room smelled of mould, alcohol and stale tobacco. The occasions when any person at that table was not carrying some sort of weapon were few and far between, and that night was not one of them.

The three men at the table who were facing the door had recognised me and knew what I was there for as Jim had notified a few of his contacts that I would be coming. The buzz of conversation that had preceded my entrance ceased. The only movement in the room was the dry blinking of their eyes that were now locked on me. I saw the person I had come for; luck was with me as he had his back to the door, which made my job much easier. By the time he had turned his head, I had removed the Beretta from my belt and grabbed him by what little hair he had and jammed most of the gun in his mouth whilst taking him to the floor. No one had moved or said a word out of respect – I liked to think it was respect, after all, I was holding a gun and they knew I was going to use it. At the age of nineteen, commanding the respect of such men was not an easy task.

While I held him at gunpoint, Conan remained amazingly composed and his eyes were devoid of expression. His calm demeanour fuelled my resentment. I cocked the hammer back on the gun and said, 'I got you now, you motherfucker. Did you really think you were going to get away with it? You are a fucking mutt'. I proceeded to beat him unmercifully on his head and face with the gun.

Something had taken control of me; I could not bring myself to stop. I got tired of hitting him in the face and he appeared to be choking on his own blood, so I started stomping on his chest, kicking him in the ribs and I even kicked him in the balls a few times for good measure. Even though he was bleeding from every orifice and looked as though he was within an inch of his life, I was still frustrated because I felt as though I could not inflict enough pain on him or humiliate him to the point where I could believe I had redeemed myself.

Even taking into consideration that I had just pressed a violent assault on Conan to the point where he had started to slip in and out of consciousness, he would not, in spite of everything, give me the satisfaction of exhibiting even a minuscule sign of anguish. By the time I was finished with him there was blood everywhere. At that stage, I figured there was only one thing left to do. I aimed the gun at his face and got ready to take the shot when, quite suddenly, I had an epiphany and lowered the gun.

I knew that Jim was going to be irate, as he was depending on me to solve the Conan predicament for him permanently but the fact that he wasn't going to be too pleased if Conan lived; had now become irrelevant to me. When I stopped and thought about what I was about to do, I somehow knew that killing him was not going to give me any sort of satisfaction whatsoever. The reality of it was that I was still very young and if I were to pull the trigger, one of two things was going to happen; I was either going to spend the rest of my life in prison or if I was not captured, the best case scenario would have me spending the rest of my life on the run; neither of which was an alluring prospect.

I kicked him in the face one last time and then spat on him before I walked out of the room. The philosophy behind what I had just done was rather simple; if I had taken his life, he would have ultimately succeeded in completely ruining my life. In my mind, what I had done was justified and even though the punishment should have been more severe, I was content that I had at least had the chance to set things right and settle the matter with Conan to some extent, once and for all. Was this some sort of enlightenment from a higher being? Had I just experienced something spiritual? On the other hand, a sense of no longer having any purpose in my life pervaded me, as the idea of retribution is what had kept me motivated, focused and fuelled for a very long time.

After the whole Conan debacle, my affiliation with Jim was more or less over and to be honest, I preferred not to be in the company of that homicidal psychopath anyway. Inevitably I returned to my old operation.

THE CLUB SCENE

Theo, one of my regular clients, suggested that nightclubs could be a goldmine; so I went along with him and his ever-present image-enhancing entourage and scoped it out for myself one night. Theo was a promoter for several underground rave venues and had conveniently organised it so that I was the regular go-to guy for most of their recreational needs; the arrangement kept me exceedingly occupied.

He lived in a house with nine women and was certainly doing well for himself, although admittedly at least half of the girls in the house were unshaven hippies. I visited Theo so frequently that I may as well have lived in that house, as there was such a high demand for chemicals in the rave scene. Theo had several alternatives when it came to whom he wanted to deal with, and he didn't worry about price. The reason I took over that market was because my product was second-to-none – and I was dependable. In that line of business, being reliable is key; if you slip just once, and for whatever reason you cannot produce the goods, you quickly become yesterday's news.

My being in that house so often was to my own detriment though, as I had picked up some new and very nasty habits. The girls who lived in the house were creative junkies and were constantly coming up with new ways to get messed up. As a result of their influence, I started to mix several drugs together and eventually found myself inventing my own drugs. As a side effect of the drug mixing, I started to lose a hell of a lot of weight and I felt ill most of the time but the way I saw it, it was collateral damage and I just wrote it off as the price of doing business.

One of the girls, Danielle, who was squatting in the house with Theo, insisted on introducing me to one of her friends. She informed me that her friend was very well connected and that she could most likely assist me in obtaining an improved quality product at a competitive price. She had apparently already told her friend about me and her friend was interested in meeting. I would have been crazy not to look into it; as a result, I went along with Danielle to meet her friend. We used my bike to get there and she directed me to a flamboyant penthouse in an expensive part of town. Upon our arrival, I was somewhat shocked when I initially saw her friend as she was clad in only a G-string, and a shady character was just leaving her apartment as though he were fleeing the scene of a crime. When I glanced over at the table, a large bowl full of condom packets and lubricants caught my attention, and it all started to add up – a prostitute.

HEAVEN AND HELL

The first thought that came to my mind was, *'What a waste!'* Her body was amazing, and even though she was a drug abuser, there were none of the usual signs in her face as she was, in spite of her drug habit, an extraordinarily attractive woman. When I looked at her arms, I noticed some track marks, which I thought was a damn shame. It was a tad distracting trying hard to look her in the face and nowhere else. It was clear she was comfortable being naked. Eventually she did put on a T-shirt but only because the night became a little cooler.

Danielle left shortly after we had arrived to allow us to conduct our business. Her contact introduced herself – her name was Alana. Being hospitable, she prepared a few lines and offered me some. I sat down with her and took her up on her offer. As soon as I sniffed the first line, I was blown away; it felt as though the back of my head had caught on fire and was about to fly off. In all the drugs that I had encountered, which were a lot, I had never come across anything as potent; I was seriously impressed.

I wanted to get straight down to business and talk about pricing; however, she was more interested in finding out about me on a personal level – and she did not ask run-of-the mill questions. I found her line of questioning unusual, as she would randomly throw in a hypothetical and then quietly analyse my responses as though she were testing me. I knew what she was doing but I played along with her mind games and answered as honestly as I could. The inquisition seemed as though it was going to last for a while, so I figured I might as well make myself comfortable. I poured myself a drink, lit a cigarette and parked myself on one of the long chairs on her balcony where we continued our conversation. I completely lost track of time and the whole night passed by while we sat and talked.

I eventually told her, 'I'm tired, I'm going to leave'. I think I was starting to come down a little. I got up and left her apartment. As I was walking to the bike, I thought to myself what a shame it was for an exquisitely beautiful and highly intelligent girl to be leading such a dark life. It was five o'clock in the morning and it was the middle of winter. I was wearing only a T-shirt and jeans at the time but in spite of that, as a side effect of the drugs I had taken, I couldn't feel the cold.

Alana and her drugs were playing on my mind a lot more than they should have. She was so seductive and I could sense trouble; however, it did not dissuade me– on the contrary – I wanted to know more.

A few days later when I went back to see her, she said she wanted me to meet her suppliers, which I thought was odd, because in that industry the supplier is your most closely guarded secret. So once I had met them, I would no longer have any need for Alana at all; however, she seemed more than happy to take that chance. I never did figure out her motivation.

Alana, riding pillion, directed me to Kings Cross – which was ground zero for the drug trade at the time – where she introduced me to three of her main suppliers. While we were there, she bought a substantial amount of 'gear'. Later, she took me to one of her favourite restaurants. After dinner, we rode back to her apartment, the roar of the bike echoing through the canyons of the city streets. It was time to try out the new drugs. She began to prepare a needle and while preparing it, offered me one; however, I declined replying, 'No fucking way!' to be exact. But she wouldn't take no for an answer so she started to work on me and, like I said, she was gorgeous. She convinced me to do a needle with her and when she pushed the plunger in, I felt so good; it was a euphoric sensation, almost as though nothing in the entire world could harm or even bother me and a sense of serene calmness came over me. I had never experienced a feeling like that before. However, once it started to wear off, I was uncomfortable and restless. It felt as though the apartment walls were closing in on me and I was having difficulty breathing. I decided to leave. I looked over at Alana and she was asleep, so I let myself out without making any noise.

Despite feeling strange, I did remember that I had to go and pick up some weed from Sam's place. On the way there, a car pulled out of nowhere into the middle of an intersection and as I was moving too quickly, I had nowhere to go but straight into the car. Seconds before the collision, I did manage to slow the bike down although it didn't do me much good as it was too little too late and I'd already run out of road.

When I smashed into the side of the car, it was with such force that the bike got wedged in the driver's door and I flew over the top. The adrenalin must have kicked in because I felt as though I had a heightened sense of awareness when I hit the ground. I didn't feel any pain; probably due to the drugs. I jumped up and ran back to the bike; the woman in the car seemed to be trapped. I managed to separate the motorcycle from her car and helped her to get out safely. Fortunately she was okay – and I had only suffered a slight gravel rash and some inconsequential cuts and grazes.

She was at fault but in spite of that, I didn't want to involve the police since I looked so dishevelled but moreover, I didn't want to deal with them in case they drug tested me. Consequently I told the confused woman, 'Don't worry about it; I'll cover the repair myself'. I picked up my bike, which looked mangled and barely operational and proceeded to nurse myself and the bike back home, albeit slowly. I had a shower to clean off the blood, got into the car and finally made my way to Sam's house.

On the way back from Sam's place, I stopped by to see Manny; he was one of my clients who also happened to own a large motorcycle dealership and workshop. I told him what had happened and he took the opportunity to sell me another bike.

He told me, 'Your bike has already been superseded; I just received the new model this week, and it has twenty percent more power!'

My response was, 'Twenty percent you say? I'll take it'.

He then asked, 'Don't you at least want to know how much it costs?' to which I replied, 'I'm sure you'll look after me, because I'm going to leave it with you so that you can give it the works'.

Manny's team of mechanics pulled the new bike completely apart and totally reengineered it from the ground up, in order to increase the overall performance. In short, the bike was being completely custom rebuilt specifically for my requirements. I had the colour changed from metallic white to a less conspicuous gunmetal grey. I also had many of the special modifications transferred over from the old bike onto the new one, in addition to some new and improved technologies.

A few weeks later, I got a call from Manny to tell me the bike was ready. When I arrived, Manny was waiting at the door to greet me with an enormous grin stretched across his mug. I followed him into the workshop and as we were walking through the showroom, Manny said, 'There is one thing I didn't tell you'. I started to get a little tense and began to think that the bike was not yet complete or something had gone wrong with it. When I walked into the workshop, the mechanics were standing around the bike, which was covered with a Castrol bike cover. They unveiled the bike ceremoniously with great pride and gratification. Manny announced, 'What I didn't tell you was that on the dynamometer test, the bike produced more power than any machine we have ever worked on before!' We had a few drinks to celebrate their success. They were extremely proud of themselves – and they ought to have been, as the machine they had created was truly an awe-inspiring work of art. When Manny handed me the bill, I realised what they were really celebrating. In spite of the astronomical invoice, I was overjoyed with the outcome. When I rode the new bike for the first time, it scared the crap out of me, and at that very moment, I went from liking it to loving it!

TWO GUNS

The new motorbike attracted a lot of attention. One person in particular who took notice of it was Damien. Damien lived at the bottom of my street and was a motorcycle enthusiast. He happened to be riding past just as I pulled up in front of my house for the first time on the new ride. He stopped when he noticed it was different. Prior to that moment, I had only known of him and we had never actually spoken; however, I had gleaned some information about him from his sister, with whom I was conducting an unusual and discreet relationship. We had met as a result of our shared interest in the nuts and bolts of computers and our friendship had blossomed. As these things happen, the friendship developed into something closer but we had to be very careful not to make it public as she already had a boyfriend who was a good friend of Damien's. In a strange kind of way, there was something going on but there was nothing going on. On a few occasions she had recited some hair-raising stories that I believed would have to be considered as far-fetched regarding Damien but I paid no attention.

He rode an extremely rare model sports bike – it was one of the few models that originally had been built for the track and later, had been modified for road use; it was a collectors' edition and was rated the most powerful in its class. In spite of that, his bike looked like it had been to hell and back many times over. It had been crashed so many times that it was mostly covered in brown and grey primer paints, which made it look like a military style vehicle with camouflage.

Damien had a beard, no teeth and hair that appeared to be close to a metre long; the clothes he wore were all black, but the worst part of his outfit was the long, black, plastic, masturbator-style trench coat. When he rode, all you could see was his long wispy hair and nasty plastic coat flapping behind him like a cape.

When he pulled up next to me he remarked, 'That's one hell of a bike!' He dismounted his cycle and gave my new ride a thorough examination, finishing with a nod of approval. When I started talking to him, it quickly became obvious that he was a fellow drug dealer. I learned he needed to obtain a large volume of amphetamines; I was also pleased to hear that he required them immediately.

I told Damien, 'I believe I may have the solution to your problem'. Without giving too much away, I wanted to let him know that I was interested in doing business. He was at least twice my age and gave the impression of being dangerous. This was reinforced when he leant over to inspect my bike again and the wind blew his jacket open exposing the two guns he was carrying, which were concealed on either side of his belt. When they caught my eye, I thought to myself, 'This guy cannot be serious – who walks around with guns in the street in this day and age?' The more I spoke to him, the more I realised there was much I could learn from him as he had been in the industry a lot longer than I had and he had already earned his stripes.

WHAT A DAY

Damien called me the following day and declared, 'I'm gonna take you up on your offer. Can you get me what we spoke about?' When I asked him how much he wanted, he replied, 'As much as you can get your hands on'. I wanted to make sure that Damien was on the level and not just another compulsive shit talker, so I figured I would start him off on a smaller quantity in order to test the waters, because I didn't want to get stuck with a large quantity of gear that I could not offload quickly. At the same token, I didn't want to give him too little because that would have offended him and burnt him as a prospective client. I went to see Alana and told her what I wanted to do for Damien. She handled it and organised my order very quickly, managing to have the gear delivered to us within half an hour. While we were waiting, she said, 'I'd like to put some money aside in order to start a much larger operation and I'd like you to be my business partner'. I didn't get a chance to hear the rest of what she had to say as my order arrived and I had to leave but I told her that I would be back later that night to discuss it.

Before going to see Damien, I went back home and found my brother standing in the street with his friends, carrying on and attracting a lot of unnecessary attention out in front of the house. I leaned in towards him and whispered angrily into his ear, 'I'm in the middle of something big and you're going to get me pinched if you stay out here carrying on like this as the police are already watching me'. He certainly did not appreciate me telling him what to do in front of his friends. I had no time for that sort of shit, so I grabbed him by his head and dragged him into the house. He got very angry because I had undermined him in front of his deadbeat, loser, freeloading acquaintances.

What he did next was the dictionary definition of insane. He was so angry about being unable to take his anger out on me, that he punched his hand through a glass window in his bedroom in a fit of anger and practically cut his hand clean off. When he saw the blood, he started to panic. All of his so-called friends ran off, although before the last one could depart, I grabbed him and took him inside. I gave him a towel and told him to start cleaning up the room as it was in a sorry state and I didn't want to have my mother annoyed when she returned from work.

I was wrapping my brother's hand up in an effort to stop the bleeding when the phone rang; it was Damien. He shouted, 'Where the fuck are you? I need that stuff right now and you can't be late!' I told him what had just taken place and he said, 'Bring your brother and drop it off to me on the way to the hospital'. The towel was not holding all of the blood because my brother must have severed a large vein or something but I also knew I had to get going to Damien's place. I ran into the kitchen where I had been preparing all the bags on the smooth marble benchtop, took the bags, raced out to the car and stuffed them in between the lining of the driver's seat in the car. Just to make life easy, instead of needing the drugs just down the street at his house, Damien wanted them delivered to him at a pub on the other side of town. I told my brother to get in. The car had white leather interior, even the dash and door trims were white, subsequently it really stood out when my brother bled all over it. I was wearing a white singlet and that too, was covered in blood.

Once in the car, I noticed that I had forgotten one bag in the house. I ran back in and grabbed it, and as I hastily attempted to shove it into the seat with the others, it broke. I had to run back inside again and make up the difference with caster sugar because I didn't have time to get any more and I'd made a mess hurrying. When I got back to the car with a newly prepared bag, I took a straw from the glove box, wedged it in between the seat and vacuumed up all the gear that had spilled out with my nose. In addition to the gear, I inhaled a lot of lint and dust that was also caught in the seat. All in all, by this time I was seriously messed up, confused, dizzy and numb.

I put the fact that I didn't get pulled over, down to divine intervention, as the inside of the car was drenched in blood and my appearance was genuinely fucked up; the car looked like a mobile crime scene. The traffic was heavy, which made me nervous, combined with the hidden drugs, my bleeding brother and the reality that Damien was in a frantic hurry! The fact that he happened to carry, not one but two guns on him, just made matters worse. I finally reached Damien and gave him his shit. He saw the car and told me, 'You'll never make it to the hospital before your brother dies of loss of blood driving the car in this traffic', and so he put my brother on the back of his bike and took him.

I went home and cleaned the car as quickly and as much as possible but it needed an entire day to clean it properly. I then rushed to the hospital to check on my brother. When I walked into the hospital, one of the nurses thought I was the one who required medical attention.

I talked with the doctors and they notified me that they were going to perform microsurgery on my brother and were confident that the damage could be repaired. I stayed at the hospital and waited until he came out of surgery, just to make sure everything was in order. The doctor's prediction was correct; when my brother recovered from the anaesthetic after a few hours, he appeared to be fine, apart from the loss of feeling and mobility in three of his fingers. They never did heal.

As I sat in the hospital listening to my brother tell his fickle friends, who had reappeared, the tall tale of how I had maimed him and nearly cut off his hand, my phone conveniently rang. It was Sam. His voice, high with tension announced, 'I've just been robbed at gunpoint! It was Robert – he was wearing a ski mask but I could tell it was him because of his voice!' Robert was one of the morons he had working for him. I distinctly remembered telling Sam to distance himself from that loser months before, although he evidently hadn't listened. I told Sam to sit tight and wait for me.

I went straight home, dropped off the car and picked up the bike as the car was starting to smell strange because of all the blood. I did make another quick attempt to sanitise the car but it was taking way too long; subsequently I just grabbed the bike and left. It was on the way to Sam's house that I saw that the bike was low on fuel, so I pulled into a service station and filled it up. When I came out of the pay booth, I noticed that Robert, the scumbag who had just robbed Sam, was standing next to a car parked on the other side of the service station; the car had three other people in it.

Just as I had noticed him, he had also spotted me and he knew where I was going and why. He abruptly jumped into the car, which was already facing the bike and started his engine. I hit the remote start and sprinted to the bike as quickly as I could. I made it to the bike and took off just in time, as the front of his car was only a few centimetres away from the back of my bike.

GRAND LARCENY

Robert was driving his BMW as fast as was possible in the confines of the service station. When I looked back, I could see the BMW logo right on my ass. I didn't even have a chance to put my helmet on, I just rode as he continued to chase me but ultimately his car ran out of breath. Once I left the service station and hit the main road, there was no way he could keep up with the bike. I knew he would not dare follow me to Sam's house as the rest of Sam's crew was there and Robert and his team of morons would have been heavily outnumbered.

Once at Sam's house, I ran in and told him what had just happened at the service station. Sam snapped, 'Why didn't you stop and confront them?' to which I replied dumbfounded, 'Why didn't you confront them?' He must have been under the impression that I was some sort of superhero or something.

Sam, Richard and I sat down and had some weed. As we were smoking I asked Sam what Robert took. Sam hesitated and pretended that he didn't hear the question, so I asked him again a few more times. Under pressure from my constant badgering he eventually said, 'Robert took our crop'. This was the crop that Sam and I had set up in a secret location a month earlier. I was fuming.

'How the fuck did Robert find out about it in the first fucking place? There's not another living person on this planet other than the people in this room who should have fucking known about that?'

Sam replied, defensively, 'I was arranging it so that Robert would buy the entire crop when it was ready'.

I said, 'So fucking what, you didn't have to show him where the fucking thing was!' As more of the sorry story unfolded it appeared that Robert had evidently figured that it would be best to take not only the crop but also the growing lights, water pumps, scales and all the other paraphernalia associated with growing and selling weed, which would have ultimately worked out to be more profitable for him.

I demanded of Sam, 'So what the fuck are we supposed to do now? I was relying on that crop and we don't have enough time to find a new place to start over'. At that stage, we were all very high. Sam very calmly said, 'Don't sweat it, it's all under control, you worry way too much'. I had no idea what he was talking about, although he seemed pretty sure of himself so I left it at that.

SMOOTH OPERATOR

I remembered that I had told Alana that I would come back and see her. By that stage, it was two o'clock in the morning but I knew she would still be up because she was practically a vampire; she slept until the afternoon every day and stayed up all night, as did I.

When I got to her apartment she was out; however, two of her acquaintances were there – I'd met them before and they seemed friendly enough. They also appeared to be 'working girls', as they liked to be called. They were helping themselves to Alana's stash while she was away and they offered me some. I joined them because I didn't want to be rude. The girls were smoking hot and one thing led to another; I somehow ended up in Alana's bedroom with the two girls but not long after we had headed into the bedroom, Alana walked in. I thought, *That's okay, there's more than enough of me to go around.* However, that's not at all that went down.

When she walked in, I already had my shirt off, a cigarette in one hand and an alcoholic beverage in the other and both girls were in the process of getting undressed. I was thinking, *Damn, life is good right now!* For some strange reason, Alana blew a gasket; she looked as though she was going to spontaneously combust. She picked up a large ashtray and hurled it at me. I got out of the way just in time and the ashtray hit her dresser and busted up a few bottles of perfume and make-up. I didn't understand what the hell was going on so I asked, 'What the fuck?'

She screamed, 'Get the fuck out of here!' to her two friends and then started searching for something else with which to hurt me. She managed to get hold of a pair of scissors. I lunged across the room, pulled them out of her hands and asked her again, 'What the hell?'

She was a little hysterical but I managed to calm her down to some degree. She spat, 'I leave you alone for a few minutes and you try to fuck my friends'.

I explained, 'I wasn't really trying; I don't know if you've ever noticed but those girls are whores and that's their job.'

I realised that what I was saying was antagonising her, therefore I strategically turned it back onto her and argued, 'Look, your job is to fuck strangers for money, and you're acting like a jealous girlfriend'. As soon as I had said it I knew that I was absolutely correct. I subsequently announced, 'This is fucking insane; I don't need this shit', lit a cigarette, grabbed my keys and started walking towards the door. She ran over, grabbed the bike keys out of my hand and pleaded, 'Sit down'. I duly sat and said, 'Talk fast, because I've just had a really long fucking day'.

She got really teary-eyed and said, 'I have a strategy on how to get out of this whole racket and I want you to be a part of it'. She appeared to be sincere and a little emotional. I felt compelled to listen to what she had to say – even though the notion of having some sort of normal life was rather farfetched; nevertheless, it was somewhat appealing. For a minute there, she had me contemplating the possibility that I could finally catch a break and simply go about living a trouble-free life.

Alana explained: 'We should combine our businesses together and just have one very large operation; if we expand we can cover a much larger area'. I started to think about it and, in theory, her idea did have merit as together we would have much more buying power.

'That's not a bad idea, although I'm going to need some time to think about it – you wouldn't believe the day I've just had; I am in no condition to make a decision like this right now'. Meanwhile, looking at her and listening to her speak, I was thinking, 'She looks so fine; in addition to that she is saying exactly what I want to hear' and a part of me wanted to say, 'Yes' to her right there and then;

although the truth of it was, for me to put that amount of trust in anyone was a concept that terrified the crap out of me. All the same I didn't rule it out altogether.

Back home, I made an ill-fated attempt to sleep for a few hours. This proved to be fairly tricky in view of the fact that I was very restless and anxious as a result of the series of events that day which kept replaying though my brain as a confused film noir. It seemed that the disproportionate amount of drugs that I had taken had also compounded the dilemma. My phone rang, and I was relieved when it did, because I needed the distraction from my own thoughts.

It was Sam. 'I've managed to track down that cocksucker Robert; we should move quickly'.

I asked, 'What are we dealing with?'

Sam replied, 'We'll need some assistance,' to which I replied, 'I'll make a few calls, and be there soon'. A few phone calls later, I'd managed to round up some of the roughest, steroid-ridden Arabs that money could buy, although most of the time the only payment they required was the chance to take part in a brawl. I then made my way to Sam's house together with my recruits. When I got there, I noticed that he had also called in some additional reinforcements. I remember thinking that the crew we had put together may have been a tad excessive for the current situation.

I saw that Sam had hired a removal truck; I couldn't help but laugh as I knew exactly what it was for. The men we had rounded up for the job filed into the back of the truck one after the other, while Sam and I rode up in the front. As it turned out, Robert was a full-blown imbecile, as he was staying only two streets away from Sam's place. I don't think that anyone had ever told him that it is not a good idea to shit where you eat.

We pulled up in his driveway, and Sam jumped out and hammered on the door. I quickly opened up the back of the truck, and instructed a few of the guys to head straight around to the rear of the house and to cover the back door; my foresight paid off, as Robert was already trying to escape from the back.

He was captured and dragged back inside. Sam then beat him unremittingly and the beating was so violent that Robert's own mother would have struggled to identify him by the end of it. Conveniently, Robert's cohorts – the same three from the service station – were all in the house at the time of our invasion. I picked Robert up, smashed his head through the dry wall and kicked him in the ass while he was suspended in the wall;

I said, 'That is for trying to run me over, motherfucker'. He stopped moving; he just hung there and I figured the blow to the head must have rendered him unconscious.

As usual, my gut feeling was accurate, as we hadn't required an entire army for such a minor job. Sam told everyone who had come along to treat themselves to as much as they could carry. Our entire crop was in the house in addition to our equipment, and while we were there, we discovered that Robert had evidently been a busy boy as he had hit many others in the same way. Everything he had taken was also stored in the house, which was great as we managed to fill the entire truck to the top. When we got back into the truck, Sam turned to me, smiling smugly, and said, 'I told you, you worry too much', and at that moment a thought struck me, and I briefly considered the possibility that he had set the whole thing up but then thought, *No fucking way!*

Needless to say, credit to the truckload of stolen merchandise, weed and extra equipment that we had seized, we made a small fortune and managed to sell the entire contents of the truck, excluding our crop, within a few days. We had become notorious, feared and, most importantly, respected once the word had gotten out about what we had done to Robert and his crew. There was no way on earth anyone was going to consider coming near us ever again. It was now known that it was not only dangerous but also very expensive to try and fuck with us. We even took Robert's furniture and clothes just to add insult to injury. Sam refused to sell

Robert's gun after the heist, he wanted to keep it as some sort of trophy.

HINTERLAND OF DEVOTION

I'd almost made up my mind about Alana's proposition. What had just happened with Robert and the fact that I hadn't seen her in a few days was pushing me more in her direction, so I made my way back to her apartment. When I arrived, she was unusually quiet, as though she was in anticipation of something. I poured myself a drink, lit a cigarette, prepared a line and then went and sat out on the balcony. She followed me out and just stood there, staring at me without speaking. I smiled and said, to put her out of her misery, 'Okay, fuck it, I'm in'. She was over the moon – she could not have been happier. Seriously, the look on her face could only be described as pure delight, she even shed a few tears of joy. Meanwhile, I was thinking, *This is awkward; I may need another drink.*

I relocated many of my things to the penthouse – I'm not sure my mother even noticed. Moreover, in accordance with Alana's plan we amalgamated our businesses and fashioned a partnership – I suppose in reality it was more like a match made in hell. I was taken by surprise at how quickly it all came together. After only having been in business together for a week, we could no longer manage the ever-escalating demand for our particular blend without help. We had no other alternative but to put a few people on in order to assist with the deliveries. Alana recruited her sister to help out with the distribution, and at the same time, I employed one of the guys from the neighbourhood who had persistently been asking me to help him start up in the industry. I mainly put him on to help with packaging, as well as deliveries.

The operation ran smoothly, as we had a high criterion when it came to selecting our clientele: we predominantly dealt with lawyers, doctors and even the occasional politician from time to time; they valued our discretion as they were high profile. Seeing that we had top quality, respectable clients, we always got paid on time; in addition to that, we could charge whatever we desired.

We were acquiring money in sums so large that when we went shopping it was frankly, outrageous. There was one instance when we went out to buy a new car and ended up buying two cars from the same dealer only minutes after we'd gotten there. We were unable to simply stop at that; on the same day we continued with our fierce shopping spree. Alana insisted that I upgrade my wardrobe; hence, we went out and bought new clothes, entirely replacing all of my personal attire. She selected the most expensive designer labels that we could find; she also did the same for herself. According to her logic, if we wanted to attract a certain standard of clientele, we had to look the part.

The amount of money we spent that day was flat-out bizarre by anyone's measure – I lost count after twenty-five thousand. The good thing was that we could spend comfortably and with confidence, as the amount of money we were earning was phenomenal; they were definitely the best of times. Apart from our arbitrary spending sprees, we essentially reinvested the money we were making back into the business in order to maintain a steady growth, and it did just that. It eventually got to the point that we were making so much money that we didn't even know what to do with it.

In the early stages of working with Alana, I could not conceive that I had very much to learn and, like most teenagers, I already felt as though I knew everything; however, I was sadly mistaken. The way Alana handled herself in business, either while selling or negotiating a price with the suppliers, was legitimately impressive. She had this way about her that made her like a dangerous drug. She worked wonders for both my self-confidence and my self-esteem as she regularly drew attention to my achievements and rewarded me for them in her own special way. I felt elevated by having my worth recognised by a poised, experienced twenty-eight year old. As a result of working together, our relationship had also developed and we'd grown a lot closer. The positive effect she had on me mentally was largely what caused the business to thrive; she made me feel like I could achieve anything that I put my mind to. Alana had also achieved her goal of putting her days as a prostitute behind her; she was earning more than enough from our business.

One night, roughly eight months into our partnership, I received a telephone call from one of my associates on the North Coast; he informed me that he had come across a phenomenal new gear that was going for half the rate that we were currently paying at the time. My previous dealings with him had all been above board; moreover, he seemed to always come good on his word. I figured that if what he was telling me was even remotely accurate, I couldn't pass up an opportunity like that. I told Alana about the call and she agreed that we needed to investigate it further. Bearing that in mind, I decided to ride up to see him that night. I took the motorbike as I wanted to get there quickly and a trip in a car would have taken ten hours; however, the bike could make the trip in six. Besides, I didn't have to worry about being stopped on the way back whilst in the possession of contraband because I was almost uncatchable on the bike, being considered by my peers to be faster than a greased leopard.

I arrived at my destination ahead of schedule so I checked myself into a decent hotel. Once I had had breakfast and a bit of rest, I headed off to meet with my contact and examine the new merchandise, and it was just as he said it would be; however, he did not have very much on hand. I took what he did have for the purpose of taking it back to show Alana. Before I walked out of the meeting, I told him, 'Organise as much as you can get your hands on, and I'll be back to take the whole lot as soon as it's available'.

PLAYED LIKE A PIANO

Even though I had only been away for a few days, I was very eager to show Alana my findings. When I got back to the apartment Alana was not there; in fact nothing was there at all. I started to fret – at first I thought we'd been robbed and Alana must be out. I found it somewhat odd that her mobile phone was switched off; I repeatedly and desperately attempted to call her but there was never any answer. I was assuming that the money would be safe, as we had taken a great deal of care to safeguard it. We had concealed it in such a fashion that no one could find it even if they turned the entire penthouse upside down. The money was in a gym bag behind a false wall at the back of the walk-in wardrobe in the bedroom. I went straight in and removed the false wall – when I saw that the money was gone, my heart sank; I looked around and noticed that all our clothes were gone too.

The reality of what had just ensued hit me like a ton of bricks. I felt my chest tighten and the veins in my wrists expand. Alana had insisted that we count the money only a few days before I'd left for the North Coast. The bag had contained a little over one hundred and eighty thousand dollars, in addition to approximately thirty thousand dollars worth of drugs.

I had just been conned on a scale of epic proportions and the fact that I could do nothing about it was making me extremely angry. She did not leave behind a single trace of her existence and had taken absolutely everything; it even appeared as though the apartment had been thoroughly cleaned. I was truly fucked, for the reason that every last dollar I had was in that bag. At first I was so furious I was almost apoplectic. I set about destroying the apartment until I ran out of stamina and finally just sat on the floor. I was devastated; I had no fight left in me, almost as though life itself had been at war with me and had finally won.

My mind had begun to wander off into a very dark place, and I considered the possibility that the name she had given me may not even have been true. All of the things she had said and done in the time we were together began flooding back into my mind and as they did, I could suddenly see all of the tell-tale signs which had indicated that I was being set up. The fact that I had been conned was not doing wonders for my ego; however, it did not hurt me anywhere near as much as having to let go of the dream of a normal life. Alana had done a great job of selling it to me; she must have used that approach because it had been obvious to her that all I wanted was to have a normal life.

As I was sitting on the floor, I heard someone at the front door; I got up to see who it was and Kirsten, Alana's sister, was standing there looking around. I shouted, 'Where the fuck is she?'

Looking bewildered she answered, 'I don't know; she called me a few days ago, right after you left, and told me not to come around for a few days because there wasn't any work'. I accepted that to be true in view of the fact that while Kirsten was working for us, Alana paid and treated her as though she was a slave. In addition to that, she was only a mule, and judging from the way Alana had dealt with her sister, it was obvious that she didn't think enough of her to tell her anything at all.

Kirsten, sounding worried said, 'I really need to find her; I need my money because I have to take one of the kids to the dentist and I have to pay the rent'.

I retorted, 'You must be mentally defective – does it look like she's coming back to you?' Seeing as I had already accepted my defeat, I handed the keys to the car to her and said, 'Here, sell this; it should give you enough money to sort yourself and your children out'. Kirsten was lucky that we'd bought two cars. I'm sure that if

Alana could have driven them both at the same time, she would have taken the second one too.

As I left the apartment, the sobering truth that not a single living human being on the face of the earth could be trusted struck home. I was bitter because I had to start over and I was resentful because I had worked so hard and had put myself through so much to make that money. Yet I was, above all, heartbroken that she didn't only leave with the money, she had managed to escape my detestable life. To dig right down to the core of it all, I was in love with two things – certainly not that gold-digging, money-hungry, scamming bitch. The first was the lifestyle; I ate with a silver spoon and drank from a golden cup but now I was going back to the beginning with nothing at all to show for it but a new bad habit to add to the list. The second thing was the idea of an easy life.

Although I felt totally destroyed, in some way this turn of events seemed inevitable. I was being punished by fate and fate was playing fair, as I deserved everything that was happening to me. Was it fate or was it the hand of God? Was God fate or was fate God? All along, I had known that I was not a criminal by nature and therefore I was going against that same nature, albeit in order to survive. I might have been living a glamorous life but even in the best of times, deep down, I was so sad and nagged by a constant feeling of despair, haunted by depression. It was almost as though the devil had got hold of me and would not let go. This incident had just made it all the more evident that I was not going to be able to escape.

With my head hung low and a grievous feeling of betrayal dragging me down, I returned home and put my other car up for sale without delay. I made a few phone calls in order to organise collecting most of the money I was owed, which wasn't all that much as most of my clients paid cash upfront. I only just scraped together enough funding to restore my original operation back to the way it was. I was feeling flat and discouraged; I no longer had the drive or desire to expand back to what I had with Alana. I had no desire to write down all these events and emotions in my journal.

What for? My controlling objective was to keep the business consistent enough to support my drug habit and keep me alive and every so often I would come across the odd job or hustle, which aided in sustaining my lifestyle.

Around that time, Sam had just moved into a large house, and I found myself spending a lot of my time there, as did many other of our associates and local drug dealers. I was abusing drugs to such an extent that I was wasted all day, every day. My tolerance to the drugs had increased so that it no longer mattered how much I took, I would barely feel the effects. My brain was undoubtedly cooked as my eyes were always crimson in colour and my speech was becoming slurred.

THE REDNECK

As time went by, I felt less and less like going out, so instead of hanging out at Sam's place, I was spending far more time holed up at home. For some reason my house was becoming a beacon for the neighbourhood loafers and junkies; they were constantly at my house freeloading, smoking my weed and eating my food. From time to time, I would charge them, which made their behaviour marginally acceptable. Richard was also visiting a lot more frequently, because he couldn't get high at home.

In addition to all this, Todd, who was one of my regular clients, was also coming around often – so frequently in fact that he was getting on my nerves. The key reason I found him so annoying was because he just would not leave; he would be there for breakfast, lunch and dinner. Moreover he would, in passing, regularly make racially derogatory comments. For instance he would part with such nuggets as, 'Let's go get a kebab; you love kebabs because you're an Arab, all dirty Arabs like kebabs.' Tact was not his strong point.

Todd was a large unit; he must have weighed in at no less than one hundred and sixty kilograms and he had some height on him which made him tend to tower over everyone else as he lumbered around. His head and his neck were indistinguishable as they were both exactly the same width, which happened to be double extra large. He was white like Wonder Bread, and had scores of unsanitary-looking freckles splattered all over his forehead and eyes; it appeared as though someone had begun spray-painting him but didn't finish the job. In my opinion, his neck was his main feature, as it was a bright and fluorescent pink; in addition to that, I could have sworn that it would become brighter, as though it were incandescing, when he was acting like a racist dogmatist, which was often. Day after day, that elephantine imbecile would come into my home and methodically eat my food, take my drugs and let out his trifling snide criticisms. He even had the arrogance to make comments on the subject of the peculiarity of the food he was eating and the drugs he was taking, but the fact that he was dissatisfied did not hinder his scoffing everything in sight.

After a while, that fat pig started to become more Machiavellian when I left him unattended. He decided to try to poach my clients right out from under me when I wasn't paying attention. He was clearly far too dimwitted to have the foresight to consider the repercussions when I found out. My clients had no interest in going elsewhere because they knew that regardless of the state of the market or how dry it got out there, I always provided reliability and quality. It also worked to my benefit that I never failed to make the time to regularly converse with many of my clients.

It was a valuable commodity, having that level of customer conscientiousness, for when Todd tried to poach them; they reported it back to me without delay. Todd had taken it upon himself to inform a few of my clients that he had a friend who could provision them with much larger deals at a fraction of the price. He also told them that his friend could give them the deals on credit for as long as they required.

I thought it ironic that Todd was making such claims, as he didn't have his own business, contacts or any means of getting anything at all; I had to assume that he was just exerting himself in an attempt to burn me, out of envy and malevolence. I should have caught on sooner, seeing that he asked me at least three or four times a week to tell him who my suppliers were! When was I going to learn not to keep hoping that trust still existed? How could I continue to be so naïve?

I had no option but to deal with him. He was lucky as I was still preoccupied with the Alana catastrophe and didn't want to spend much time dealing with trivial items such as he was. For this reason, I wasn't too harsh on him; I cut him off in a straightforward manner.

I waited until there were a few people over, as there were others who needed to hear the message, and just as Todd was going to reach for some weed, I pushed his hand away and announced, 'No weed for you; this weed is for people who have a spine. Now get up and get the fuck out of my house, you're no longer welcome here!'

He stood up and asked, 'What's your problem?' to which I yelled, 'You heard me. Get the fuck out – don't make me tell you again. You know what you've done, you low-life fucking snake'. He got up and walked out. As far as I was concerned, that was the end of it with that prick.

The following day, I was hanging around at home with Richard; we were playing video games, when my brother ran in and shouted, 'Someone is in the backyard trying to steal the plant!' I had a little plant growing in the backyard just as a pastime; it was by no means going to make me wealthy, so I was not too concerned but there was the matter of principle. In the backyard, I caught a glimpse of one of Todd's friends trying to pull the plant out of the pot. He noticed me coming and abandoned the plant to make a run for it. I picked up the closest thing to me, which happened to be one of the bricks that the pot was originally resting on, and I threw it at him. I managed to get him on the back of the neck while he was jumping over the fence; unfortunately, it dropped him on the wrong side of the palings where I didn't have easy access to him, and he had an accomplice waiting for him in the laneway on the other side in a car, who aided his escape.

THE CHIROPRACTOR

I went back inside, grabbed the phone, and called Todd; amazingly, he had the balls to answer the phone and talk to me.

What the fuck do you think you're doing?' I yelled at him.

'I've no idea what you're talking about', then he hung up on me. I don't think Todd realised it at that stage, but he was playing a particularly dangerous game; he must have mistaken my previous lack of action as a sign of weakness.

Shortly after that, I received a few calls from clients. While I was talking to one of them, the bike alarm went off. Unusually, I had left the bike at the front of the house rather than putting it in the garage as I normally did. When I hurtled outside there was nobody there, although I heard a car a few streets away take off. I recognised the distinct sound of that particular car, as it had been modified; it belonged to another one of Todd's friends. I was furious to discover that the bike's steering lock had been broken; on top of that, the barrel for the key had been damaged, as they had used a slide hammer, which meant that they had come with the sole intention of stealing my bike. That was a very serious offence, which called for some drastic retaliatory measures.

By that stage I was truly seeing red, as all I had done was feed that feral animal, and I had treated him with courtesy and respect up until his well-deserved eviction, and even that had been conducted with remarkable restraint on my part. For no apparent reason at all he had decided to wage a war on me. I was becoming obsessed with my need for retribution, although I didn't let it take control of me. For the next few days, I carefully and covertly set up surveillance across from his house and waited for him to eventually return home. My call must have alarmed him somewhat, as he appeared to have disappeared off the face of the earth. I knew he would return sooner or later, because all of his belongings were there.

When he ultimately arrived back at his home, he got out of his car and looked around to ensure he was not being watched, although he didn't spot me. He appeared to be hesitant and distressed as he got out of his car, which in my opinion, is the demeanour of a man with a guilty conscience. When he felt confident that he was in the clear, he made a run for it; prior to that I had never seen an obese person run so fast. It was uglier than it was funny; the bottom part of his body was moving really fast like a duck under water, and the top part followed like a big, saggy waterbed that didn't have enough water in it – it was almost as though he was moving in sections. I promptly left my hiding spot and crossed to his front door; I couldn't see the point of knocking, as he was clearly not going to let me in. Opportunely enough, he had only closed the screen door behind him. When I reached the door, I could see Todd's brother standing there. Before I had a chance to say anything, his brother abruptly said, 'Todd's not here'. His short, dry and rude response did not sit very well with me in my current mood; hence I kicked the screen door in and destroyed his nose with my helmet. I hit him with such force that the helmet actually broke. Todd's brother blacked out instantaneously. I ran upstairs to Todd's bedroom, which was locked and commenced kicking that door in too. When the door finally collapsed open, I saw Todd standing there with a baseball bat in his hand in front of his bedroom window. He snarled, 'What are you gonna do, you stupid, filthy Arab?' Without even stopping to think, I charged at Todd and pushed him through the glass and out of the window. Conveniently for him, he landed on the roof of his car rather than the pavement; due to the fact that he was such a fat fuck, the impact broke most of the windows.

I walked downstairs and dragged him off the car by his mangy, unkempt orange hair; he was crying like a little girl and repeatedly gasped, 'Please don't hurt me'.

'You brought this on yourself you fat cocksucker'. He had chosen the wrong person to fuck with. I stood over him with my foot pressed into his face, called Sam and instructed him, 'Bring a few guys, and come see me right now'. I gave Sam the address and he showed up within minutes, as he didn't live very far away.

Sam helped me drag Todd back into the house, where I beat him senseless for at least half an hour. Sam belatedly came over and stopped me, saying, 'Hey, one more blow and you'll kill him'. I sat down and lit a cigarette. Meanwhile, Sam and the guys had searched Todd's house and they were very thorough. When they moved into the garage, they discovered a plantation. When I walked in, I could not, at first, come to any conclusions about what I was seeing. Todd had never mentioned anything about it to me at all, although it did start to make a lot of sense. That would have been the motivation for his sad attempt to steer my customers away.

Upon closer inspection, it turned out that his plants were all males, which meant that they were absolutely useless, just like the fat prick who planted them. I thought that it was hilarious; I actually could not stop laughing at what Todd had done, as that donkey had jeopardised his life for sterile plants. Needless to say, we took all of his equipment and anything else of any value that we thought we might be able to sell. While I was looking around, I came across a bolt action hunting rifle and a box of bullets; I decided to keep those particular articles for myself.

I loaded the gun and slid the bolt into position. At that point I walked over to Todd, who was still crouched, cowering, on the floor, and put my foot on his oversized neck, pressed the rifle into his face real hard and said, 'Hey Sam, I have no alternative but to finish this fucking guy, because I'm positive that he just won't quit'. Todd started begging again, 'I will leave, I promise, you'll never see me again'. Sam reasoned, 'That's fair enough and if he does come back, I'll kill him myself, no ifs, ands or buts about it'.

While we were still at Todd's house, Sam got hungry. He opened the fridge which was empty so he opened the pantry and it was full of canned spaghetti, bottles of vegemite and a few loaves of bread. Sam called out to me, 'How the fuck did that prick get so big eating nothing but canned spaghetti on toast?' I told him, 'That stuff is packed full of carbohydrates; besides, I think it may be genetic, just look at his neck, that shit is downright freaky'. Once we had concluded our discussion regarding Todd's dietary habits, we packed the cars with what we had looted and left.

A few weeks later, I coincidentally ran into the ass-pirate who had attempted to steal the plant from my backyard. I spotted him at a club; he was leaving while I was making my way in. He stood out because of the large Band-Aid he was wearing on his neck which was concealing the injury that I had caused when I threw the brick at him. When he noticed me, his demeanour indicated that he wished to seek recompense for what had happened in my backyard. As we stood at the top of the stairs, he actually had the cheek to approach me and say, 'You're not so tough without a brick are you?'

I said, 'On the contrary, I'm actually tougher'. Without delay, I grabbed onto his face and pushed him down the stairs head first – it happened so quickly. It was a long flight of stairs; hence it took him a while to tumble all the way to the bottom. When he finally arrived at his destination, it appeared as though he had been badly injured. It caused a bit of commotion and the crowd that was in front of the club started to gather around. I did my best to blend in with the mob and become a bystander; I rushed over with the rest of the faction as if I was concerned for his wellbeing or inquisitive as to what was going on. When I reached the bottom of the stairs, I exclaimed, 'My goodness, are you okay?' and I said it loud enough so that the people standing around could hear it. I then leaned over him, as though I was about to assist him, and quietly said, 'Listen here you motherfucking mutt, if I ever see you or any of your friends in the neighbourhood, you will not get off this easy again'.

Following that little event, Todd must have moved house or left the country, because I never saw or heard from him again. Come to think of it, I never saw any of his friends either. It appeared as though my message had finally gotten through. After this, I began to distance myself from a lot of the low-lives, losers, deadbeats and scum that I used to keep in my company, which limited my social circle to quite a small number. What had happened with Todd reiterated and reaffirmed the cold reality that the notion of trustworthy people was purely a myth. The dealings that I had with my clients had become very sparse in nature. In addition to that, I reduced the amount of contact that I had with people in general to such a degree that I was practically living in seclusion.

MULE BOY

I was drawn out of my solitude when one of my clients approached me and requested my assistance. His name was Hugo and he had a tiling company; he claimed that he was on the verge of losing the business, as his apprentice had just left him in the middle of an urgent job. I was extremely reluctant to assist him but I agreed only because he had a distinct air of desperation about him; he had a family to support and relied solely on his business to do that.

From the moment I got there, the job didn't agree with me. On my first day, he made me haul large buckets of sand and bags of cement up the stairs of a seven-storey building as, naturally, he happened to be working on the top level. I had to endlessly repeat the process over and over again throughout the course of the day. I perspired profusely as I toiled with those damned buckets, while Hugo just sat there comfortably and laid the tiles.

After a few days, it began to get on my nerves. What made matters even worse was Hugo's morning ritual, which consisted of him taking several lines of speed, removing a mirror from his pocket and proceeding to spend at least twenty minutes gawking at his reflection. He would then stop, look at me and say, 'My eyes are beautiful; don't you think my eyes are beautiful?' I found his actions and comments to be very peculiar and not a little narcissistic. Who did he think he was?

Only a week into the job, I started to become convinced that I was just a few buckets away from retiring. Hugo helped hasten my verdict while he was having his lunch. He sat on the stairs with a few of the other tradesmen who were working on the site and started to show off. He turned to me while I was in the process of carrying the buckets up the stairs and called, 'Hurry up mule boy, move faster!' I freaked and my anger was almost uncontainable; however, I managed to stay composed and kept quiet. I proceeded to the roof with the buckets but then departed from routine and dropped them from the very top of the building onto the roof of his car. The heftiness of the sand buckets completely demolished the vehicle. I grabbed a shovel and made my way back down the stairs. Hugo queried, 'What was that noise?' I told him, 'You have a convertible now,' and whacked him with the shovel; I got him square in the face. He was such a bitch that he actually started to snivel.

'Now you can carry the buckets yourself, mule boy', I told him and mentally crossed him off the list of my clients with a flourish.

PRIVATE DICK

Spending so much time alone gave me cabin fever. I figured that it was time I did something productive so I enrolled to study at the best tertiary education supplier available; I settled upon becoming a private investigator. I figured I might be able to do some good for a change, in an attempt to try and atone for the loathsome and evil things I had done and metamorphose from being the totally unwholesome creature I had become to a worthwhile and useful member of the community. My philosophy dictated that it would be a somewhat rewarding and worthwhile job, as I could specialise in finding missing people and return them to their worried families.

For the next two years, while the drugs business was more or less running itself, I completely committed myself to my studies and put my heart and soul into it; as a result I reaped the rewards of my hard work and devotion. I was awarded high distinctions for all of my assessments and I topped the state in nearly every exam. Once I had completed my studies, I remember feeling somewhat pleased with my accomplishments. The fact that my certification clearly indicated that I had finished with high distinctions only added to my overall sense of achievement. The next and final step in obtaining my private investigator's licence was a visit to the local police station where I would register, thus enabling me to commence work in an official capacity.

At the police station, I was greeted by a morbidly obese, malodorous and sloth-ridden police officer; he looked as though he could have been Todd's father. I handed him my paperwork with a huge smile and said, 'I am here to get my licence'. The police officer accessed his computer and within seconds joyfully replied, 'Your application has been rejected'. I immediately became agitated and to make matters worse the bad news appeared to be giving the police officer in question a great deal of unnatural gratification. However, I simply bit my lip and asked, 'Why has my application been rejected?' He replied, 'Because you have a criminal record'. His brief answers and obvious pleasure were not helping the situation or my level of agitation one bit; nevertheless, I pushed on and asked, 'Is there anything I can do to resolve this issue?' He said, somewhat triumphantly, I thought, 'No'.

At that point, I was only seconds away from dragging the cop over to my side of the counter and beating him to a fine pulp right there in the police station, which would, unfortunately, have been detrimental to me. I said, 'I understood that a background check was done by the course provider before I even started to study, just to make sure this sort of thing would not happen'.

He looked back down at his computer for a few minutes, and then, without even looking back up at me, announced, 'There appears to have been a clerical error; your name was misspelled in the system. You should not have been allowed to do the training in the first place'.

I replied, 'Well it's too late – I've done it now, and short of a frontal lobotomy I cannot unlearn it. Besides, I was a minor when I got my record, surely you must have made a mistake or two when you were young? I say let's work together and find a solution'. His response was to indicate the way to the door with a flap of his pudgy hand.

ON THE EDGE

I was devastated and exhausted in light of the naked truth that I had misapplied my time, money and effort – and it was all for scratch. You'd think I would have become acclimatised to that type of scenario by then; yet it had completely crushed me. Over the next few months, my drug intake tripled; my mental state declined to such an extent that I eventually went into an abyss of deep and dark depression. I felt as though I was losing my will to live, and possibly even my mind; my response to this was to become increasingly reckless.

There was a shortage of weed for myself and my clients, which meant me heading up the north coast. I knew of a place where I could always get some; approximately a nine-hour ride from my home. In an effort to make my voyage a little more amusing, I consumed an entire bottle of Absolut vodka before I rode up.

It was a miracle that I got there in one piece; was someone "up there" looking after me?

I was feeling weary when I arrived and decided to stay for a few days in order to recover. It was a secluded area which did not have any main roads running through or even near it. The people who dwelled there were a very small and intimate community and the fact that they were so off the beaten track left them free to live like carefree hippies. During my stay there, I experimented with some of their drugs; I even sampled their magic mushrooms; intense and I hallucinated terribly. The hallucinations were incredibly vivid and I could not make them stop no matter how much I tried. It was an overall terrifying experience, almost like being stuck in your worst nightmare and not being able to wake up. What made matters even worse was the fact that the area where I had ingested the mushroom was in close proximity to the edge of a cliff and I was walking around unaccompanied, under the influence of an extraordinarily potent hallucinogenic. In hindsight, how on earth did I not end up walking straight off the cliff? I would almost have to chalk that one up to divine intervention.

It seems likely that the bad trip was prompted by my already being in a very bad and sad place mentally. If I had had even half my wits about me or cared at all about my survival beyond that day, I would not have eaten the mushroom.

The experience left me feeling drained and mentally broken; I only just had enough zeal left in me to return home. The ride back ended up being a treacherous ordeal as I was caught in a very heavy storm while experiencing nightmarish flashbacks, which was a relapse side effect commonly caused by the mushrooms. That ride felt as though it was the longest ride I had ever been on in my life.

It was soon pretty obvious that I found taking risks, living dangerously and cheating death were the only things that made me feel remotely mortal. Within no time at all I had reached a stage where I was basically trying to commit suicide on a daily basis; surviving would make me feel like I had achieved something great. I had proved to myself beyond a doubt that if it is not your time to die, you just can't force it. Meanwhile, at the back of my mind was the constant thought rolling around that not one of my so-called friends, and certainly not my mother, cared enough about me to even notice that I had reached rock bottom which deepened my feeling of desolation. I was so alone.

Risk-taking became a way of life for me; I would experience a drug overdose at least three times a week – I was on firstname terms with a number of the doctors and nurses, and when I rode my bike there was no longer an inbetween on the accelerator – it was either all on, or else the bike was parked. I even managed to get my hands on an old revolver and every so often I would put a bullet in it, give it a spin and engage in a one-player game of Russian roulette. Hearing the click of the trigger and actually having lived through it was beyond doubt an amazing feeling; it was almost like a pure adrenalin hit and an overwhelming sense of relief all rolled into one. The best part was the calm after the storm. My heart would race more than usual until finally an overwhelming peace and serenity would wash over me. Winning the game of life and death was more addictive than any man-made drug, so much in fact that I gradually became obsessed with the constant pursuit of finding new and improved ways to recreate that feeling all the time.

MENTOR

Every so often, I'd ride with Damien and the more time I spent with him the more I began to realise that we actually had a lot in common. For instance, he rode in a very similar fashion to me, which was like an all-out kamikaze suicide mission. In addition to that, he too was a computer enthusiast and his absorption in the machines prompted the rekindling of the all-consuming interest in computers that I had formerly had, and I swiftly got back up to date. We used to spend hours on end in a tiny room at the back of his house, which was filled wall to wall with computers, and we would just work on them. He was running at least six computers at a time for his own personal use, which I thought was impressive. He did the occasional random IT job from time to time for people he knew, which eventually gave me an idea.

I didn't have any official qualifications; however, I managed to work out how to build a computer or laptop from scratch; in addition to that, I taught myself the vast majority of the software packages that were popular at the time. Watching Damien work had motivated me and given me some new ideas.

I then started doing odd jobs for people I knew and made a bit of money from it but I was mostly doing it because it distracted me from the reality that the whole world was a rotten, morally corrupt and dark place to try and survive.

It didn't take Sam that long to catch on to what I was doing and he sought to exploit my skill, as he often faced the dilemma of what to do with stolen laptops that were locked. Before long I had become the go-to guy for all of his laptop unlocking needs, even when they were locked deep in the hardware. Once I was established as a laptop unlocker, I began to receive follow-up requests for further software and hardware upgrades and started making reasonable money out of it.

In those days the internet was not yet at a stage where it could render adequate assistance, therefore I would have to consult with Damien when I came across a problem I couldn't decipher. In the time that I spent with Damien, I began slowly to discover that he had a very dark and troubled history although I couldn't be absolutely certain of what he had done; however, I did know that he had done a long stint in prison.

The more time I spent in Damien's company, the more bizarre he turned out to be. One particular incident occurred when I went to visit him in order to acquire some computer software. He walked out of his room wearing nothing but high heels and a pink scarf! What added to my dismay was the repulsive and nauseating fact that he had his dick tucked in between his legs, to make it look as though he had a vagina.

'What the fuck is the matter with you?' I asked but he just laughed. It made me uncomfortable to even be in the same air space as him, as he had just redefined the connotation of the word fucked. He, on the other hand, didn't seem to be more than usually concerned with his outward appearance, as he continued to walk outside and quite calmly walked down the street. He actually walked all the way to the local shops and started talking to people. It seemed as though he had no inhibitions or self-respect whatsoever. No attempt was made to stop him – where were the cops when you actually needed them?

One night when I was home alone, I was feeling a little bored so I decided to go for a ride to the casino and play the blackjack tables for a while, in order to pass the time. On the way there, I saw Damien in the street; he waved me down and asked me where I was going and when I told him, he announced, 'I'll come with you'. Conveniently he was dressed appropriately, which was a relief but as soon as he put the key in the ignition of his bike, he got a call from his sister.

'I have to pick up my sister from a club on the way in; she can come with us to the casino'. I remember thinking, Great; this is going to be awkward, as she was Carmen, the sister with whom I had had the discreet and exceedingly confusing relationship. I followed Damien as he went to pick up Carmen, and as it turned out, she was nowhere near the shortest route to the casino. When we finally reached the club, she jumped on the back of the bike with her brother but almost immediately after we had started moving again, a police siren chirped behind us; we both took off as soon as we heard that sound.

At that point I lost track of Damien as we'd split up and gone in entirely different directions. I stuck to the back streets and kept the bike in a high gear so I would not make too much noise, in order to evade detection. For some reason, there were a lot more police patrol cars on the road than usual that night and they seemed to know the route I was taking and had set up a roadblock on the darkest possible road. By the time I saw the roadblock I knew that it was too late to stop or turn around so I pulled the bike up, removed my helmet, and lit a cigarette as I had an idea it was going to be a very long night. The cop walked over to me, pulled me off the bike and slammed my head onto the hood of his car. I dropped my cigarette and the cop grabbed my wrist and started bending it behind my back until it felt like it was going to break. He demanded, 'Where did the other bike go?' I asked, 'What other bike?' He responded by slamming my head into the car again.

I said, 'Look man, I don't know who that guy was; I just saw him riding and decided to ride with him for a while'. The cop got out his ticket book and proceeded to write one citation after another; in addition to that, he cancelled my licence on the spot. I managed to attain a few thousand dollars worth of fines for violations that I didn't even know existed, which left me feeling somewhat petulant.

The cop finished writing the tickets and said, 'You can no longer ride the bike because you don't have a licence'.

I said, 'I wouldn't dream of it', and while he was still standing there, I pulled out my phone, called Sam and told him, 'I'm going to need you to bring your tow truck and come and pick me up', and I told him where I was. Sam replied somewhat surprised, 'What the fuck are you talking about, what tow truck?'

I replied, 'So you can't get here any sooner? Okay then, no problem, I'll see you when you get here'. I hung up the phone and told the policeman, 'I just called a friend who has a towing business; I'll have to wait until he arrives and tow the bike home for me'.

I waited a minute or two until the police car was out of sight, and then I got the hell out of there. For the most part I stuck to the back roads and made my way to Damien's house. I happened to run into him on the way back, as he was also taking the back streets. We were not very far from the neighbourhood when I caught up with him.

We rode back to Damien's house together, in order to finally drop off Carmen. She jumped off the back of his bike, and what happened next was wrong on so many different levels that I cannot even begin to express it. Carmen removed her helmet, walked over to her brother and commenced kissing him in a freaky just-about-to-have-passionate-sex kind of way. I felt as though I was going to be sick and rubbed my eyes, just to make sure they were not playing tricks on me. What I was seeing was regrettably accurate, which indicated to me that they were both very disturbed. I did not even say farewell, I just started the bike and took off as their moment seemed as though it was by no means going to end any time soon.

GANGS OF SYDNEY

A few weeks after that weird evening, my brother was walking home with some of his friends when a number of intoxicated Torres Strait Islanders must have arrived at the conclusion that it would be savvy to relieve them of their money and shoes. Damien was concluding a drug deal at my place when my brother arrived home bleeding and shoeless, and was not happy that such a thing had taken place in his neighbourhood, as he was immensely territorial. He asked me to wait a few minutes and then follow him to his house. He wanted to sort it out. When I reached Damien's place, he was in the process of loading a handful of bullets into two large chrome revolvers, which he then stowed away in their customary position in his belt. In addition to that, he had concealed several throwing knives in his boots. He then grabbed hold of a bag which contained a shotgun, shells and various other weapons – some of which I had never seen the likes of before – and slung it over his shoulder.

I was thinking that the night was undoubtedly going to end in disaster, as the drunken Islanders were all assembled in a park that was very close to the local police station but the fact that the police station was in such close proximity did not trouble Damien in the least, most likely quite the reverse.

He had a large four-wheel drive parked out in front of his house; he jumped in, and I followed suit. When we arrived at the park, Damien drove the four-wheel drive up onto the grass and made a beeline for the biggest Islander in the group. I was under the impression that his intention was only to scare them a little;

however, that did not turn out to be the case at all. He did not stop or even slow the car down until he had in fact hit one of them. Before I had had a chance to blink, Damien had leapt out of the car and started wielding his guns – he even fired several random shots all over the place. This was apparently so intimidating that the police didn't care to venture an investigation.

Meanwhile there was a bunch of hefty drunken Islanders scrambling, screaming, weeping and hiding. Damien grabbed the one who was lying in front of his car, as a result of having been run over, and dragged him over to a picnic table in the park. He then started pounding his head into the table with the handle of the largest gun. Once he was finished doing that, he pulled a knife out of his boot and held it so close to the Islander's face that he cut him slightly. He told him in a deliberately slow voice, 'The only reason I'm gonna allow you to live, is so that you can let the others know that if I ever see any of you in the neighbourhood again I'll finish the job'. I watched in awe as he then jammed the knife into the table next to the Islander's head.

I was learning a great deal from Damien and taking into consideration the reality that he was a deranged psychopath, this made him an exceptionally unfavourable influence on me at that point in time. I was beginning to see how the mechanism of true evil actually operated and how easy it was for people in his circle to commit random acts of wickedness. For me, this was moving on from my previous experiences where the violence I had perpetrated on others had been something I saw as justified – either as protection or as retribution. Damien was into violence purely for the pleasure.

GRAVEL RASH

A few months later, I was out delivering a package to one of my clients and I was in a mad rush, for the reason that I had to be in several different places that day. I tested the limit, pushing the bike past what the laws of physics would safely allow – my belief was, and still is, that the only way to know what the limits were was to go past them and so, while I was riding round a corner, I was moving way too quickly and the bike came out from underneath me. I slid down the road and regrettably, I was only wearing jeans and a T-shirt at the time, not being a fan of the regular protective riding gear. As a result, I lost a great deal of skin from my knees and forearms as I slid along the road. Eventually my headlong slide was stopped by an oncoming car when my head became wedged between the front wheel of the vehicle and the road. If the car in question had advanced forward by even one more centimetre, it would have broken my neck and killed me instantly. Was this another case of my guardian angel being there for me or what?

I was losing a lot of blood. Consequently, I was rushed to the hospital, where I was put under anaesthetic while they repaired my busted up knee and tended to my injuries. My habit of camouflaging the gear in innocuous looking gift-wrap proved its usefulness, as no nosy nursing staff investigated it while I was unconscious and it was still there waiting for the client who had to come and pick it up from the hospital.

When I came round, I began looking for my clothes; I couldn't find them anywhere. Eventually, a nurse came in to check up on me. When she had finally given up on trying to tell me that I had to stay in overnight, she told me, 'A grimy-looking, bearded man who was covered in tattoos came in and took your clothes, and he left with them.'

I asked, quite justifiably I thought, 'And you just let him take my clothes?' The nurse shrugged disinterestedly, although on second thoughts, I didn't know many people who would dare say no to Damien – I knew that it could only have been Damien, as he had a defective and perverted sense of humour. I also knew where he would most likely be; across the road at the hotel. There was a bar there where he played pool and drank every so often. I had no alternative but to leave the hospital without any clothes in order to find him and recover my garments. As I crossed the road, my ass was hanging out of the hospital gown and as a result, I was getting a little bit of a back draught and a few wolf whistles from nurses taking a smoke break outside the hospital.

When I walked into the bar, it turned out that I was right. Damien was there and in the process of playing a game of pool. When he noticed me, he started laughing and pointed at the bar, where my clothes were in a neatly folded stack. While getting dressed, Damien started causing some trouble in the hotel. He was getting ready to take the next shot in his game of pool, when a large biker approached him and asked, 'Do you know how many more games you are going to play?' An innocent enough question but the expression on Damien's face had altered; he had taken offence.

Damien apparently didn't think the biker's query merited any response other than to look at him with cold, dead eyes. He sat down on the floor next to the pool table and removed one of his boots, followed by his sock; he then took his sock and put a pool ball into it. At that stage, the large biker had already walked away and had his back turned; Damien took the opportunity to assault the man with his sock. As soon as the sock connected with the biker's head, he went down and was out cold; in addition to that, a pool of blood started to form around his head. The unconscious biker's friends happened to be at the bar drinking and when they saw what had happened, they rushed over to assist their friend and to straighten out the matter with Damien. Damien's face lit up, more or less like a child who had just gotten exactly what he wanted for Christmas. It was as though he merely wanted justification in support of instigating a brawl. There were three other bikers and each one of them was at least twice the size of Damien. I was surprised at the outcome, as Damien went crazy and took all three of them down without sustaining a single injury.

Damien wisely fled the scene almost immediately after the last biker hit the floor; I quickly finished getting dressed and got the hell out of there too before the police started to arrive and ask questions. I had to limp down the street and catch a cab, as my knee was still in a great deal of pain. Meanwhile, Damien was flying on adrenalin and had apparently gone for a ride in an attempt to calm down and, as a result, ended up having an accident.

FALSE STATEMENT

The next morning Damien came to my house and announced that he wanted me to tell the police that I had witnessed the accident but I wasn't comfortable with doing that, and besides, I was loaded to the eyeballs with drugs and painkillers because of my own collision. He pleaded, 'I really need your help – if there are no witnesses, I can't get the insurance money to fix the bike'. Feeling sorry for him, I capitulated. 'Fine, what do I have to do?' He took me out to where the accident had taken place and I think he may, as usual, have been high on something, as he explained what had transpired in a fashion that did not make a lot of sense.

I went to the police station with the dodgy information that Damien had provided to me and began to tell them what I had witnessed, with apparent confidence and unwavering certainty. The police officer who was taking my statement stopped me and said, 'Did you know that you can be charged for giving a false statement?' I quickly started to back-pedal in an effort to talk my way out of a predicament that was rapidly becoming oppressive but didn't make much headway with the officer who made it clear he did not believe one word.

I left the police station thinking that Damien was a fucking idiot as, once the police had revealed to me what had actually happened, I knew that the details he had provided me with were entirely incorrect. When I got to Damien's place, it turned out to be lucky for me that he was strapped to some sort of apparatus and was hanging upside down while a chiropractor was in the process of treating him for his back pain. When I told him, that the information he had given me was all out of whack and that the police wanted to charge me for giving them a false statement, he didn't react very well at all. Struggling to release himself from the harness, he screamed, 'Get the fuck out of my house!' I couldn't be bothered arguing with him, so I left without saying a word.

I didn't hear any more from Damien while he was recovering from his accident but a few weeks later he climbed in through my bedroom window when I was asleep. He took a pillow and held it over my face with enough pressure on it to suffocate me. I got one of my arms free and managed to hook it under his leg and flip him over and before he even knew what was going on I was standing over him, gun drawn and pointed at his forehead. It was fortunate for me that I was mistrustful enough to constantly sleep with my gun close to the bed.

Seeing the gun aimed at his head, he began to laugh maniacally and said, 'What's the matter with you? I was only playing. I need you to get me a few ounces of gear, and I need it fast'. I moved away and let him go.

He got up and said, 'I'm impressed that you're able to handle yourself like that. With my guidance I think you can be even better'; but I knew beyond a shadow of a doubt, in my mind and in my heart, that he was there for one purpose and one purpose only, and that was to murder me. The only reason he'd changed his tune, was that I had unpredictably overpowered him. I had come to this conclusion in light of the fact that he hadn't mentioned one word about what had happened with the bike. You see, his bike was chiefly a standard topic of conversation between us, and he would normally introduce it as a code to re-affirm our association, every time we spoke. On that particular day, he didn't, which is what gave him away. Despite everything, I overlooked his attempt on my life, as I was still somewhat intrigued by him and felt as though I could still learn from him, not to mention the fact that I was making better than average money off him at the time.

However, I couldn't simply leave the situation with Damien unresolved, as I knew he would make one attempt after another until he eventually killed me. I had to get that psycho off my back, therefore I approached him and suggested, 'Bring the bike to me, and I'll take care of getting it repaired for you'. I had no intention of making his bike brand new again; my plan was to basically restore it back to the condition it was in before the accident, and make it functional again in order to get back on a good footing with Damien. I ordered the parts necessary to make the repairs; I then removed the damaged components from his bike personally.

For some reason, unclear to me, the fact that I was working on his bike began to make Damien feel uneasy; he brought a truck to my house and collected his bike, as well as all of the parts that I had painstakingly ordered. The odd thing about his actions was that he didn't offer any sort of explanation as to why he had taken the bike back, nor did he tell me where he was taking it, or what he intended to do with it. I felt as though I had done my part in order to set things right with Damien, particularly considering that it was a rare vehicle and locating the parts was an absolute nightmare. I believed the whole witness shambles was finally squashed and behind us and we never mentioned it again.

I still had my own motorcycle to tend to, as it had been damaged in my accident. When I took it back to the shop that had initially built it, Manny and his team of mechanics had looks on their faces as though they had just lost one of their own children. After a quick inspection Manny said, 'The damage appears to be mostly superficial; I think she's going to make it' to which I replied, 'That's a relief, how long is it going to take?'

'Give it a couple of weeks, as I have to order some parts and besides, it's a custom colour so it's gonna need extra work'. I felt confident leaving it in his care, as he had never disappointed me.

THE CONSULTANT

A short time later, Damien paid me a visit and informed me that one of our mutual acquaintances was in the process of setting up a new law firm. He said, 'I'm going to need your assistance; I've got a huge networking job ahead of me, and this guy wants to deck out the place with some real high tech shit'.

'Sure, why not?' I thought it'd be a good opportunity to gain some knowledge on setting up networks. Damien was being paid amply for the job; I, on the other hand, was providing my services purely as a favour to Damien. The solicitor who owned the office also happened to be one of my clients, which made the fact that I was helping him free of charge satisfactory from my point of view as I felt as if I was helping out a friend. The job itself lasted a little over ten days and I'd have to say that I believe that it was carried out flawlessly by anybody's standards. The set-up was state of the art for its time; the entire office was automated, and I was seriously impressed with the outcome.

My satisfaction was, however, short-lived. Not long after we had completed the job, a situation presented itself that highlighted to me just how rotten, dirty and despicable the bulk of humanity was. Adam, the degenerate anal discharge for whom I had set up the office, out of nowhere, began to spread rumours and innuendoes about me. These concerned my livelihood, being slurs cast upon the quality and quantity of the drugs that I supplied. He also drove clients away by claiming that the gear was laced with bug spray and had lead weights in it to make it heavier.

I was more than a little peeved as, not only had I set up that cocksucker's office at no cost to him, but I had also referred the majority of his client base to him, which was the reason that he needed a bigger office and more staff in the first place. I was in fact deeply confused, as he had chosen to reimburse me for helping him by attacking me personally as well as my livelihood.

For some reason he was under the impression that he could put it over me just because of his friendship with Damien. I rang him to confront him about the rumours. When he answered the phone I asked, 'What is this I hear about you telling stories about me – is there some sort of problem that I should know about?' to which he replied, 'I'll say whatever I want to say. Why, what are you going to do about it?'

One part of me wanted to resolve the issue peacefully out of respect for Damien; however, the evil motherfucker in me could not let that happen. I told him, 'You'd better think really long and hard about the next words that come out of your mouth, motherfucker'.

He wasn't scared or threatened and replied, 'I don't give a fuck about you or what you think you can do'.

'Then I'll answer your question now as to what I'm going to do about it. I am going to destroy your business, and then send you broke. Once you are homeless and living in the street, I am going to break both of your legs and remove all of the teeth from your head one at a time with a pair of pliers, you piece of shit-fucking, mutt cocksucker!' and then I hung up on him.

Approximately half an hour later while I was looking for my pliers, Damien's brother showed up to purchase some weed, which was not at all out of the ordinary, as he was a regular customer. On that particular stopover though, he had a hidden agenda. He was Adam's best friend and was there on a reconnaissance assignment in the hopes of obtaining some information pertaining to my next move regarding Adam. When he realised that I wasn't going to give him anything interesting to report, he said, 'If it comes down to it, my loyalty is with Adam'. I replied, 'I respect your decision, and wouldn't expect anything less from you; however, Adam has crossed the line and has to be dealt with accordingly'.

URBAN WARFARE

Once Damien's brother had left, I picked up the phone and made a few calls. My first was to Sam. When he answered he told me, 'I already heard about it, and I have started to make the necessary moves to round up a few people in order to deal with it'. After I had spoken to Sam, I finished making the rest of my calls and later that night all the players gathered at Sam's house to discuss our next move. My suggestion was rather straightforward. I addressed the group and explained, 'This is what's going to happen. Tomorrow morning during business hours, we're going to walk into Adam's office and break his bones right in front of his staff. Once we've finished doing that, we're going to remove anything of any value, and destroy what we can't take on the spot. On top of that, from this day forward, no one will ever use his services as a lawyer again'.

Not long after we had concluded devising our plan, I received a call from Damien. 'We need to talk. Meet me at the hotel now.'

At the hotel – the same one where Damien had beaten up the bikie, which was basically his home away from home – he was already seated at the bar smoking and drinking. Before I even had a chance to sit down, he announced, 'I don't want you to go after Adam'.

I sat down, ordered a drink, asked the bar tender to give Damien another one of whatever he had been drinking, and calmly said, 'We both know that can't happen. If I let him get away with it, I'm going to look like a punk. Besides, that ship has already sailed, I've already made the arrangements'.

Damien then picked up the phone, called Adam and commenced coercing him to apologise to me over the phone. He also told him, 'I want you to go back to everyone that you ran your mouth off to, and undo it'.

He paused; I figured that Adam was trying to weasel his way out of it as he was, after all, a lawyer. Damien suddenly raised his voice and shouted, to the bemusement of the other clientele, 'Hey fuck head, I don't give a fuck how you do it! You can tell them that you are a fucking idiot with a big, fucking mouth for all I care – just get it done right now!' Damien then handed me the telephone. Adam began, 'I'm uh… I'm sorry for the misunderstanding…'

I quickly cut him off and said, 'Damn right you're sorry, you piece of shit! You've no idea how lucky you are. Damien has just saved your sad excuse for a life, and as far as your business goes, you no longer have one – you have been boycotted!' and hung up on him. I called Sam and told him, 'Cancel the strike on Adam – I'll explain later'.

I was still feeling as though the situation had not been adequately resolved as I wanted and needed vengeance. I told Damien.

His response was, 'Personally, I most probably wouldn't have let it go. Let's just say I owe you one'. In the circles that I ran with, having a favour of that nature up your sleeve was highly beneficial so I felt slightly mollified.

Thinking back on those years, life was so much less complicated. You see, back then, resolving issues of that nature was a far simpler process: if, for any cause, someone was out of line or disrespectful in any way, he or she would be dealt with unhesitatingly. The repercussions of such conduct varied from broken legs, all the way through to extended periods of intensive care in a hospital bed. Existing in such an environment also had its downside as there was no one you could trust. All my acquaintances were drug suppliers and the clientele who consisted mainly of junkies. The females in that scene were cold and ruthless as they wouldn't give you the time of day or even piss on your face if your teeth were on fire, unless you had something of value to offer. I discovered the hard way, that that fact held true for the majority of people. I was beginning to feel like the ghost of human kindness past.

OFFICE POLITICS

Michael, one of my regular clients at the time, was employed at a large supermarket. His job was to pack the shelves at night. He had started to acquire higher volumes of drugs from me, as he saw an opening to resell it to his colleagues at a marked-up price. They purchased the amphetamines in order to assist them to stay awake and get their work done throughout the night, and the weed to take the edge off the amphetamines and enable them to get some rest when they arrived home in the morning. They had climbed on the drug seesaw that was the backbone of many a dealer's business.

Michael caught me at a moment when I was sufficiently high to be susceptible to his bullshit and he persuaded me to come and work nights with him at the supermarket. Even though my previous experience attempting to work at a regular job had been by no means pleasant, I took him up on his suggestion nevertheless. I figured it would do me some good to get out and have some "ordinary" interaction with new people, as my mind had reached the state of being constantly in an exceptionally dark and ugly place.

I decided to conform to popular demand, as I had started to consider the possibility that things had gone as bad as they had for me throughout my life due to the whole "what goes around comes around" logic. I felt that if I did what was socially deemed as the "correct thing", my luck would somehow change. Man, was I wrong.

When I originally started, although the labour was quite physical in nature, I didn't mind it too much as the atmosphere was fairly laid back. At the time, the company was managed by a few

Arabs, which meant that at least half of the staff was also of Arab origins. The remainder of the staff was Anglo-white, and for some mysterious reason, the two groups practised total segregation, preferring no company at all to the company of a member of the other group.

Light duties such as stacking toilet paper were predominantly handled by the Anglo team as they were rather delicate and rumour had it that they would have injured themselves if they were to lift anything heavier than a bag of cotton balls! That whole situation didn't play out well with the Arab team who worked there, as they too were a lazy bunch by nature and simply preferred not to perform any back-breaking activities, although they were made to do it in any case.

A few weeks after I'd started working there, my curiosity got the better of me. I felt as though I needed to unravel the mystery and finally understand why such social constraints existed between the Arab and the Anglo teams. One night, before the meal break had concluded, I returned to the shop earlier than the rest of the staff. I then secretly hollowed out one of the shelves holding boxes of tissues and hid there, as the shelving was conveniently just large enough for me to stow away snugly inside unnoticed – I had no worries about being observed on CCTV as the company was too tight to spend money on them. I then restacked the tissue boxes from the inside, thus cloaking myself from sight. My intention was to listen in on the Anglo team's discussions and in fact to see if they did ever speak at all, seeing as they had barely strung two words together during the coffee breaks.

Initially, I believed that my idea was sound and had its merits – bearing in mind I was using a lot of drugs in those days. In fact, it turned out to be one of those things that would have been best left alone, as my findings were far beyond disturbing. I regrettably learned that they were of the opinion that all Arabs were slimy, malodorous, stingy and vulgar and had no ethics or self-respect. They had also established that Arabs were of inferior intellect and therefore should not have any rights. I also recall them referring to the Arabs commonly as "feral animals".

Interestingly enough, the faction of Anglos in question consisted of elderly people; for that reason I found it to be staggering and almost beyond belief that they could be so ignorant. It also appeared as though the group actually believed everything that they were saying, as I could hear the conviction and commitment in their voices. In light of the new information that I'd discovered, I decided that I would distance myself from that particular group, as I had no desire to associate with racist, white supremacist Klanspeople. By the same token, I also limited my contact with the Arab team, as they continuously unloaded all of their duties onto me. I was back to exactly where I started – in seclusion. I figured it was best to leave each to their own, and at the end of the day, opinions are like assholes, everyone has one, as they say.

J.R. Rothwell

CAMEL TOES

It wasn't long before the company inevitably removed the Arabs from their management positions and replaced them with Anglos. The new manager was a middle-aged crusty, white woman, who wore a bodysuit made out of spandex, which, unfortunately, vividly accentuated every drooping crevice in her old floppy carcass. Her camel toe would be best described as being the same shape and size as a toaster, the kind that takes four slices of bread at a time. Her name was Dianne.

Dianne's first order of business was to employ a multitude of Torres Strait Islanders. Although unaware of it at the time, in due course it became common knowledge that the huge black men were employed purely to serve as an entourage of Dianne's personal fuck puppets. There were eight of them and their sole purpose was to please her whenever she required it, which was apparently a lot. She had five black children from four different fathers and she intended on expanding her family unit.

Her "service" men were peculiarly massive and each one of them looked meaner than the last. She permitted them all to work on light duties, because she needed them to keep their strength up in order to pound her old sagging backside. That was the first time I had ever worked in such an environment and was unaccustomed to the office politics and bureaucracy of it all.

Dianne, in common with the other Anglos at the store, appeared to have a profound detestation for Arabs in general; I believe it was because she couldn't manipulate them with her furry cheque book. She eventually made existence nearly impossible for the Arabs who worked for her, so much in fact, that they would just leave on their own accord – a technique known as "managing them out of the company". The Arabs were expected to move an unrealistic amount of stock in a preposterously small amount of time and they would receive verbal and written warnings if they didn't meet her farfetched expectations. That resulted in job loss for every last one of them still hanging on despite Dianne's damaging treatment, except for Michael and me – and I put my survival down to being a glutton for punishment who followed every single ridiculous rule even if it physically hurt. It made me sad to see the job losses occur, as the majority of the people she was affecting had families and needed their jobs in order to support them. None of that mattered to Dianne, as she needed to make space for more large black men to come in and service her ancient body.

At that time, Michael, the punk who recommended that I work at that shit hole in the first place, decided to participate in the politics game as well. One night, he arranged for one of my clients to come to my house and throw herself at me. Now normally, I would be accommodating but this particular bitch was notorious for having every sexually transmitted disease you could think of and then some. Everyone I knew who had ever been with her, had had to start making regular visits to a sexual health clinic for treatment of some sort. Bearing that in mind, I declined her offer and turned her away.

The very next day, as soon as I got to work, Michael began to tell everyone the account of how an exotic and beautiful woman was thrown out of my bed because I didn't want to have sex with her. He then proceeded to notify anyone who would listen, that he supposed there must be "something wrong with me". He had a good laugh at my expense for at least the next month or so. I was starting to see a pattern develop. I noticed that Michael had started to take shots and make snide comments about me and then sent that grimy, disease-infested bitch to my home, knowing full well that I would not touch her, just to set me up for a story, in the hopes that he could humiliate me enough at work, so that I would simply leave. I never determined his motive for this act nor if he even had one.

Apart from Michael, I was the last-standing original employee and, like the others, I was forced to resign from my full-time job and become a casual. Dianne preferred it that way, as she could get rid of employees whenever she wanted to as casual employees typically do not have many rights. Working at the supermarket actually suited me just fine, as my house was constantly watched by the police. Clients would recurrently meet me there throughout the night in order to get whatever they needed and besides, I was also robbing the place blind in order to make up for the mistreatment. I stayed on as a casual and kept working, although being up all night while doing some serious lifting, and then sleeping during the day was starting to take its toll on me.

THE GAME

While toiling away at the supermarket, I started working with a dwarf-like guy named Nick. He was a tiny Greek man, who had a chronic case of small man syndrome; he constantly boasted about how dangerous he was and the countless people he had beaten in fistfights. He avoided having to take sides in the Anglo/Arab schism by even-handedly disliking both groups and distributing his copious negative comments equally to both sides. I have to admit he was moderately entertaining – reminiscent of a cartoon character, and therefore, more often than not, I listened to what he had to say.

He started hanging out at my place on a regular basis; we did the usual stuff, which was primarily smoking pot and playing video games. One night, out of boredom, we decided to go on to an internet chat site, and while we were there, we started communicating with some random women. After having chatted to one of them for only a short while, she insisted on meeting us and at that particular moment I saw some potential to have some fun and was inspired.

By nature, my mind tends to wander from time to time and if I ever come across something that I really enjoy, for example a favourite food or favourite song, I keep eating it or listening to it until I can't possibly take it anymore – you could say I had an obsessive temperament. Unfortunately, in those days, when it came to women, I simply couldn't draw the line.

The following day, I went to the computer store with Richard and Nick, where we purchased three brand new laptop computers. We then transformed finding eligible women on the internet into a three-player game. The main objective of the competition was to hook up with as many women as we possibly could. It was a good game, since playing the game itself was the reward. I swiftly discovered the means to set the game up in my favour; I wrote a small script that worked from within the chat program. It was quite straightforward – the program asked a succession of questions such as: What is your age? Your sex? Your location? Depending on what answer was returned, the program would then either let the user proceed to the next round of questions, or alternatively delete and ignore them if they were not female, too old, or in a remote area.

The next stage for the lucky lady who met the criteria was a request for a photograph of herself. The software automatically ran several generic, although charming, pick-up lines that I had painstakingly crafted. I discovered that being funny was the new black when it came to impressing women and my pick-up lines were invariably witty. Once I had made the girl laugh, the rest was plain sailing. I couldn't believe how effective my software actually was, as after only having run the program for a few hours, the computer would gather a substantial list, in the hundreds, of photographs and telephone numbers of eligible girls within relatively close proximity. Then all that was left to do was filter out the less appealing ones and as a result, I would be left with nothing but qualified prospects.

It wasn't all fun and games, as every so often a weirdo would slip through the cracks. A classic example of such an occurrence was Tina. When I had initially met her at the outset, she conveyed the impression that she was normal, apart from an awfully atypical sense of wittiness. We got along exceptionally well and the fact that we had both lived in Boston gave us common ground. We went out on a few occasions, and everything seemed fine while we did the usual things, such as dinners and movies. She did tell me that she had already been married several times which I considered that to be somewhat odd, as she was only in her early twenties. However, the deal breaker for me was the night I spent at her place. I woke up in the morning and could hear water running as Tina was taking a shower. I figured I would keep myself busy by flipping through her photo albums. I opened the first album, my heart sank, for what I saw was incomprehensible – the entire album consisted of hundreds of photographs of sleeping men. Upon closer inspection, I observed something protruding from behind one of the photographs.

I removed the photo to reveal a plastic slide, which had what appeared to be human hair concealed within it. My suspicions raised, I carried out an even closer inspection on myself and discovered that there were two perfect rectangles of hair that had been removed from each of my legs. I panicked and wasn't sure exactly what to do. In the end, I replaced the albums back the way that I'd found them and got the hell out of there before she finished taking her shower. That was the last time I heard from her but the strangest part of that particular incident – the thing that has puzzled me to this very day – is the fact that the hair has never grown back in those spots on my legs since it was removed.

This unhealthy behaviour on my part continued for extended periods of time, as I was winning the game, with much credit to my unique software. Richard and Nick started to protest and were certain that I was in some way cheating. My response to both of them was, 'Don't hate the player – hate the game you pack of bitches!' It didn't take me long to become obsessed with the game. I had my mobile phone connected to the laptop and wore earphones from the laptop in my helmet while I rode so that I would know the instant I got a new hit from a potential prospect. Back in those days, it was an expensive exercise as a mobile phone call would typically cost a fortune and the internet in that era was mainly dialup, which was also charged by the hour. I had both the mobile phone and the internet connected twenty-four hours a day. To my mind, paying the overly exorbitant bills was totally justified, as it gave me the edge I needed in order to prevail in the game.

SHOW STOPPER

What happened next, not a soul, including myself, ever saw it coming. I was working at the computer, revising a new version of the script while one of my clients was over picking up some weed at the time. Nick was also there; he was playing video games. I received a reply from a girl named Angie on the internet. In addition to her reply, she had sent through a photograph of herself which stopped me dead in my tracks; at that very instant the game was over. I flipped the laptop around and showed Nick and my client the photo and announced, 'I'm gonna marry this girl'. Her hair was the most amazing shade of red and was long and curly, framing small, exotic features. She looked small but athletic and had that gorgeous olive skin. Her eyes were so open and innocent.

Nick responded, 'Yeah, sure you will. Have you got any more weed?'

I don't know how I knew but I was certain that I would. I asked Nick and the client to leave immediately as they were distracting me.

Once they'd left, I spent several hours chatting to Angie and was encouraged in the belief that there was a remote possibility that a decent person existed out there by what I was hearing. She seemed innocent and had never set a foot wrong in her entire life and from what she said, she also appeared considerate and gentle, which were qualities that I had never come across in a human being before. It was considerably out of the ordinary for me to divulge any facts pertaining to myself or what I had done; however, in this case, I was completely upfront and frank about everything. I didn't hold back one smidgen; I described the monster that I had become in explicit and vivid detail. Bearing her background in mind, most people in her situation would have run for the hills; however, she didn't. I gave her my telephone number and told her that it would make me happy if she would call me. I also insisted that she draw a little happy face next to my number, which would serve as a reminder of how happy I would actually be when she made the call. A few weeks went by and I had heard no more from her; I assumed that I must have scared her off by being too honest.

Just the experience of having spoken to such a person had given me some much-needed optimism, in spite of the fact that she didn't call. For the first time in ages, I wanted to write something about her in my journal. For once I could write something positive and with promise; I'd never done that before.

I began to question all my long-held beliefs about myself. Maybe I didn't need to be that evil person any more. The idea that such genuinely good people might actually exist was enough to give me a new lease on life. I decided that I needed to make some changes and my first order of business was my appearance. Consequently, I visited the barbershop for the first time in many years and told him to cut my hair, which was in the region of being half a metre long and shave off the beard.

Richard had decided that he too needed a change when he met a girl from his home country. He actually followed her all the way back to Russia after only having spent a few days with her! He claimed that the main motivation behind his departure to Russia was to go there in order to obtain degrees in genetic engineering and quantum physics, which I thought was ridiculous as, prior to meeting that girl, he had never expressed any interest in furthering his education. It was much more likely that he was continuing his pattern of subordinating his will to whomever he was attached to at the time and he probably thought that quantum physics would impress his new girlfriend! I was even impressed, as it is quite a transition from drug abuser to genetic engineer and quantum physicist.

TIDES OF CHANGE

Changing my appearance had some remarkable side effects; for example, when I walked into stores, I no longer had a convoy of shop assistants following me around to ensure that I was not going to steal something. While I was out shopping for new clothes, as part of my attempt at transformation – everything I had in my wardrobe was predominantly black at the time – I received a phone call from Angie. I was bowled over as she said, 'I would like to meet you in person'. Apparently the happy face next to my number on that little scrap of paper had been playing on her mind. That and the prospect of being paired up for life with one of her relations by her parents, which I later learned was supposed to be her fate. When I eventually met the proposed suitors, I could empathise with her.

I returned home, switched on my laptop, loaded up the social networking software and began to systematically and methodically block and delete the entire list of women that I had accumulated over time. Destroying that list was somewhat liberating and gave me a sense of that chapter in my life being closed once and for all. Nick, however, was feeling disgruntled to some extent as he felt a sense of loss, seeing as he no longer had a worthy adversary in the game that we'd created, with Richard out of the picture as well. It literally was a brand new beginning for me.

When I met Angie for lunch, I'm not sure exactly how to put it into words but we sat and talked as if we had already known each other for a lifetime. There were none of those awkward or uncomfortable silences that you typically encounter when meeting someone for the first time. When I saw her in person, I have to admit that she looked even better than the photo she had sent me. She had an unforgettable exotic quality about her as well as a kind and friendly disposition. She was an angel.

We continued to see each other for a while and the more time that I spent with her, the more I wanted to put my old way of life behind me and strive to do the right thing; well, at least society's version of the "right thing". I had no way of knowing it at the time but moving – from what I had become – into being a regular civilian, would not come without severe consequences. I was going to pay the price and then some.

Because of Angie's ridiculously strict family unit, we had no alternative but to see each other in secret. Angie eventually presented a scenario to me where we could see each other regularly without being faced with such concerns. In her culture, it was traditional to be engaged before a man and woman were permitted to speak to each other in a public place; insubordination or failure to comply with the regulations was punishable by various methods of physiological and psychological anguish administered by the occultist Gypsy community. It didn't take me long to reach my conclusion, as I'd already fallen hopelessly in love with Angie and it became crystal clear to me as to what had to happen next. I made a decision that was going to affect a lot of the people in my immediate circle at the time. I asked her to marry me.

I planned the proposal meticulously as, for the first time in my life, it really mattered to me that I did something right for someone who actually deserved it. It was a whole new experience for me and I was having some trouble getting my head around the idea that someone else's happiness meant more to me than my own. Choosing the ring was the easy bit – it had to be a pink diamond as Angie was a fan of that colour. I racked my brain to come up with a pleasing scenario for the proposal and in the end decided to channel my inner romantic – which I was hoping was in there somewhere – and, sure enough, I woke up one morning with a plan.

I invited Angie for a bike ride and took her way up into the mountains where I had booked a log cabin. The cabin was purpose-built for romance as it came with chocolate-covered strawberries, champagne and a hamper of ready-prepared luxury food. After we'd eaten in front of the wood fire, I popped the question and offered the ring. Even though I was fairly confident she would accept, I was ready for anything in the way of her reply, as up until that point, my life to date had more than prepared me for knock backs just when it looked like happiness could almost be within my reach. When I saw the tears glisten in her eyes, I thought, 'Oh shit – this is it. I must have messed up somewhere in the planning stages', but it turned out they were tears of happiness.

She accepted.

SAY GOODNIGHT TO THE BAD GUY

My next stride was to disband my entire business, which I knew was going to upset quite a few people who felt that they were entitled to take advantage of it for some indefinable reason. I had considered separating it evenly and allocating each person a piece, however, that idea was unacceptable and I decided that it would be safer for everyone concerned if I did not do that, as it could potentially have created conflict or possibly even a small war.

Ironically, it was my clients who surprised me with their unpredictable reactions; some of them actually threatened to kill me or members of my family if I didn't continue to supply them. As I was turning a new leaf and changing my ways, I let the threats and comments slide and put it down to them being frustrated junkies.

Angie and I then began making arrangements for our new life together. While that was taking place, I began to sever all of my ties with my clients, which was causing a stir with my affiliates. The element of this process that most disappointed me was the fact that, after an era of allegiance, service, riches, transgression and struggling through the toilsome times, nobody wanted to even know me anymore. Once the money ceased to come in, I ceased to exist. The most startling aspect of it was the grim reality that it was not even a gradual decline in the friendship; they more or less cut me off on the spot. Admittedly I was one of the uppermost earners and my closing the business would have impaired them to some extent financially. I remember feeling disillusioned at how fiscally based our association truly was; it had become obvious that, from their point of view, I was as only as valuable as my last deal.

As I had decided to do what was deemed socially correct, my perspective changed when I returned to work on the day following the marriage proposal; I decided to take it a lot more seriously. I approached Dianne and requested that she give me my full-time position back, as I was going to get married and needed the additional hours.

Dianne rejected my request without any hesitation whatsoever, although she did say, 'If you want a full week's worth of hours as a casual, you have to do all of the heavy lifting, and you have to do it on your own'. At that moment, the notion of what work was all about suddenly become a horrible reality. For the first time ever I had been given an ultimatum and had no choice but to accept it. That whole state of affairs did not sit well with me at all, as I was being exploited and there was not a damn thing I could do about it.

CAREER MOVES

Within a few weeks of embarking on the new duties, Dianne appeared frustrated; probably because I'd survived. So, in an effort to make my nightmare additionally unbearable, she assigned one of her large black fuck puppets to push me to my limit. That was, hands down, by far the most exhausting physical activity I'd ever endured. Never before had I experienced such physical pressure and that includes carrying tiles as the mule boy. I was responsible for throwing hefty twenty-kilogram boxes two metres into the air to a large Islander who was sitting at the top of a high ladder-trolley; I had to repeat that process continuously for nine hours straight without a break if I wanted to maintain my hours. The vigorous and non-stop activity inevitably caused muscle and nerve damage in my back; however, I just pushed on and worked through it. To this day, it hurts like hell.

I decided pretty swiftly, that there had to be a healthier approach to making a living, as there was no feasible way I could have withstood that sort of punishment for much longer. On top of that, starting my new life of redemption in such an environment, surrounded by people with sad and burnt-out souls was not exactly encouraging. The people who worked in the supermarket didn't trust anyone or anything. When I told them about my recent engagement, they accused me of lying. It was almost as if they were oblivious to the outside world; their world was the walls of the supermarket.

I spent a few weeks looking for work during the day which was a little tricky as I was working through the night every night of the week. I managed to hold it together and eventually found one.

When I returned to work later that night at the supermarket and before I even had an opportunity to give notice to anyone that I would be resigning, it turned out that Dianne had already made some preparations of her own to persuade me to do just that. She was of the opinion that I could still be pushed even harder, even though she must have already identified that no matter how much pressure she applied, she was not going to get much more out of me, as I was already at my physical capacity. However, it didn't stop her from trying. She made the necessary arrangements for one of her large henchmen to attack me in the supermarket when there was no one around. At first I was puzzled, as he appeared to be doing me a kindness by swapping tasks with me so that he would be undertaking the box throwing and I the catching. However, I was soon disillusioned as he instigated the attack by throwing the heavy boxes at me much quicker than I could possibly catch them; it appeared to be giving him some twisted sense of pleasure, as the assault seemed to amuse him.

As a result, I fell off the ladder and was lucky enough to land on my feet. Once I'd found my bearings, all thoughts of my new, reformed approach to life temporarily left the building and I shouted, 'What the fuck is your problem you big fucking baboon!' Being the brute he was, he pushed me and due to his sheer size, the shove was strong enough to knock me down. I fell onto an empty pallet that was lying on the floor, and it felt as though I'd been hit by a freight train; I then heard him charging at me like a wounded bull. By chance, one of the planks of wood on the pallet had become unfastened when I had fallen on to it. I picked up the piece of wood as I stood up and without even thinking; my old instincts kicked in. I turned around and swung it as hard as I could. He was out cold.

He bled a lot; however, he was still breathing. I had to shift the overgrown savage out of the aisle as I was fretful that he would, in due course, regain consciousness and then kill me. Once I'd ensured that nobody was watching, I dragged him into the fridge on a pallet-jack and locked him inside. I then went into the office and told

Dianne, 'Take your job and bash it up your ass sideways. You should also bash a few rolls of toilet paper up there as well, in order to take up the slack'. She immediately called out to the gorilla who was, unhappily for her, laid out in the fridge at the time, in order to come to her aid; however, he was, of course, in no condition to reply. I walked out of there and never looked back. Actually, it was highly cathartic.

BEYOND THE GRIM LANDS

Meanwhile, I was trying to understand my prospective in-laws. I had not yet met them but the preparation that was involved in the first meeting with them was ridiculous; beyond any stretch of the imagination and required extensive amounts of groundwork! Angie was of the opinion that it would be beneficial for me to meet her brother prior to meeting her parents, in order to break the ice gradually – and also so that her brother could advise us on how to proceed with her parents. The fact that we had to go to so much trouble was setting off some alarm bells for me.

When I initially met Angie's brother, my first impression was that he appeared to have an enormously over-inflated opinion of himself, almost as though my being allowed to converse with him was a divine privilege. His name was Balthazar. Although he was Angie's brother, they did not bear any resemblance at all, as Balthazar had large, fear-provoking and ubiquitous teeth. Add to that, scores of unsightly moles, he had smaller moles growing out of his primary moles. However, what alarmed me the most was the non-existence of his top lip yet he had freakishly large gums!

Balthazar was married to a chronic drug addict – I could spot a drug user from thirty paces. To be fair, she had an incredibly legitimate excuse for abusing the drugs as her husband regularly verbally abused her and the drugs were merely a coping mechanism. Upon my arrival into their home, she proceeded to tell me a long, rambling story and that very same story seemed to last the entire duration of my visit; a few hours! This may be hard to believe but the story itself was about garden hose fittings and an assortment of ways of linking them together. For the life of me I could not work out whether she was either stoned or retarded. Her story was incredibly boring and as a result, Balthazar would sporadically abuse her with such lines as, 'Hurry up and tell your story, you idiot', or such great classics as, 'Shut your mouth, you're boring everyone, no one cares'. I felt bad for the lady, as, apart from being mentally challenged, she appeared to be a genuinely nice person. I wondered why he allowed her to use the drugs, as he seemed such a control freak. Perhaps he felt it would be too demeaning to have to admit to himself that she needed drugs to cope with the life he was inflicting on her.

When we finally got down to business, Balthazar began coaching us in a tortuous manner on how to present ourselves when we meet his parents. The references he made, and the general thesis I was taking away from his dialogue, was that we were to conduct ourselves as though her parents were gods, and we were merely lowly servants who were not worthy of being in their presence. Balthazar's sense of reality was so distorted that it was chilling, as he actually believed that his parents were sovereigns and were entitled to be treated accordingly. I remember thinking, *'What the hell am I supposed to wear for my trip to Buckingham Palace?'* When he rattled on about how high and mighty they were, I could actually hear the fervour and conviction in his voice. If what he was saying was at all accurate, he would have actually been a duke and his wife the princess! By the end of our discussion, I was feeling exasperated and mystified. I did not like his shitty undertones; however, eventually he did offer to assist us, and said, 'You don't need to worry; I'll come to their house later in the day and back you up'.

It took me a few days to assimilate all the information that Balthazar had filled my head with and then, dressed smart-casual, having agonised over what would be appropriate for this "royal" meeting and trying on and discarding half a dozen outfits, I made my way over to the farm where Angie's parents lurked.

The entire family was standing at the front door, which I thought was a little insane. I walked in and introduced myself to them and had barely had a chance to sit down before Angie's stepmother, who was the self-proclaimed ruler of the world, commenced conducting her interrogation of me. She was most certainly, beyond doubt, the most frightening creature I had ever had the misfortune of encountering. She was wearing a tattered old tracksuit, which looked as though she had found it in a dumpster; in addition to that, she was wearing shiny formal men's shoes. Her hair was almost a long-lost memory, and what little she did have was unkempt. I had seen homeless alcoholics with better hairstyles. I don't think her teeth had ever seen a toothbrush, as there was a build-up of fungus on them; her face was too horrid to even describe. It was like looking into the face of death itself.

In a high-pitched, glass-breaking shrill, she screeched, 'How much money do you have in your bank account? Is your cock circumcised? Is your family decent? What do you do for work? Do you know how to read? Are you willing to take a blood test?' as well as many more private and embarrassing questions. Throughout the entire interrogation she gawked down at me through her nose, with an expression on her face as though she was struggling to defecate. I suppose I handled it pretty well, considering. Angie's father just glowered in the background, nodding his head from time to time while the stepmother conducted her grilling.

The frustrating thing though was that no matter what answers I gave her, she would never be satisfied; I wasn't royal and that was that. Luckily for me Balthazar arrived just as I was running out of breath. As soon as he walked in, I felt reassured, as he had previously informed us that he would be there to offer us some support. To my dismay, his first words were, 'You're Christian aren't you? What are your kids gonna be if you get married?' Before I had a chance to reply, he jumped in and said, 'Don't just sit there like an idiot; answer the question now!' I was drained, frightened and a little disgusted to be honest. He seemed to think it was acceptable to treat me in the same insulting way that he treated his wife.

I tried my utmost to get along with the family for Angie's sake, although it proved difficult considering they were ignorant, petty and basically, peasants. It resulted in Angie and I feeling extremely stressed. The irony was that as far as Angie's parents were concerned, I was an ordinary working-class guy who'd never done a wrong thing in his life and to this day, that is still what they believe.

They have never actually met the "real" me. I couldn't tell them that I rode a motorcycle because, in their narrow minds, anyone who rode a motorcycle had to be a troublemaker; however, in my case it would have been true. Consequently, I borrowed a car in order to visit Angie. After a while, I no longer had access to that particular vehicle and, as a result, I was inevitably forced to get rid of my bike. I went to a car dealership and was very hasty as I had no time to waste. I did a straight swap and traded my bike for a car. I did it so quickly that I ended up with a piece of crap. I may as well have swapped it for magic beans. Watching them load my bike onto the truck was the equivalent of someone hacking my heart out of my chest and then feeding it to me. However, Angie meant a lot to me, and I knew that if I wanted to make a future with her, it had to be done.

While in the process of trading my wonderful bike in a desperate, but futile attempt to get the self-proclaimed queen to accept me, I received disturbing news. I learned that Angie's parents were frantically bringing their nephews and other various oddball relatives into their home in an effort to arrange a prospective husband for Angie. The fact that she was already engaged to me merely added fuel to their plan to rid themselves of me once and for all.

At that point, any remaining respect for them completely evaporated although I kept my "game" face on, as we were close to being liberated from their tyranny. Angie's family was a gypsy occult and had the customary occultist gypsy narrow-minded point of view. They came from a village that was located in a country that I had never heard of and can't even prenounce. With a population of approximately forty natives, the only group they were permitted to interrelate with or marry were the people from their own tribe; as you can imagine, the gene pool would start to become fairly shallow after a while. They had, in fact, referred to me as the "outsider" on many occasions. In their culture, respect was not something that was earned; they merely demanded it simply because they had grown old. For example, if an occultist gypsy was a sixty-year-old convicted serial paedophile, public masturbator, rapist loser, a younger person would be forced to demonstrate to him or her, high levels of admiration and respect because of the age gap, which is ludicrous. Another tradition that I didn't agree with, was the fact that you had to refer to the elder gypsies as, my lord god; failure to do so was not tolerated in any way and was considered a serious offence. Angie was the first in her community to ever go out and interact with an outsider, and she couldn't simply stop there could she? She had to go one step further and marry the outsider – she more or less took the bull by the horns.

I believe the fact that I was a foreigner – by not being from their tribe but also born overseas, was by and large what irked them. I also believe they had worked very hard to get to the stage where they had become royalty within their own minds, and I considered that they may have not taken a liking to me because I was an outsider and would not recognise them as the "royal family".

Meanwhile, I was doing considerably well in my new occupation with my newfound motivation and as a result, was fortunate enough to have collected some rather sizable commission payments for my hard work. The commission came in just at the right time, as it was much needed in assisting us to set up for our future. At that time, I also had some cash hidden away in various locations left over from my earlier money-making activities.

I loved spending all of the money I had at the time on Angie, as I believed that I needed to show her some of the finer things that the world had to offer, bearing in mind she had lived a secluded life under a very authoritarian regime. She had been concealed in a remote area with negligible exposure to modern civilisation, which I thought was a severe and outrageous injustice, not to mention inhumane. Before I met Angie and rescued her from captivity, she had never eaten food that consisted of more than two or three meagre ingredients, such as boiled potatoes and salt. In addition to that, she had never had any exposure to non-occultist gypsy people; even the television in her home had been modified to receive foreign channels through the use of various satellite dishes.

A MARRIED MAN

Angie's parents stipulated that I organise and pay for an excessively elaborate wedding ceremony which would cater for the occultist gypsy community; in addition to that, I had to make provision for the fact that they were "royals"; whatever that meant. However, I wasn't too concerned because, as I saw it, it was a small price to pay in order to commence my new life with Angie. So I did exactly that; I put on a wedding which catered for all of the occultist gypsy village peasants, although I was a little disheartened in light of the fact that only four people attended from my side while all one hundred of the gypsy community crowded eagerly into the reception hall. We had to use their hall, even though it was not the most salubrious of venues because it was close to the gypsy community; they refused to exert themselves by travelling to the delightful country house setting that Angie had dreamed about for her wedding. It saddened me that the few people I had invited because I regarded them as bona fide friends from my earlier days, didn't bother to turn up or even respond to the invitation but I guess it rammed home the fact that they had no more use for me.

The wedding itself was a spectacle, as Angie's totalitarian family had commanded that she incorporate all of their traditional occultist gypsy heathen rituals into the wedding. The ritual that alarmed me most was the "virgin blood" dance. The ceremony was supposed to signify a virgin's blood on her wedding night. I found such a ritual to be vulgar and barbaric; however, I had no alternative but to go along with it. The bride – who in this case was Angie – and the bridesmaids were forced to perform the ceremonial blood dance with a red-covered urn in their hands. While a horn that sounded like a broken car alarm was played, they danced as if they were possessed by badly-coordinated spirits. The urn was passed in a seemingly random order from one person to the next, until the bride would, in conclusion, have to hold it up and present it to the pagan blood god, before destroying it by smashing it on the floor. The wedding took all day, and in all, there were four or five rituals but my mind has mercifully succeeded in blocking most of them out.

On the up side, Angie's white wedding dress was beautiful, almost managing to do justice to her, and the kiss after the vows has become legend to the girls in her family. Mind you, that could have had something to do with the fact that they all had to marry their cousins.

We had people show up whom I had never met before, nor ever saw again after the wedding day. Meeting and greeting some of those people was jarring, as the names were so far out of the ordinary; I nearly sustained injuries trying to pronounce them – it was almost as though saying the words correctly involved contorting my face and having parts of my tongue removed. I ultimately decided that it would just be easier to nod and smile, as I didn't want to offend anyone by saying the wrong thing!

By the time I'd finished paying for the wedding, furnishing our home and spoiling Angie rotten, all the funds from my prior business were gone. At the same time I had just completed finalising my dealings. I was literally flat broke and had to start over with nothing to my name. It was as though someone had changed the rules in my life and I had no choice but to learn how to play by the new ones, and it was extraordinarily tricky to get used to, as I'd become accustomed to wanting something and obtaining it immediately.

SUBTERFUGE

I now focused on my new job at the electronics shop and committed to it with heart and soul, as I figured that I'd be there for a while.

Ed, one of the other sales assistants – who apparently wanted to be my new best friend – was being particularly supportive and helpful while simultaneously, the store manager took a sudden dislike to me. I couldn't understand why and when I questioned him, he assured me that there was no issue and that I had nothing to be concerned about. Based on my previous experiences with people, I should have seen the signs, his physical appearance was deceptively normal apart from his oversized oblong shaped head and his very beady bird-like eyes. His hair looked as though someone had glued a soiled kitchen sponge to his head, there was also something that was just off about him, almost like he was short of a few chromosomes.

I eventually figured out that my new friend Ed was telling the manager that I'd been talking about him behind his back, the fact that it wasn't true meant nothing. I didn't know the nature of that game at the time, as I was accustomed to dealing with things in a more direct way. I came to the understanding that just because people worked in a professional industry, it didn't necessarily mean that they had any integrity, were honest – or had any backbone. In fact, it appeared as though common criminals and drug dealers were far more honourable and upfront in how they conducted their business.

As a result of his actions, Ed became the store manager; he became a slave driver and constantly reminded me that every sale I made was effectively making him richer as he creamed a commission off the top of everything I sold. He even had the gall to say, 'Go out and make me some money!' every time I went out to assist a customer.

It wasn't long after Ed had taken over that one morning, while we were setting up the store for trade, two masked armed robbers stormed in to hold us up. To illustrate that they were serious, one of them hit a staff member in the face with the butt of his shotgun, which rendered him cataleptic. Once Ed realised what was actually happening he immediately soiled himself. I quickly took a few steps back as a puddle of urine started to form around his feet and a nasty smell filled the air.

Ed just stood there, stunned and too terror-stricken to move a muscle. I turned to him and quietly said, 'You want to be a manager, go ahead and manage. I think these gentlemen may require some assistance.'

They were not the smartest crooks around as they were wearing stockings on their heads the entire time whilst inside the store, where there were no security cameras. The nylon pantyhose were so tight that at times, it almost seemed as though they were going to suffocate! As soon as they got outside, in plain view of the external security cameras, they ripped off their stockings and unsuspectingly posed for the cameras. Needless to say, they were captured only a few days later.

BLOOD ON MY HANDS

The following day, while cleaning up the mess that the robbery had created, I received a call from the police. At first I assumed that the call was in relation to what had happened in the store but they started asking me questions about my mother and my brother. They then told me that there had been an incident and that I would have to come in and identify bodies or something of that nature, to be honest I couldn't really hear much of what was said after that because I was feeling dizzy, nauseous and my ears had started ringing.

I made my way to the police station and was then taken into a room to identify the bodies. When they pulled the sheet back on my mother's face I threw up all over the floor. Her body was in a very bad shape, as though she had been hit by a bus. I was taken out of the room and given a chance to clean myself up before I was basically forced to return and identify the other body. This time they did not pull the sheet down and I was instructed to identify him by the tattoos on his arms. When I saw them, I threw up again.

Once I confirmed that it was in fact my brother on the table, I was taken to another room at the station where I was questioned for several hours. I was asked every question they could think of as I was the remaining member of the family.

While I was with the police I asked some questions of my own. It turned out that I could not identify my brother because he had been shot in the face multiple times, and from what I understood, my mother was shot when she rushed into the room to see what was going on.

I immediately began to piece it all together in my mind. My brother had taken my old room and the bed was positioned so that his head was just under the window; which meant that those bullets were intended for me.

I then remembered that some of the junkies who had previously threatened my life, used to collect their drugs from that very same window, and after thinking about it a little more, I started to think about everyone who I had pissed off by closing down the business. The whirlwind of shit that was going on in my head made me feel like I was going to get sick again, although I stayed in character, seeing that I was surrounded my law enforcement.

I didn't mention any of this to the police, as I didn't want to make matters worse than what they already were, if that were at all possible; however, I did visit the crime scene a few weeks later and what I found confirmed my suspicions; the shooter had taken his shot from the window and then shot my mother while still standing outside.

That reality weighed down on me like nothing anyone could imagine. I was responsible for the murder of my own family and would have to carry that with me for the rest of my life.

Having my family wiped out all but broke me. My first notion was vengeance, but the sad truth was I had made way to many enemies over the years to be able to pin it on any one person or group as much as I felt I needed to, and I wasn't about to go on a killing spree. It would have more or less destroyed my relationship with Angie, as I had learned from my obsession with hunting Conan for all of those years, the end result is just not worth it, and will not bring anyone back.

It only ended up turning me into something I never wanted to be and ended up being a complete waste of time. I figured I only had one shot at this life and decided not to waste any more of it chasing after ghosts.

I did not mention my brother very often in all I have written, and for good reason. I did my utmost to protect him and keep him sheltered from the life I had led. I knew that he looked up to me and the little exposure he had to my life hastily started to lead him down the wrong path, thus every time I spoke to him I painted the foulest possible picture and turned what I did into a horror story, eliminating all the perks and benefits from the equation, and it seemed to have worked.

Before the bullet that was intended for me had taken his life, he was studying to become a doctor, and worked two jobs to put himself through medical school, while doing charity work every time he had a chance, that made the situation all the more catastrophic and pushed me further down into my dark depression. I did keep it well hidden from the rest of the world though, I had to, as I learned early on that showing any kind of weakness or despair would result in being eaten alive.

Limited Options

After a month of grieving, I had no choice but to return to work as finances dictated. Upon my return I was relocated and given a so-called "promotion" which came with several conditions attached and the manner in which it was presented it to me was demoralising. I was told that I was being given a chance to "prove" myself but really, it was only because no one else wanted to work in that particular store! The powers that be, then advised me that there would be no increase in my wages until I had proved that I was worthy. Although they did not feel it necessary to mention it at that particular point, I was later notified that the commission structure had been reconfigured in such a way that the sales people were paid an inadequate amount and the sales manager was no longer entitled to any more commission whatsoever. They had also changed the regulations so that the store manager, who doubled as the sales manager, was required to be in the store seven days a week, displaying a complete disregard or ignorance of the bare minimum health and safety requirements.

On top of that, my personnel had been cut down to a small fraction of what it was when Ed was in charge. For me, the icing on the cake was the fact that I was expected to double the store's revenue in order to be considered for a pay review – when the chain of which we were a part – had opened a new superstore only two streets away and had advertised it like mad. The superstore had effectively lured all of our customers away.

I remained committed to my work and gave the company all that I had. I had no choice. The truth was, I couldn't afford to take the time off and look for another job and we had no one to turn to for help.

As a result of whatever Ed had done to put me in the bad books with management, I was visited twice a week and ordered to rearrange the entire shop, which involved moving the shelving and all the stock. That procedure took two full days and as I had to do it twice a week, it didn't leave me much time to look after the business itself. I tried to get the staff to help me but they were worse than useless – I'd been assigned a few of the local drug addicts – and doing it all myself actually saved time. I eventually started working seven days a week and would start early in the morning and leave late at night in a desperate attempt to catch up. I was blessed with a wife who hated not seeing so much of me but accepted the necessity. However, I wasn't sure how much longer she or I could take it.

THE AMBASSADOR

It was all going downhill quickly but it accelerated one day when a member of the gypsy sect came into the store looking for me. He said that he was Angie's uncle and that my in-laws had recommended a visit to me for anything electronic that he may need. This was news to me, as I could not recall hearing of, or seeing him before that moment.

He told me his name was Farquad and it was pretty obvious that he was not bothered about his appearance. He was morbidly obese and wore tight, chequered tracksuit pants with a pirate-like, ruffled shirt tucked into them. He topped it off with a mustard-coloured suit jacket. He also had on really old and dirty tennis shoes, which did not match. In addition to all that, his clothes appeared to be unwashed and unironed. He also stank. Even his glasses were covered in rust, mould and grit and were held together by masking tape. His hair was so greasy that there appeared to be motor oil oozing out of it. However, what stood out the most was the nauseating breath coming out from under his thick, dirty, flea-ridden moustache. He was truly deficient in anything that was decent or natural.

He then began to tell me how important, intelligent and financially well-off he was. I just acknowledge his ramblings and listened. He rattled off a list of items that he wanted to buy for his son; mobile phones, computers, personal digital assistants, navigation systems and an elaborate car stereo system. I remember thinking that, if what that oily gypsy was saying was in any way accurate or by some remote possibility factual, he would have effectively made me my store's budget for the month all in a single transaction. However, I doubted it and although I do not like to "judge a book by its cover" in his case, it seemed to be a safe bet.

Like most of these freaks, he spoke very broken English. After wasting several hours of my time, insulting my religion and telling me how great he thought he was, he finally cut to the chase and told me his real reason for being there; he merely required some speaker wire and ultimately demanded that I give it to him free of charge. Shocked and angered by his demand, I advised him that that would not be possible, for all the obvious reasons. He proceeded to inform me that he was highly esteemed and regarded as an ambassador in the occultist gypsy community and that if I did give him the wire for free he would tell the entire occultist gypsy community what I'd done, they might be more accepting of me and come to me for help.'

Appealing as the offer was, I still declined. After several hours of haggling and making me hate life, he ended up leaving without buying a thing but before he left, he announced, 'Money is no object, I'll be back and when I return, I'll pay cash for everything!'

The next day I fell ill, and decided to take a day off in order to recover. Prior to that day, I hadn't taken a single day off work for any reason in over two years. I was lying in my bed sweating with a fever, when I received a phone call from Anthony. 'The banking for the day didn't balance and I couldn't find the invoice for the speaker wire that Farquad said he paid you for.'

Apparently, Farquad had visited the store while I was away and, according to Anthony, Farquad had said, 'I am the manager's uncle and I have already paid him for a wiring kit; I have just come to pick it up.' Anthony claimed that he had tried to call me but couldn't get through and so stupidly, Anthony gave Farquad the wiring kit, not even having the intelligence to ask for an invoice.

I eventually explained the situation to Angie and told her the story of a man who had represented himself as her uncle, and how he had by some means pilfered a wiring kit worth several hundred dollars from the store. Angie knew at once who I was talking about but said that he was a distant relative – not her uncle. However, as Farquad had previously mentioned, he was in fact regarded as being the almighty, all-knowing overlord of the occultist gypsies. I also came to learn that most of the occultist gypsy community sought his advice on significant issues, such as etiquette, values and religion, which explained a lot. Farquad the bottom-feeder, as leader of the community, was apparently at our wedding and despite his outlandish attire, I had managed to completely miss him bearing in mind that I did have a lot to take in that day!

After a great deal of inconvenience, Angie managed to get hold of Farquad's telephone number and took it upon herself to call him. She mentioned to him that we would be grateful if he returned to the store and paid for the item, as my not being able to account for it would have effectively jeopardised my position within the company. Farquad's response to Angie was, 'I am offended that you have called me at my home and are questioning me regarding this.' He went on, 'I have paid your husband for the item with cash; he must be the thief.' I happened to overhear the conversation, as Angie was speaking to him on loudspeaker, and I was livid and interrupted, 'You're a fucking liar and a peasant, and I'll pay for what you have stolen out of my own pocket, you fucking lowlife skid mark. I hope you fucking choke on it.'

Farquad couldn't simply leave it at that. He decided to take it further and waged a holy jihad on me. In fact, he had the nerve to write a lengthy letter of complaint about me to the company's head office. He was unrelenting about his cause and corresponded with head office several times in a mammoth effort to guarantee that the letter would actually make its way through to the board of directors. His letter depicted a fictional version of the story; he also made several recommendations such as my removal from the company or as a minimum, that I should at least be demoted for treating him disrespectfully

For the life of me, I couldn't understand why any member of Angie's family would have sent someone like that to see me; he was renowned for causing specifically that type of nuisance. The more I dug around, the more stories came out about that asshole and what he'd done to other people just like me. It saddened me sad to think that the need for Angie's parents to suck up to Farquad actually outweighed their own daughter's interests, as hindering my career or interfering with my livelihood would hurt Angie just as much as it would hurt me. Farquad actually had a lawyer who worked with him full-time, whose sole occupation was to write letters of grievance to various companies on behalf of Farquad, in an attempt to get refunds for items he had either purchased or stolen. When this new information came to light, I couldn't believe that someone could be so petty as to endeavour to put together a career out of cheating people in retail stores.

When I confronted my in-laws about what had happened and asked for some guidance, they kept silent, which was a first for them. It dawned on me then that it was some form of fanatical *modus operandi*, as they refused to give any information pertaining to Farquad at all. When I asked them what he did for a living, again their reply was not to reply and all my further questions were treated in the same manner; they remained mute. However, I did notice that when I initially informed them about what Farquad had done, the news appeared to bring them a great deal of joy and had a soothing effect on them. I was distraught and my opinion of them fell even further.

The main reason for highlighting this revelation was because it was out of character for my in-laws to be silent or at least to not voice their opinions which were invariably aggressive and directed at me.

I remember once suggesting to my mother-in-law an accountant, as I was pleased with the work he had done for me but her evil response was, 'If you're such a big man that you need an accountant, why aren't you rich? You haven't even finished paying off your mortgage yet!' She proceeded to abuse, insult and emasculate me for the better part of an hour. On another occasion, I recall having a discussion with my sister-in-law who advised, 'If you ever go out with my parents, you must always pay for everything, as they would be deeply offended otherwise, and it is a serious offence in our culture to not comply.' However, fortunately that never became an issue, as for some unknown reason it was unacceptable for them to travel outside of a two-kilometre radius around their property, and there were no special dining facilities which catered for their unique needs inside that radius. My father-in-law had his own style of humiliating me. He would wait until there were at least five or six scabby old occultist gypsy men at his home and would then poke his old finger at me and belt out comments such as, 'If it wasn't for me, he'd be nothing!' I was bemused by his statement, as he'd never done a single thing to help me in any way whatsoever

About a week later one afternoon, at home after, work, I went into the kitchen and started to prepare dinner. Angie was due home later. While cooking, there was a knock at the front door and without first checking, I was greeted by a large man wearing a ski mask which had a huge beard hanging out from the bottom of it. Before I had a chance to even think, he pulled out a knife and stabbed me in the middle of my stomach then ran off.

My first instinct was to close the door and lock it, and once I had done that, I realised that I was losing a lot of blood and collapsed. I was struggling to move, and all the phones were on the other side of the house. I knew my mobile phone was my best chance because I would not have to stand up to get it. I figured if I could just get to my desk in my office I could reach the phone which was next to my keyboard and call an ambulance, I would be okay.

I started dragging myself along the floor, and barely made it half way across the kitchen before I was no longer able to move. I was delirious from the blood loss, but thought what if they came back to hurt Angie. So I wrote 'be careful your uncle did this' on the wall in my blood which was seeping from the open wound before I passed out.

I woke up in the hospital the next day, and the first thing I saw when I opened my eyes was Angie standing there looking terrified, stressed out, but still very attractive. I was in a lot of pain, but it appeared that Angie was in even more pain. I remembered what I wrote on the wall and thought 'crap!' I wasn't expecting to live long enough to deal with the fallout, otherwise I would not have written anything at all, and I would have handled the situation on my own terms.

Angie was hysterical and told me that she thought I was dead, she then told me that we were safe, because she had contacted the police and put an apprehended violence order against her entire family.

WORKING HARD FOR THE MONEY

Somehow, I assumed that my life experiences to date, would have been enough to toughen me up and prepare me for just about anything that life could through my way; man, was I wrong. As it turned out, trying to make a "legitimate" living or pursuing a career required qualities and skills I apparently do not possess.

Retrospectively, what frame of mind one is in at any given moment, determines cause and effect –and in my case – having just buried my only family and with my wife's family wanting my head on a stick, I was desperate to succeed; to prove them wrong. Added to that, my family's welfare and livelihood was solely my responsibility. I was okay with that fact; however, employers and colleagues seem to have a special sense whereby they could smell my fear and desperation, almost the same way a shark senses blood in the water.

I only wish someone had advised me that to leave behind a profitable life of crime in order to earn legitimately, was not a good idea. If survival was reliant on one's income, I doubt there are any career advisers out there who could handle that type of scenario.

I discovered early on in life and throughout my career, that the majority of people who work in so-called "legitimate" jobs are fucking hypocrites. If any of them were to ever learn that someone was a drug dealer or a shoplifter for instance, they would regard them with disdain. Another thing I picked up on is, unlike the criminal world, people are far more expendable in a professional setting. As soon as an employer believed it would be in their favour, by even a fraction of cent, to not have an employee around, that employer would kick ass. As far as fellow employees go, in most cases, it meant walking around with a target painted on your back so that they knew where to put the knives in. The earning potential and resources in the work environment are also substantially lower, which means greed will ultimately break the back of any deal or relationship in one way or another.

I'm not saying it's all bad, and the reality is that for most, it is a necessary part of life. It is, however, an ongoing challenge for me to try and get my head around how it all works. I did manage to work out a few key factors; such as, in the workplace, it appears that you're only seen as a plus or minus on a ledger, you either have something to give, or something that someone wants to take away. I also learned that unlike criminals, professionals will never tell you what it is they want directly to your face, it is normally done through a twisted game of lying, cheating stealing, manipulation and outright backstabbing. Being a criminal was so much easier because it was honest and direct; anything that wasn't, was dealt with by means of swift and severe punishment, which tended to keep people honest.

The main difference and by far the most disturbing is that nobody in a professional setting will accept any form of friendship; no matter how sincere or legitimate. Most people in those situations live in constant fear that at some point in the future, it could result in having to give a discount, special treatment or it may just put them out-of-pocket! What a sorry state of affairs we live in and how scary and ugly is a section of humanity. In simpler times, the not so common criminal would welcome you with open arms, and you became more than just a friend, you became a family member and so every now and then, I ask myself, why does doing the "right" thing feel so wrong?

Anyone reading this may have gathered that I am ever so slightly, cynical, bitter and jaded; however, it is not without good cause.

I spent many years of my life jumping from one terrible job to another, all the while getting screwed over on a scale of titanic proportions. I don't want to turn this into a résumé as I get weary just thinking about it but I do need to mention one particular job that highlights my point of how fine the line is between legitimate earnings and the reality of being a crim. My colleagues at this particular organisation were fascinating to say the least; you could say they were "freaks".

THE NEGOTIATOR

At the outset, I believed that I had taken a job with a reputable company. In hindsight, I should have done some research before accepting the position. Once past the point of no return and already in way too deep, I learned that the company had previously traded under a different name and had been closed down by way of law, a few years earlier. After some belated research on the internet, I managed to glean that a class action had been filed against them which involved hundreds or possibly even thousands of disgruntled and badly burned customers. Digging deeper, another informative article via the internet, implicated that dirty politicians had not only looked the other way but endorsed the concept in order to improve the company's image and help with public relations for a cut of the profits.

I was hired as a sales representative and my role consisted of visiting clients only once and offering home renovations to people who had credit issues by providing refinancing solutions on their existing mortgages.

As I was fairly new to working in that particular environment, it didn't occur to me, during the hiring process, that something was amiss. I was informed that I would be required to use my own car; pay for my own fuel and purchase a laptop and phone which would be strictly for work use. I was also informed that to begin with, I would be offered the bare minimum wage permissible by law. The upside was a commission structure, although I was told that they were not at liberty to tell me what it was until I had been working for them for at least six months.

I suppose the only lesson in this is that, in work situations there is always compromise although in this particular case, it began with how little I would accept, and the meagre conditions I would agree to work under; until eventually I found myself compromising my principles altogether.

AMAZING GRACE

The first person I met at my new establishment was Grace, my manager. Her first words to me were, 'I'm your boss and you'll do whatever I tell you to do and you better never forget that.' Not sure why, perhaps it was her belligerent tone but I just nodded. That introduction was enough for me to form my first impression; which was that she was a crazy bitch who clearly was disconnected from reality.

After spending only a few more days with her I managed to put together a rudimentary psychological profile on her and my findings were, that she was predominantly angry because of her total lack of appeal. She was devoid of any personality, imagination or commonsense but above all, she was bitter and twisted because she knew that she was unrefined; putrid, cunning, insecure, envious, repulsive, uneducated and manipulative. Attention she craved and sought after and woe betide anyone who stole the show from her!

Grace was manipulative. Just for the sake of being evil she would revel in creating problems for people by using gossip and deception, then would sit back and enjoy the fallout while everyone around her turned on each other as a result of what she had orchestrated. I, for one, could never understand her logic or motivation as there was no benefit or end game.

Her attitude to everyone was condescending which resulted in a depressing atmosphere and I personally felt myself drowning whenever I was in her presence. I never once saw her smile.

Grace was a morbidly obese pig. Her face was large, round and bumpy, sort of like an "off" watermelon that had been dropped from a height onto concrete. Her eyes were deep set, cold like a dead fish and evil but it was her nose that was the main issue. It projected out a great distance from her face, then hooked downwards at a ninety-degree angle, then hooked back towards her face, resembling a medieval weapon. Her hair was insane and a little intimidating. I am no expert but it appeared that she had tried to have it chemically straightened but somewhere along the line, the equipment they had used must have malfunctioned because the result resembled a nest which would have been a suitable home for small birds or large insects.

She did love her fashion though; according to her, everything she wore was current designer runway model clothing yet I always thought that someone ought to advise her to consider switching designers as her choice of attire unfortunately always drew attention to her oversized and very disproportionate body; they were at least three or four sizes too small. Being short, stumpy and broad, her ass was located just below her shoulders which was a problem as conventional pants would not cover it up, which then left it exposed. It was hairy and tragically, one could not escape encountering it! Unsightly protrusions of bulging blubber bubbled out over her already disproportionate frame – the tight clothing made her look like a condom full of walnuts. She really was the full package.

Due to her incredibly low self-esteem and dejected outlook on her own sad existence, in addition to the obvious insecurities about her swine-like appearance, she paid to have glamour shots of herself made and then hung them all over the office for everyone to see.

For the life of me I couldn't figure out why they didn't airbrush her hairy ass out of the photos or at least shave her first.

No doubt anyone reading this may have detected a slight hint of animosity in my part towards Grace; it is not without good reason though.

Early on in our working relationship, she told me that I would have to be her "silent manager", again being new in the industry; I was unfamiliar with the term. What it meant was, I was required to not only fulfill my duties but was expected to do her job as well, although I would have to do it in secret and take no credit or remuneration, hence silent manager.

This plan of action then freed Grace up to work more closely with the director and gave her the time she needed to perform her various unsanitary duties, such as face time with his crotch, handling the unmentionables and oral duties. I may have omitted to mention this before but Grace was a whore, and did not let the fact that she was married, stand in the way. She needed to constantly advise everyone that she was from a strict Muslim background, though she regularly threatened some of the call centre staff with their jobs or deportation if they did not have sex with her in her car on demand.

THE SILENT MANAGER

The silent manager liability turned out to be more than I'd bargained for. The first task I was delegated was the grand responsibility of being Grace's personal therapist. I'd only been working there a week when, early one morning, I was approached by Grace (a misnomer if ever there was one) who appeared to be experiencing some sort of psychotic episode. She roared at me, 'Get your car and meet me out front in one minute!' She knew my car was parked at least ten minutes away; however, I did try to get back in one and ran like hell. As soon as I pulled up in front of the office, she jumped into the car and slammed the door so hard I was surprised the window didn't shatter. I was then ordered to drive.

'But where to?' I asked.

'Just drive,' she muttered.

It was a little daunting as she appeared to be out of control and made me drive from Sydney city, all the way to the mountains, which took a few hours. During our bizarre road trip, I gathered that she was having paranoid delusions that one of her boyfriends might have been cheating on her.

During her mental breakdown, she started shaking her fists while talking, screaming and crying simultaneously and I was horrified to notice little spots of froth in the corners of her mouth. Her make-up was melting from the sweat and tears but after a while, I thought she must have worn herself out because it suddenly went quiet. At that stage I took advantage and mentioned that I was tired and hungry and suggested that we get something to eat. We walked into a café, sat down and ordered some food. At that point, she began again to behave erratically; Grace had completely lost her fucking mind. She proceeded to beat her hands on her chest so hard that her jewellery actually drew blood and as if that wasn't bad enough, she started to literally tear the hair out of her head while simultaneously letting out incomprehensible screams, which sounded as though she was being tortured.

I was stunned and embarrassed but I do remember thinking that her bird-nest hair style suddenly made a lot of sense. I also realised that I was by no means qualified to deal with that type of shit.

Another part of my job as a silent manager was keeping up staff morale. The following day after our "trip", Grace got to work early and made a bee line for the Ladies without greeting any of the staff. Seconds later, we heard the tell-tale sounds of snorting. Everyone could clearly hear what was going on as the walls were paper thin; she was in there doing lines of what she later told me was coke. She eventually came out, watery-eyed and sniffling and then ordered one of the telemarketers to join her in the toilet cubicle where he joined her in even more snorting! As they exited the restroom together, the telemarketer proclaimed proudly, 'Last night we fucked like champions!' and pointed his finger at Grace.

If that wasn't unprofessional enough, Grace went to her car and returned with a portable stereo. She started playing some sort of tribal music that had been modified to sound just as crazy as she was and discarded her top so that she was only wearing a bra and skirt and proceeded belly dancing on the desks in the middle of the call centre while people were trying to work. She then called out to the call centre staff and instructed them to cheer her on. They applauded her by clapping, although most of them were a little confused and very frightened. The scariest part was the look on Grace's face; she was so angry, livid, while belly dancing her way across the room. I ducked outside for a smoke and to try and forget what I'd just witnessed, although Grace managed to find me and started crying and wailed, 'I've tried everything to motivate them as you just saw but nothing seems to be working!' She then ordered me to "motivate" them. For a minute there, I was worried that I was going to be asked to take my shirt off and belly dance, however, I was fortunate in that she agreed to let me use my own methods.

Shit, I had my work cut out for me; on top of the frequent counselling sessions, motivating a team of people who were being sexually abused and regularly threatened; I also had strict targets to meet.

Grace also ensured that it would be entertaining for her to give me at least five appointments a day which were all two hours apart. A successful deal took approximately one hour to complete the paperwork alone and in many cases, I would have to drop everything and return to the office to meet Grace when she demanded it. Taking all of that into account, I was working close to fifteen hours a day.

In hindsight, I must appear to have had rocks in my head for entertaining anything Grace had to say and not telling her to smash her job up her bony ass sideways. However, there were two reasons I had to stick it out; the first just reconfirms my previous sentiments in that my livelihood was totally dependent on my job and I couldn't afford to go looking for my dream career (both literally and figuratively) and had to take into account my previous work experience. The second reason was that I was baffled as to how the fuck a business that was being run by that fool, was not only self-sustaining but extremely profitable and I think I stayed and put up with her shit, mainly to find out more about how it all worked because they were obviously on to something.

THE FAMILY GUY

With all that had been going on at work and then having to bury my family, Angie and I had agreed to wait until it had all settled down before starting a family. I realised that if we kept waiting for the "perfect time" it was never going to happen – is there ever a perfect time? We wanted to do something different and make the process a bit more fun like a trip around the world and fingers crossed, by the time we got back, hopefully Angie would be pregnant.

Apart from borrowing the money for the trip from the bank, there wasn't much planning involved. We pretty much boarded a plane and took off. I did bring my journal along as I thought the trip would definitely be noteworthy.

Europe was outstanding – more so than any other place I visited; the culture was diverse, the history awe-inspiring and the food awesome. We began the European portion of our adventure in London where it was cold, windy and gloomy. It was January and we were told that the weather did not get much better than that. The people there always seemed to be in a frantic hurry; even on weekends, which meant you couldn't stand in one place for too long or you'd eventually get knocked over. That being said, the UK was still my favourite place in Europe. Being a technology enthusiast and admittedly at bit of a geek, London catered to my every need. The stores carried technology items that I knew were not going to be available in Australia for several years. I was like a kid in a candy store!

From there we made our way to France where we gazed at the Mona Lisa, ate frogs' legs and snails, bought loads of perfume and visited the Moulin Rouge which was one hell of a show.

Angie fell in love with Italy and is today, her favourite place on the planet. Of course we could not visit Venice, without taking an iconic gondola ride while sipping mulled wine.

In Rome we visited the Vatican City and while looking at the architecture, something deep inside me stirred. Not sure what or why but I was in awe and felt humbled. Wandering around the streets, Angie spotted an out-of the-way secluded restaurant, not far from the Vatican. Local singers and an accordion player entertained us while we dined. After dessert, our waiter brought us an odd-shaped bottle and explained that it contained a "very special" drink which was handmade by the monks who lived in the mountains of Italy; he then asked if we would like to sample it. Of course we would and upon closer inspection, the fluid in the bottle was bright yellow, even brighter than highlighter fluid. Apparently, it was customary for the waiter to pour that particular drink directly into one's mouth from the bottle, we figured why not, when in Rome. I tilted my head back as the waiter poured the mystifying drink down my throat. When I swallowed, I could feel it burn its way down through my abdomen like acid and it did not stop burning until it had made its way down to my pooper. By then it was too late to warn Angie; she'd already started drinking it. The effects of that drink were immediate. Hallucinations accompanied us all the way back to the hotel although we have no recollection of how we got there!

Fortunately we recovered by the following day and Angie went on a shopping spree through Rome, which could only be described as obscene – we visited one clothing boutique after another until the credit cards were thrashed.

Amsterdam was intriguing, the availability of weed back then was no secret; however, what we were not told was its high quality. Our first few days in the Netherlands were spent doing the proverbial touristy type things; we tasted wines and cheeses and visited the Anne Frank house. Towards the end of the week, as anticipated, we went to sample some of what Amsterdam really had to offer.

We had been advised not to leave Amsterdam without seeing a "special adult" show. That spectacle demonstrated to me that no matter how many outlandish, crazy and fucked-up things I've witnessed; there would always be something out there that could eventually trump it. The club at which the show was held was dark and sleazy, it had rows and rows of undersized movie theatre-style seats and each seat had its own cup holder. It felt dirty and unsanitary and the floor was sticky. Without any introduction or warning, the show commenced. A tall, black man walked out on to the stage – naked. He had a dick that was bigger than a Pringles can, just hanging there for everyone to stare at. A minute later, a thin blonde woman followed him onto the stage and lay down on her back on a rotating mattress, which was located in the middle of the stage. The black guy then mounted her and started to pound her as though he was trying to excavate a tunnel. The woman lay there inert, unenthusiastic and not the least bit phased by what was happening. Once he had "finished", as a special feature, he stood up and blew on the first row of people in the audience! They fondled his "junk", cheering him on. I felt so uncomfortable and relieved that we were sitting at the back of the club. If that was not demented enough, a well-endowed Asian woman walked out with a banana in her hand. She sat on the edge of the stage, peeled the banana and gingerly placed it in her vagina, she then started inviting random people from the audience to come and take a bite from the banana! With each bite, the banana got progressively shorter until there was nothing left but a small nub. I turned to Angie and said, 'I don't know about you but I've seen enough, let's get out of here before I get called to eat that last piece of banana!'

Walking out of there was a huge relief and as we had nowhere in particular to go to, we traipsed around the streets until we eventually came across a coffee shop. The first thing that caught my attention were the large, glass displays which had rows upon rows of sweets, pastries and cakes but upon closer inspection, I realised that they were not typical sweets. They were jammed packed full of drugs. I was ridiculously excited and must have spent about an hour in that place just admiring the "desserts"; we eventually reached a decision on which sweets we wanted, made our purchase and headed back to our hotel.

We'd skipped dinner and so decided to eat the sweets! There was no immediate effect – none at all and I remember thinking to myself that maybe everything I'd heard about Amsterdam was just hype. Angie ate one and said, 'What a scam, can't feel a thing.' That was an odd comment for her to make because up until that moment, Angie had never tried any type of drugs before, she'd not even smoked a cigarette, which meant her tolerance was lower than mine. There should have been some sort of reaction as the sweets seemed to contain more hash than any other ingredient; they were dark brown, almost black and very bitter.

We later realised that there had definitely been some sort of delayed reaction as we don't remember falling asleep but woke up the next morning unclothed, tangled and twisted up in each other in sort of a pretzel-like shape. Our faces were white as snow and we spent the first few hours confused and disorientated.

BACKDOOR BOB

After our wonderful trip it was back to work, and Grace. She had a few surprises in store for me. Her two brothers, Neil and Bob had been hired – to be her assistant managers – both of them! So, she had two assistant managers and one silent manager; I was starting to wonder how she *managed* to do anything. The first order she barked at me when I got back, was to train Bob in sales and management as Neil was not 'yet ready' to start work. I was extremely reluctant as he was huge and sleazy.

He was tubby but not like any regular plump person, it seemed like he was soft and wobbly with a doughy centre; more like a jellybean. He wore very thin glasses and had very large and saggy titties that appeared to be losing their fight against gravity. His face resembled a Mr Potato Head figure with most of the pieces put on the wrong way. I found his lack of a neck the most alarming, as it made it nearly impossible for him to turn his head. That guy put the sex back into convicted sex criminal.

Within nanoseconds of meeting Bob I found him very annoying, and repulsive, mainly because without delay, pleaded with me to take him to a brothel. Apparently he was too uncomfortable to go on his own. He said he wanted to go because his wife was very ill with brain cancer and as a result, was incapable of having sex with him as often as he would have liked. Just about every time he brought it up, I advised him that he should be ashamed of himself for proposing to do something like that because it was an act of pure evil.

I later learned through other members of his family that his wife was perfectly healthy, and that he had just concocted the entire story to get sympathy from his co-workers and in order to get someone to help him deceive his wife. Apart from looking really depraved, Bob had no facial expression at all, and a wit so dry you could sharpen a knife on it, he was overflowing with self satisfaction almost as though he had single-handedly put an end to world hunger. I discovered reasonably quickly that he was a pathological liar and I suspected that he may have been afflicted with chronic masturbator's disorder, if such a thing exists. I am no expert but when I noticed the obvious underlying mental illness, I started to connect the dots and figured that it must have been hereditary.

Bob's desperate need to constantly and unrelentingly lie to everyone he ever spoke to at any given opportunity was very irritating and made me want to slap him in the face as hard as I could. I think that in his feeble mind he must have believed that he was achieving something impressive. His dilemma however, was that the target audience could for the most part see straight through his lies, as he was not at all skilled at his craft.

As I had been instructed to train him, I took him along on an appointment with me but before we walked in, warned him that at the first hint of trouble I would take over and conclude the meeting myself. Up until we reached the front door everything was going well but no sooner were we inside when Bob introduced himself with a fake name, I think he did that primarily because he was a fucking idiot. I supposed he believed that misleading the customer from the outset, he would have a better foundation to build his bullshit on. I was pretty sure he caught onto the fact that I was less than impressed, but he chose to ignore it, his misrepresentation was so unashamedly obvious that the customer immediately tuned into it and became defensive, and tensed up. I had no alternative but to arbitrate. I quickly apologised and asked Bob to leave, recovered the relationship with the customer, sold the deal and returned to the office. Bob must have called Grace while he was waiting for me outside, because when I returned she was enraged, took me into the boardroom and commenced swearing at me. She accused me of 'costing my gorgeous baby brother a deal with your lies and you haven't yet taken him to a brothel!'

At that point, I scratched my head and tried really hard to figure out what was happening. She then barked on about if I wanted to keep my job I should take him and as punishment, pay for him!

I figured I would make the job a little easier and more economical for myself, I made a few calls and tracked down a contact from my previous life who worked in the sex industry, she owed me a few favours since I bailed her out and got my hands on large volumes of amphetamines for her on very short notice more times than I could count. When we turned up at her place, I took her aside and told her the situation, and that I would not normally bring a depraved weirdo around, and ask that sort of favour of her, unless it was important.

I waited outside for the better part of an hour, all the while wondering if anyone else ever got themselves into preposterous situations such as the one I was in, or if it was just me. He returned to the car with a smile from ear to ear. He insisted on giving me details no matter how much I pleaded with him not to. I had to turn up the volume on the car stereo, pulled the button off and threw it out of the window.

Back at the office I received a call from the girl I had taken him to see. She asked me, 'Was that guy a *friend* of yours?' to which I hurriedly replied, 'Absolutely not! Regrettably I do have to work with him, why do you ask?'

'Well, he is a total freak. He demanded that I strap on a massive dildo and sodomise him with it, and afterwards he rolled up into the foetal position and started weeping!'

My reaction was, 'I really wish you hadn't told me that'.

THE LINE

The next day, one of the girls who worked in the call centre asked to speak to me in private. We went to the boardroom where she locked the door and drew the blinds. I asked her what she was doing but she was reluctant to speak and then her eyes started to tear up. I sat and waited until she eventually broke down and told me that Bob had cornered her after work when she was alone in the office and that he had forced himself on her. He also told her that he liked "little girls".

'Why are you telling me this? You should go to the police!' I shouted.

She replied sobbing, 'I can't go to the police because I'm not in the country legally and I'm afraid they will deport me, and Bob and Grace both know it.'

It felt like my blood was boiling inside my veins. I had no idea what I was going to do but told her I would figure something out and advised her to go back to work. I sat in that boardroom for two hours with my head in my hands, just thinking about what had happened. I was also considering that I was bound by the promise I made to Angie, when I told her I would not participate in anything criminal ever again, which was serious, as it was my word.

I left the room and started looking for Bob with the intention of only talking to him, but was told he was out on appointments for the day. I called Bob and asked him to drop what he was doing and to come straight back to the office because we needed to talk, then I hung up. He called me straight back and tried to warn me about ' …

not ever hanging up on him again …' Not sure exactly what he said after that because I'd already hung up the phone.

He didn't get back until much later. I was the only one still at work and was in the parking lot smoking a cigarette when Bob's car pulled up. He got out of his car and was muttering something about him having to teach me a lesson, show him respect and all that bullshit. All logic, reason and the promises I had made suddenly disappeared like smoke in the wind.

I looked him straight in the eye and roared, 'Who the fuck do you think you're talking to? Over the last week you have had me pay to have a hooker fuck your ass and now you've raped a girl in the call centre!'

He stared back at me silently and then spat out slowly, 'You can't prove anything, and she'll never tell anyone because she'll get deported.'

I grabbed his head and smashed it into the hood of his car, hard enough to break his nose and knock out a few of his teeth. When he fell down, I pinned him up next to the tyre and kicked the crap out of him. With the little energy he had left he started laughing and said, 'I think she liked it; I'm gonna to do it again.' Without thinking, I pulled his pen from out of his shirt pocket and stuck it in between his ribs. I then whispered closely to him, 'This was a mugging, if you ever mention this again there will only be two outcomes; the first is, I finish the job I started here, the second is making your dildo fetish public and I will personally go to the police about the rape. Do you know what they'll do to you in prison when they find out you like little girls? It would make what happened here seem like a fucking picnic!' I then took his phone, dialled emergency and left it on top of him, removed the pen from his side which resulted in him bleeding profusely and went home.

While driving home I couldn't help but wonder if the ambulance was going to make it to Bob before he bled out. I also knew that I had come way too close to crossing the line, nearly taking a man's life but for some reason it didn't affect me as much as I thought. I did worry that the weight of everything I'd been through in my life was crushing down on my humanity and compassion, gradually killing them off.

When I got home, Angie greeted me with, 'We have to talk'. Dinner was ready, so we sat down and poured some wine. I was nervous that someone had already phoned and told her about my fracas with Bob but it wasn't. Angie was pregnant. I was overjoyed but a part of me was deeply concerned, in light of the day's events. I didn't know if I still had a stable income let alone my freedom. I had every intention of telling her what had happened, but decided that now was not a good time.

After a sleepless night I made my way to the office, fully expecting to be greeted by the police and handcuffs. However, Grace was at the front door when I arrived and as soon as she saw me walking towards the office she ran towards me and my first thought was 'Shit! Here we go.' Tears and hysteria covered her face as she cried that Bob had been attacked and stabbed and was recovering in the hospital. He would not be returning to work because of the trauma the assault had caused him and that from the hospital, he was going to be checked into a psychiatric care facility because the treating doctors determined he had schizophrenia and could be a danger to himself or others. The only idea going through my mind while she was prattling on hysterically was this could not have worked out any better if I'd planned it.

Noxious Neil

Before I had a chance to absorb or even appropriately take pleasure in the good news, Grace informed me that she wanted me to train her other brother, Neil. She warned me that Neil was "special" and had "special needs". At that point, I was certain the entire family was "special".

When Grace first introduced me to Neil, I had to exercise a great deal of self-control to hold down my amusement. Neil was a Cambodian transsexual, who could have gotten a job as a circus freak. It was evident that he had spent many hours under a plastic surgeon's knife. He had attached over-sized silicone breasts to himself and appeared to have had his face manipulated to such an extreme; he looked frightening.

"Her" hair resembled a soiled kitchen sponge that had been glued to her head. His miniskirt was ridiculously short and it was impossible not to see the large bulge in the front. His pecker was obviously still intact. His eyebrows had been shaved off and replaced by what he must have thought eyebrows were supposed to look like. The makeup he wore was outrageous, my guess is he must have poured a pile of make-up onto a table and then slammed his face into it and hoped for the best, if he was aiming for the evil clown look, he was certainly going the right way about it. A keen visitor to the gym, he was large and muscular and looked like a condom full of walnuts.

Out of courtesy I attempted to introduce myself but Neil abruptly replied, "Who the fuck are you and what do you want?"

His voice was as soft as a woman's. It seemed that I had my work cut out for me, and it was going to be a challenge to say the least.

The first day on the job with Neil was surprisingly normal. I got him to sit in the boardroom and read the scripts, policies and procedures that Grace made me write for him, which was great because it allowed me to put some space between myself and Neil. I really needed to get some of my own work done, as keeping my job heavily relied on achieving sales targets, and to do that I had to give up little luxuries like toilet and lunch breaks, which was a pain but a necessary sacrifice especially in light of the fact that I was soon going to be a father.

My most treasured part of those days were when I could, on the rare occasion, escape from Grace long enough to buy a coffee. Once, while waiting for my coffee, the girl who Bob had assaulted was at the café ordering her lunch. She came over to me and hugged me and said, 'I don't know how I can ever repay you for what you did.'

'I don't know what you're talking about,' I replied.

'You made Bob go away,'' she said.

'I really wish that were true, but I had nothing to do with what happened to Bob.' She smiled as if to say, 'Yeah right, I don't believe a word you're saying', and walked away. I felt uncomfortable, as she had just become a loose end, and the reality was that if she ever mentioned it, people would start doing the sums and it could blow back on me, conversely there was nothing I could really do about it.

At work the next day, I was expected to take Neil out on the road with me and teach him how to present. He showed up to work wearing an overly low-cut revealing camisole in an effort to accentuate his rubber cleavage which made everyone sick. Nobody knew where to look; it was horrible to be honest.

On the way to our first appointment Neil received a call and during the conversation he was explaining to whoever he was talking to about the tremendous burden it was always being lusted over, and how every man "she" meets, just has to have her/him! I struggled against bludgeoning myself with something or beating my head against the steering wheel until I passed out; instead, I decided to just go to the happy place in my mind and tune out of the conversation altogether.

Neil's phone call ended before he had expected it to, so he decided to use the time to tell me his life story which was to my great dismay. He did clear up a question I had though, he'd been adopted, which explained why he was Asian and Grace and Bob were not.

Neil then went on to tell me stories which were grandiose beyond any stretch of plausible reality. She started off by telling me she'd been a Venezuelan super model for a few years, but gave it up because the travel and glamour of it all got too much. Then he went on to tell me that his birth parents were royalty and that one day he would inherit an entire nation which would ironically make him a queen. There were many more stories but as far as I am concerned it would be a waste of paper and time to write them down. I do have to hand it to him though, most people lie for the sake of lying and it's usually tediously monotonous but at least Neil's lies were novel.

When we finally walked into the appointment, Neil's performance was disconcerting. We met with a middle-aged business man and Neil immediately began to flirt with him. The client was obviously also some sort of freak; he actually reciprocated and went right along with it. There were a few times when I considered hurting both of them, but somehow Neil managed to close the deal on his first time out without any help from me whatsoever. I was impressed and confused at the same time. The good news was that I had concluded my training with Neil.

Neil certainly began making a name for himself in the business but when his sales targets fell behind, his skirts would get progressively shorter and at one point, I was concerned he would be walking around in a belt!

If that wasn't enough to worry about, Grace wasn't exactly making my life easy either. He had orchestrated it in such a way that Neil would be given appointments which were in convenient locations, with people who had potential. I would be given what was left over, which meant I had to work a great deal harder to get the same result, which was not fair but seems to be usual workplace practice.

A few months later, when Neil got comfortable and settled, he started to exhibit some strange behaviour, as if he wasn't strange enough already. A classic example of such conduct was the time he decided to harass one of the girls in the call centre.

He casually walked over to her and asked, 'Do you have a mirror in your pocket?'

The girl appeared to be confused by the question, as was I and replied 'No.'

Neil continued, 'Because I can see myself in your pants'. He then took it one step further. He picked the girl up and threw her over his shoulder, then put his hand up her dress and grabbed her holiest of holies. While he was doing that he said, 'I want to brush my teeth with your toes.' I could not believe what I was seeing and froze. I wasn't sure what to do because how often does one witness a large transsexual holding a girl up in the air then sexually assault her? But within seconds, I got up from my desk, and shouted, 'What the fuck do you think you are doing, put her down now!' I thought to myself, *What the fuck is it with that family and the call centre staff?*

Neil put her down but the poor girl was understandably hysterical and sat on the floor motionless but sobbing. I helped her up and asked her if she was okay but that set something off in Neil's feeble and twisted mind. He verbally attacked me, his voice gradually changing from a woman's voice to man's voice while he spat, 'You have just made the biggest mistake, embarrassing me in front of the entire call centre like that, by the time I'm finished with you, you'll not be able to support your family, you'll have to give that baby you have on the way up for adoption', she/he then added, 'you'll be lucky if you can get a job in a kebab store cutting the onions!'

Grace walked in half-way through Neil's rant and did nothing to stop it. The abuse lasted for about twenty minutes, and once it was over, he left with Grace for a two-hour lunch break. When they returned, Grace's face was putrid and I could tell she was shaking as she headed for her office; not a good sign. She ordered me to the boardroom (again) to wait for her. She was the angriest I had ever seen her. I initially thought she was angry with Neil, but that was wishful thinking on my part.

She screeched, 'If you *ever* talk to my family like that again I will make you disappear, I have the power to put you out of a job just like that!', snapping her fingers. I knew that logic dictated she could not get rid of me that easily, because there are not many people out there who would work sixteen hours a day for minimum wage, especially under her tyranny and those meagre conditions. I was worried nonetheless because I also knew logic very rarely factored into anything that crazy bitch did, I was happy with the situation but as far as just shutting my mouth and accepting what I was told went, it was becoming habitual nonetheless.

She then went on to notify me that there would be a substantial delay on my wages as business had been slow, and the director had over spent from the cash reserve or something like that.

Feeling hysterical and angry I argued, 'How am I going to live; my pay barely covers my expenses and mortgage repayments as it is, plus I have a baby that is due any minute, who is going to be expecting to eat, and I figure he may like eating so much that he may want to do it again the next day as well!'

'This is not a good time for me, I'm very stressed out because of what you put Neil through and what's more, when I got home last night I found my girlfriend going down on some random woman whom I'd never met, they'd used all my drugs which meant I had to spend the entire night without any sex or drugs!'

Was she expecting sympathy? At that stage I interrupted and said, 'Hey, I'm sorry, I'm not following, in what way exactly, has this got *anything* to do with my not getting paid?'

She looked at me blankly and left the room. Her phone rang as she was walking down the hall. She stopped dead in her tracks and said, 'I'll do it now', turned around and came back into the boardroom. She looked nervous and hesitated to speak. After a minute or so she finally said, 'The director wants you in his office; now.'

THE DIRECTOR

Up until that point I had no idea who the director was as I hadn't met him nor did I realise that he worked in the same building. His office was at the very top of the building with its own private elevator.

Security had to escort me and when I got to his door, I was greeted by even more security. The guards all wore black suits and wore ear pieces – his own secret service or what. *What on earth could he be so paranoid about?*

I was authorised to enter and, once inside, was immediately struck by the grandiose of his office. Compared to Grace's office which was so small – she had to go outside to change her mind – his was luxurious.

He offered me a drink and seat. At his private bar, he poured me a fifty- year-old single malt scotch and said, 'I witnessed what you did to Bob.'

He'd observed it all from his window, high up in the sky. At that point my heart nearly stopped but I did my utmost to stay composed because he was watching me and looking for a reaction, and from experience, I knew that a guy like that would have eaten me alive if I gave him half a chance.

Steadily, I asked him, 'Okay, what now? You obviously want something or I would've already been dealing with the consequences.' He began telling me about the true nature of the business which not only caught me off-guard but made me uneasy. In other words, if I ever outlived my usefulness after having heard what he told me, I wasn't going to live to ever tell anyone about it.

In carefully selected words, I was informed that the business was not what I thought it was; the customers do *not* actually receive what they had been led to believe. The quality of product that they see displayed in the showrooms or brochures is all misleading. They buy into a flat pack version of it, and end up with a mortgage so large that they could never possibly finish paying it off in their natural lives. I wanted to punch him in the neck because I was destroying at least three people's lives every day without even knowing it.

'Why are you telling me this?'

'Because some of the customers are disgruntled and seeking retribution,' he replied flatly.

'Hmm, hence your little fortress here,' I remarked, taking a sweeping glance at his office, to which he replied, 'Precisely.'

'What has any of this to do with me and what happened with Bob?' I asked him calmly.

'I liked the way you handled yourself that night and I need an enforcer,' he answered curtly.

Taken aback, I said, 'Look, this is not what I do; surely you could find someone else who does this for a profession?'

He replied, 'No, and from what I saw this is very much what you do; besides, you know the business as well.'

'What happens if I refuse this offer?' I asked.

Quietly and softly, he said, 'All you have to do is get up and walk out, but keep in mind that I will be an eyewitness to an attempted murder.'

He didn't have to say any more as he was not exactly being subtle about the fact that he was blackmailing me. I figured I may as well take a shot at taking something away from the meeting and commented, 'I know for a fact that if I did this kind of work anywhere else I'd be earning a hell of a lot more than minimum wage.'

His reply was immediate. 'No problem,' and upgraded me to a six-figure salary package on the spot.

'Okay, what do I have to do?' I asked.

'Wait for my call, I'll give you a name, time and a place and you'll have to get the work done that day, no questions asked.'

I stood up to leave when he stopped me. From under his desk, he pulled out a business compendium and handed it to me. Inside was a brand new gun with filed serial numbers, a silencer and an envelope filled with bullets. I zipped the compendium shut and started walking out of his room when he asked me, 'Why did you do it?'

My reply was immediate. 'He raped one of your employees.' I let myself out.

Based on what had just transpired, I knew I was heading home to another sleepless night. I stopped by an all-night chemist and picked up some sleeping pills. Next door was a liquour store. The scotch would aid the sleeping pills.

While I was driving home with a box of sleeping pills, a bottle of scotch, a gun, a silencer and a laptop in the front seat of my car, I felt haunted and wondered how it was even remotely possible for fate to keep bringing me back to the exact same place, when it was the last place I ever wanted to be, no matter how hard I tried to avoid it. The devil has got hold of me again, against my will. *Will I ever be free of this?*

Back at home, a large part of me wanted to tell Angie what was going on but I simply couldn't for so many obvious reasons. Besides, how on earth was I to word it? 'Hey Angie, how was your day? Guess what? My boss just blackmailed me into becoming his personal assassin because he saw me try to murder one of my co-workers with his own pen.' No. Not a good idea.

I felt trapped. I was a prisoner or slave to my own contrivance. On the other hand, a new, so called opportunity to provide for my family had presented itself. I did think for a minute that I could just change occupations; however, the problem there was that I couldn't afford the time that it would have taken, and even if I did find something quickly, I still had the blackmail swinging over my neck like a sword.

After dinner that night, I carefully found somewhere to hide the weapon then took two sleeping pills, washed down with a glass of scotch. For most people that would equal a coma. I am clearly not "most people" and have built up a resistance over the years from my days of drug abuse. Even after all that I still had a restless night, the demons fighting me all the way.

The next day at work felt awkward and the day brought heaps of anxiety but in order to keep up appearances I had to do my usual job, all the while anticipating the next phone call from the director.

A few weeks went by where I heard nothing at all, though I did have to contend with Neil, Grace and their bullshit politics. Every time I did anything, they wanted to know about it. I felt like I was under a giant microscope and I did not like it. One would think that making sales for the business would be a positive angle, although as far as Grace was concerned, the more successful I was, the more the tall poppy syndrome would flare up, and the more she would feel the need to cut me down, which again is a common practice in Australia. I have actually seen business owners sabotage their own business because they didn't want to see their employees succeed.

Grace was spiteful and angry, and I don't think it was because she thought she was worthless but because she knew she was worthless. She got off by bullying me and the rest of the staff and no degree of punishment that cold-hearted bitch could have ever dished out, was ever going to be enough to gratify her.

BAD GUY COMING THROUGH

A couple of days later, while driving to an appointment, he rang.

'Drop everything. I need you to persuade one of our clients not to take legal action against the company. I'll send a few guys to meet you at the job for back-up.'

I tried to explain that I didn't need any assistance and preferred to handle it on my own but he wasn't up for negotiation. I was told that it was going to be like this for the first few jobs; he then gave me the address and hung up.

I turned the car around and returned home to collect the gun, get changed and grab some gloves. The address the director had given me was the client's business address which was a mechanics' workshop. The shop was full of customers and staff so I waited in my car across the street and tried to stay out of sight. I figured, since the "mark" was the owner of the business, he would have been the last to leave; getting him alone was my objective. While sitting in my car, impatiently waiting for the time to pass, I noticed three motorcycle enthusiasts pull up at the far end of the street. Clad in patched leathers, I knew that they were club members, although not a club I was familiar with.

I walked to the end of the street and introduced myself. They followed me back to my car where we all waited in silence. Several hours later, towards the end of the day, the coast looked clear and as far as I could tell, only the owner was still inside. It was time to move in.

I told my "new friends" to follow my lead but they advised me that the director had told them they were only there for back-up; to make sure the job got done. I could not hide my sarcasm, 'Great!' and made my way to the door. It was closed and had already been locked. I knocked on the door and the "mark" opened it announcing, 'We're closed' and as soon as he looked over my shoulder and saw the bikers, immediately tried to slam the door in my face. I jammed my foot in the doorway and without thinking, grabbed the back of his head and used the door to break his nose. Once inside, I noticed there was an office upstairs and asked the biker thugs to take the "mark" to his office. Not only did they take him there, they also used some cable ties they had found in the workshop to bind his hands and feet.

I explained to the half-conscious man the reason for our little visit and that my business associate did not appreciate having legal action taken against him.

'D'ya think you're scaring me? This changes nothing! Your boss ruined me financially and he'll pay for it and now he's added assault to the list of crimes!' he spat.

'I really wish you hadn't said that,' I replied. I had to stop for a minute and think. I could see that the bikers were carrying weapons and unless I came up with something quickly, my man was going to end up dead at their hands.

I removed the gun from under my jacket and shouted wildly, 'Do you think this is a fucking game?' While attaching the silencer to it, I aimed for a part of his leg that I knew wouldn't cause any permanent or substantial damage as far as a gunshot wound goes, and pulled the trigger without hesitation. I picked up a framed photo of his family from his desk, and asked one of the bikers to shut him up and take his wallet. I smashed the photo frame, removed the photograph and pulled his driver's licence from his wallet.

I explained to him that it could all end right now or get a hell of a lot worse.

'We have your home address and a photo of your family so I suggest that for their sake, you do the right thing and forget about any further legal action!' He eventually agreed to my terms. I cut him loose, placed his phone in front of him and said, 'I suggest you get your nose looked at,' and left.

As I drove away, I felt unbelievably sick. *What had I done?* I pulled over to the side of the road and had to just sit for a while. I was experiencing some sort of anxiety attack and my hands were shaking too much to drive. I felt dizzy and got out of the car and threw up. When I got back into the car I noticed a missed call from Angie. I called her back, and as soon as she answered she said, 'My water just broke.'

THE COLOUR OF LIFE

I was a forty-five minute drive away from home. I turned the car around and drove like a man possessed and made it home in less than fifteen minutes. I must've broken every road rule imaginable during that trip and remember thinking, *Shit, if only I had a bike now; it sure would've shaved off some valuable time.*

I drove Angie to the hospital. She went into labour as soon as we arrived at the maternity ward and remained in labour for the next twenty-four hours. Twelve hours into it, I tracked down a doctor to ask why it was taking so long and if everything was going to be all right. The doctor advised me that everything was fine, and that nothing was going to happen for a while; consequently, I took that opportunity to go outside for a coffee, a cigarette, and a much-needed break.

I made the mistake of turning my mobile phone back on; I had thirty-six new messages and ninety-nine missed calls from Grace. While going through the messages, the phone rang which startled me. I certainly wasn't expecting any calls, as it was past midnight.

It was Grace. 'Your taking time off now is not good for the business; at this rate you will be lucky to even have a job to come back to.' I couldn't believe that she could be so inconsiderate and just downright insensitive to what was happening; she knew damn well that my wife was in labour. I'd already advised Grace beforehand that I'd be away for two weeks from the time my child was born.

Grace's messages were ominous; one could even say threatening in nature. They were actually starting to make me feel somewhat stressed, so I turned my phone back off. However, she was lurking in the back of my mind as I knew, beyond a shadow of a doubt, that I would have hell to pay when I returned to work.

Approximately twenty-two hours into the labour, the doctor returned to check on Angie and discovered that the baby was in the breech position. He then presented us with two options, both of which could potentially result in a catastrophe. We were notified that it was preferable that the baby be delivered by caesarean; however, that scenario was not brilliant as Angie has scoliosis, which is a condition where the spine is curved from side to side and the procedure could render her paralysed. Our other option was to deliver the baby breech thereby risking its life, as there was a possibility of asphyxiation.

We were given an entire one minute to decide on how to proceed. Throughout my life I have been faced with innumerable difficult and stressful decisions; however, that was by far unlike anything else I'd ever had to contend with. I actually started to feel woozy and was having trouble collecting my thoughts, when suddenly, the 'bad', deep down inside me surfaced. I grabbed the doctor by his coat lapels and said, 'Save them both, like it is your life that depends on it,' in a tone that indicated I was not playing, and that there would be a problem if he was not successful. Calmly, he replied, 'I understand how hard this must be on you; I'll do everything I can.'

The doctors rushed Angie into the operating room; they had decided the caesarean would be the best way to go. However, with the doctor's newfound motivation, he chose an alternative and much safer method to administer the medication that was required for the caesarean.

The operation was relatively brief. I was instructed to sit behind a curtain while the doctor performed the surgery, therefore I could not see what was happening. However, I was later told by Angie that the look on my face throughout the surgery was one of sheer terror.

Prior to that moment, it is fair to say that I had never witnessed a miracle. I had always seen the world in black and white or at best, in faded opaque colours. I watched my son lie on that table and take his first breath, his little body gradually turning from blue to red, the transition occurring progressively from his chest and slowly expanding outward towards his extremities; the transformation didn't stop even when he had finished changing colour. It was as if the entire world had suddenly become brighter and more colourful for me. The feeling was so vivid, overwhelming and downright amazing that I even teared up a little. The doctor handed me a pair of scissors and asked gently, 'Would you like to do the honours and cut the umbilical cord?' I grabbed hold of the scissors but as I was so rattled with overwhelming emotion, my hands were trembling so much that I cut the doctor's finger while cutting the cord!

I was over the moon with joy and couldn't leave my son's side for one second. I must have gone two whole days without sleep, just staring at him. He became my own personal miracle, and I suddenly knew, after having lived such a hard, troubled life, that I had at long last found my purpose; it was him. And I would do everything in my power to not let his story be anything like mine.

I used my son's birth to motivate me; he had effectively become my second wind, inspiration, and the strength that I required to soldier on and strive to be the very best man that I could possibly be. I felt an overwhelming urge to work harder and a burning desire to succeed, in order to secure a future, and moreover, a better life for my son than the one that I had been forced to live myself.

CORPORATE WARS

By the time I got back to work, Grace had hired about a dozen new people to fill in for me. They were all, in one way or another, related to her and it scared the shit out of me. My history with her family was not good.

Before I even had a chance to settle in, the director called me up to his office and congratulated me on the baby and told me that he hadn't got a chance to commend me on a job well done with the 'mechanic incident'.

'Thank you,' I replied, to which he advised that there was another job for that had to be dealt with, that day!

He went on to explain that business was doing poorly and the survival of the company hinged on the acquisition of a competitor company's database which contained all of their client and financial information.

'How, exactly, do you expect me to do that?' I asked him.

'Not to worry, I've a plan I've been working on for a while now, and I have people on my payroll who have been strategically placed within that company.'

Once he'd given me the finer details, I went home, where I spent some time with my son until his naptime. While Angie prepared his bottle, I discreetly made my way outside and into the shed, where I assembled the gun and made my way to the rival company's headquarters.

At the reception desk I was greeted by a young girl who was wearing hardly any clothes and was chewing gum like a cow on heat; her whole mouth flapped while she talked on the phone to one of her friends. I waited patiently for about twenty minutes for the conversation to end, and as I turned around, I noticed that a line had started to form behind me. Her discussion left nothing to the imagination. She was oblivious to everyone and everything as she prattled on about being at a club where two guys tried to fuck her, and quote, ' … and I was like, whatever, and they were like, whatever and I told them that I like to chew gum and that.' She twirled her hair with her fingers as she babbled on.

Eventually I interrupted her and asked to see one of the girls who worked there, creating a fictional story that I was her boyfriend, and that I needed to speak to her regarding a personal matter.

When my "new girlfriend" arrived at the reception desk, she put on a show for the receptionist and took me through to her office. On the way there I did my best to assess the situation and realised that the company had taken their security very seriously, because there was not a single door in the building that could be opened without a security access swipe card, I also noticed a few armed security guards and a lot of surveillance cameras, although what stood out the most and was a real cause for concern, was the presence of yet another motorcycle club. My guess was that they were the rivals of the club that I had previously worked with.

I had to make my way up four levels of the building using the fire escape in order to get to her office. Once in her office, I was expected to collect the data on a memory stick or a compact disc. However, that was not the case. I was presented with a large document storage box that was so heavy; she struggled to slide it across the floor.

'You have got to be kidding me! How am I supposed to walk out of the building with a box, undetected by the surveillance system and in one piece?'

'You don't have to worry about that, we've got one of our own people working in the security room and the system is being shut down and restarted for maintenance as we speak'.

The Devil's Grip

It all appeared a tad too easy. Why the hell would I be sent on a job that was so straightforward, when he could have had a courier pick the box up? I picked up the box and began the walk down the stairs, when half-way down near the second storey of the building, one of the doors opened and I came face to face with a security guard who just also happened to be using the fire stairs!

'Where d'ya think you're going with that? Stop right there and show me what's in the box".

The situation suddenly turned shit-side up, and there was not much likelihood that I was going to be able to talk my way out of it but it did not stop me from trying. I pretended I couldn't speak much English and said, 'Thank you, but I can carry this down on my own'. Unfortunately he didn't buy it and drew his radio with his left hand from the holster on his belt which must have activated a building-wide alarm because it immediately set off a siren. I had no choice but to retrieve my weapon while still trying to hold on to the box. Taking a chance, I tried to push him back using the box just to get him off balance, which caused him to stumble and fire at me; luckily it only hit the box with the files in it. I fired a few rounds at the ground near his feet, and started running down the stairs, leaping over three to four at a time, all the while keeping an eye on the doors at each level.

At last at the bottom, the bloody door was locked! No doubt the alarm had activated it. I aimed at the lock and shot at it but unlike in the movies, the door did not spring open! The sound of doors opening in the stairwell above me and running footsteps, were closing in. What to do. Keep firing at the door or save the bullets for when the troops arrived. I chose the lesser of two evils, turned to the door and emptied the entire clip into the lock and then, just like in the movies, the door swung open.

I ran for the car, threw the box inside and made my way back to the office. I delivered the box to the director in person and asked him, 'What the fuck was that all about? They had an army over there and you sent me straight into the middle of it!'

'You'd better shut your mouth or have you forgotten how this arrangement works? You will do what I tell you to do!' He was right; I was trapped and felt distressed because every job I did for him kept pushing me in deeper and there was absolutely nothing I could do about it.

Between juggling Grace's workload and the director's secret missions, I was tired and the reality of what was happening was hurting me. As selfish as it sounds, I thought if I caught a bullet during one of those jobs, I could at least get some rest. That being said, I knew I could not give up, would not give up because I also knew that if I wasn't around, my son would ultimately suffer my fate.

Isolated Incident

One morning we were called into work early. Grace had an announcement to make and wanted everyone to be there for it. We gathered in the meeting room.

Grace looked so excited that bubbles of white foam formed at the corners of her wrinkled mouth. The expression on her face was one of the proverbial cat and the cream. When the last person walked in she proudly yelled out, 'The director has decided to leave his wife, and we are going to get married,' then pulled her hand out of her pocket to present to us, her over-sized ring.

While she was still talking, I drifted off for a moment to consider why anyone would consciously make the decision to marry such a grotesque creature. After she received her tepid obligatory congratulations and applause from the staff, I was beckoned to stay behind.

She closed the door, turned to me and said, 'I don't know what you've been doing for my fiancé, but you should know that I will have even more power and that things are going to change around here, so you better watch your back.'

My reply to her threat was, 'That is physically impossible', but the joke was lost on her.

Being the pack of unconscionable tight asses that they were, they did not invite a single person from work to the wedding, but apparently still had over seven hundred people attend. I don't know why Grace found it necessary to inform everyone that she was going to delay the honeymoon until she made some changes to the business.

Changing me was part of her plan and after being summoned to the director's office, I knew something had altered as this was the only time that he did not pour me a drink. He announced that Grace had found out how much I was earning and was not happy about it.

He went on to advise that because of that, my salary level would drop but the job specification would remain the same!

Gobsmacked and unbelieving, I asked him, 'Why are you doing this to me? I've done everything you've asked of me, I have never expected any special privileges, and have shown you nothing but loyalty and dedication.'

He replied, 'Look, I left my last wife because she refused to suck my dick, and unless I keep Grace happy and give her what she wants, I'm afraid she will stop doing it too.'

'Wow, this is classy, you just fucked me over for a blow job.' I wanted to keep going but I was mindful of the gun in his desk and the fact that Grace was his wife. I was not happy with the turn of events, I had to summarise it in my mind, and the bottom line was that evil prick had made it virtually impossible for me to support my family because he was a depraved man who was married to a cocksucker.

Unfortunately the exploitation did not stop there; he added that I would have to conduct my business for him at nights because Grace no longer wanted him using up any more of my time during the day.

I became lightheaded when I realised what his new proposal really meant. Firstly, I wasn't sure how I was going to do anymore when there were already not enough hours in the day, and the true horror in the story was when I realised I would have to go into people's homes late at night and threaten them in front of their wives and children.

'Whatever, it's not like I have a choice in the matter anyway.' I did stipulate that if Grace ever found out about the arrangement or the nature of what I was doing for him, it would be the deal breaker, and he agreed.

When I left that meeting I felt defeated, not just by the director but by life in general. I also felt that the part of me that made me human; the essence of me was dying a slow death as a result of the accumulation of bad events, rottenness and the greed of evil people. I believed my life was difficult, and often wondered if anyone else ever felt the same way, or maybe that I was simply not strong enough or adequately equipped to deal with it all.

The worst part of the situation was that I didn't want to hurt Angie, she had already been alienated from her family because of me and I would not allow her to suffer any kind of pain but the way things were going, it would only be a matter of time.

Not having any real family or friends you can trust is not easy when facing such challenges, and people can tune into that when you are desperate. Grace certainly picked up on how much I relied on my job and how flattened I was, because as soon as I arrived at the office the next morning, she began to voice loudly her achievements and drew attention to them by causing a huge commotion. Boasting about her success in ensnaring the director did not wash with all of us and we had no choice but to tolerate her belligerent behaviour. I never could understand why she continually felt the need to break my spirit and confidence and her managing to manipulate the reduction in my salary was her way of kicking me when down.

This kind of larceny seemed to have no end, no matter where I was. The central theme of everything in this business seemed to meet the standard of evil, greed and stupidity, but the truly fascinating thing is, just when you think you have reached the limit of rottenness and malevolence, along comes someone who can stoop that little bit lower.

ALLERGIC REACTION

When Grace announced that she was all set to go on her honeymoon, I relished the prospect of some peace. The idea of the director and his fantasy dream cock-whore fuck-slut Grace being out of the country for a few months was a huge relief, although, that reprieve was short-lived. Grace had put Neil in charge and knowing our history, I couldn't imagine that we were going to benefit from working together.

The first thing Neil did was buy a journal, for the purpose of collecting information about every single thing I said or did in order to twist it and somehow use it in a manner that would be detrimental to me in the future. He took great delight in telling me too. My response was to keep quiet.

I digress. One of my many other responsibilities was to listen in on telemarketer calls, to ensure they were saying the "right thing" to the customers. Using a feature in the telephone system called call-barging allowed me to listen without anyone's knowledge. The company justified spying on the staff by labelling it a quality control measure.

On one occasion, I intercepted an exceedingly unsettling call that caused me grief no end. Neil was sitting at one of the telemarketer's desks and was on the phone to her specialist. When I first heard the conversation, I thought it was work related, until I heard her say that her penis had had an allergic reaction to the cocaine and a rash had started spreading back towards her vagina, balls and then anus. I was tangled up and not exactly sure what to do; there must be something wrong with me because I didn't hang up the phone until the doctor said, 'Your herpes might be flaring up from the stress.'

I knew then that I had heard enough and hung up. I couldn't help but wonder how she could have had all of those parts in that order, and then for some reason I tried to figure out what to call them, was it a Mangyna or a Vageenis; either way it seemed highly unusual.

Neil heard the phone click when I hung up and immediately stood up and lost his fucking mind. He sprinted towards me accusing me of eavesdropping. I tried to explain that it was part of my job and that wasn't he being a little hypocritical using someone else's phone and desk? He continued to abuse and yell, stormed off to the IT department and pulled the phone records. He/she then called the police, and told them that I had abused him/her.

The police pulled me aside and took my statement. I recited the details of the phone conversation, including the names that I had come up with for Neil's genitalia. They left giggling, which exacerbated Neil's state of mind. He walked over to me so that she/he was less than a meter away, pulled out her pink mobile phone and called his lawyer. He was going to sue me for everything I had.

Once off the phone, he/she spat out, 'My lawyer is the best and by the time she's done with you, you and your family will be living on the streets!'

I had heard those threats too many times before and it was starting to get on my nerves. Sighing, I replied, 'Do what you have to do.'

He didn't like the fact that I was antagonising him and started shouting and yelling again, going about him being the greatest con artists that ever lived. I couldn't handle him being in my personal space anymore and took refuge outside with a cigarette. My phone rang and shit, was I surprised to hear from Timmy. He was calling from prison. Timmy explained that he'd really screwed things up as he had taken a shot at some police officers and had now lengthened his time in prison but that the main reason for the call, was to inform me that he'd heard that there were people looking for me.

The bikers from the rival company were conducting an investigation and were apparently getting close to figuring out who and where, I was. Timmy said that he knew who it was as soon as he heard the story, and that it was only a short matter of time before they finished connecting the dots, and caught up with me. I realised that I'd been lied to, and that the security cameras were never shut down, and that the director had set me up to take the fall for his data, because he knew that someone would want to eventually seek reprisal.

I was a "wanted man" and had to think fast on my feet, because I knew how it worked, and knew they would not stop with me. They no doubt would have come after my family as well, just to send a message to anyone else who considered trying anything. I asked Timmy if he was allowed visitation, which he was, I ended the call and went back inside. Neil then informed me that his lawyer had just called him back and told him he had a solid case against me. At that moment, a solution had presented itself.

THE DEVIL'S GRIP

It appeared as though the life of crime that I was so desperately trying to avoid was not going to let me go as easily as I'd hoped. If I wanted to survive, I had no choice but to stay connected.

The following day after my call from Timmy, I made arrangements to visit him. I was fortunate because I got to sit down with him within a few days; as opposed to the usual procedure of paperwork, followed by a prolonged waiting period before one is even given a time and date.

Upon arrival, I was directed to the meeting room where Timmy was seated. Before I even sat down, Timmy looked around him and then leaned in towards me. 'I need you to do something for me'.

I replied, 'So do I'; however, I was concerned about what he was going to ask of me.

'You go first,' he instructed. I explained that he needed to reach out and let whoever was looking for me know that I was only a mule, and that in order to make things right, I would deliver the person responsible for the administration of the company and moreover, the one who ordered the job to be carried out. I did not expect his response. 'What the fuck! Have you turned rat?' he spat at me.

Immediately I leaned in towards him and spoke harshly, 'Are you out of your fucking mind? The person I'm going to deliver is a huge problem who needs to be handled, as it was a "two birds, one stone situation".'

'Do you have any idea what this will mean? Everything's final you know and people are gonna get hurt,' spat Timmy.

'Yeah, I know but I'm not about to let my family get hurt so let's do it!' I replied in a whisper.

'Tell me what you need me to do.' I was expecting the worst case scenario like retribution or something along those lines. Although it seemed I got off easy, he apparently had some money hidden and just wanted me to collect it and deliver it to his wife; big relief.

Back at work the next day, I allocated the appointments for the sales representatives and then left to carry out my own appointments. Concentration was difficult and as soon as I was finished, I headed back to see how the situation was manifesting. I pulled up in front of the club house where the bikers, who worked for the rival company, were. I got there just in time to see Neil walk inside but no sooner had he/she walked past the roller door, than someone hit him over the back of the head with what appeared to be a shotgun. The roller door was then lowered. As I drove away, it occurred to me that it sucks to be Neil, because I'd made sure he was carrying some of the stolen documents in his briefcase, for them to find.

From there I headed back to visit Timmy's wife where she lived in witness protection. I picked up his bike keys in order to make good on my end of the deal. Apparently, the people who were holding his money were under strict instructions not to hand it over unless they saw his bike. The added bonus of that job was that the money was located roughly six hours away, and I hadn't ridden in a while so I welcomed the opportunity to get back out on the open road and catch some bugs in my teeth.

The ride gave me some time to finally stop and think. I racked my brain trying to come up with a solution as to how to handle the director, as there was no possible way I was going to go into people's homes and threaten them. Also, the Neil situation was weighing on my conscious in the worst possible way, and it was a heavy burden. The way I saw it, his crimes did not fit the punishment, which is not my way, and the fact that his blood was on my hands made it so I was having trouble thinking about anything else no matter how hard I tried. That sort of situation changes a person, and getting away with it only made me feel worse. Although I took some solace in the fact that if I had not acted, then my family and I would have ended up dead, or worse.

As I neared my destination, I discovered that Timmy's contact proved to be a challenge. He was hard to find because he was in the middle of nowhere, in a caravan. When I eventually found the trailer home, I tried to take a peek inside but couldn't see anything because the windows were too dirty. While trying to quietly clean a small portion of window in order to get a better look, I found myself surrounded by iguanas! *What the hell was this guy doing out in the middle of nowhere by himself?*

Then before I even got a chance to properly assess the situation, it started raining heavily. I decided I may as well get it over with now, rather than conducting my investigation in the middle of the night while it was raining. I knocked on the caravan door and was greeted by a large bald and intimidating man covered in tattoos of skulls, demons and snakes, and before I had a chance to speak, the tattooed beast stuck a sawn-off double-barrel shotgun in the middle of my chest while shouting, 'Why are you riding Timmy's bike?'

'Shut the fuck up and get me the money now, you little bitch' to which he did not bat an eyelid and replied, 'But of course sir'. He lowered the shotgun and invited me into his humble home, where he made me a coffee, gave me a towel so that I could dry off the rain, and more importantly, handed me the backpack containing Timmy's money.

I drank my coffee and had a few cigarettes, while we sat and discussed the socio-economic constraints affecting competition and regulatory reforms in developing countries. As I left the trailer park, it occurred to me how although he looked like a savage, he was more hospitable than the vast majority of people who lived in the city but I also considered that it was a good thing that I'd remembered the words Timmy told me to say, because even if there had been the slightest variation, I would have ended up with a big hole in my chest that night.

DAYLIGHT

Work over the next few weeks, with nobody around, was peaceful. I actually managed to triple the yield and profits started to soar in the short time everyone was away. I wasn't sure why I did it, it wasn't as though I was going to be compensated or even acknowledged for it, but it gave me a feeling of contentment nonetheless.

My typical daily routine did feel like an endless cycle. I got up, went to the office, collected my appointments, and then spent most of the day driving to them. Once that was done I would return to the office to follow up on whatever needed to be done, then would spend a few hours on paperwork and general administration, which would allow me just enough time to get home and sleep, only to start the process again the next day.

That all changed the day Grace returned from her honeymoon. I remember walking in after an appointment one day to see her standing in the office and looking frantic as usual. With arms flapping like a frightened bird, she squawked, 'Where the fuck is Neil?'

'I've no idea. He came in one day, picked up his appointments and that was the last I heard from him. I haven't been able to get through to the mobile phone either.'

'You're all fucking useless', she snarled.

I didn't react nor reply; though it best to give her some space to simmer down. I'd grown accustomed to her erratic personality, and recognised that anything I would have said would have set her off even more. I attempted to walk away from the hostile situation, when she asked me, 'Where the fuck d'ya think you're going?' Then insisted that I update her on how the business was performing.

I told her the good news about the increase in profits and instead of being pleased; this news seemed to push Grace well and truly over the edge. She started to have some sort of seizure, and tried to scream so loud that no sound was coming out at all, she was also turning blue as she perspired profusely. I wasn't excessively concerned as I'd seen similar behaviour from her so many times before, but on this occasion, she started scratching her own face! When she could finally speak again, she whispered, 'You piece of shit, you tripled the profits? Do you think you're better than me? Well you're not, you're nothing!'

She ran over to my desk and swept everything of mine onto the floor, including my laptop. She then added, 'Let's see how good you are now minus a job, and don't bother going to your precious director for help because he's dead!'

'What did you say?' I stopped her. Staring at me wildly she replied, 'You heard me, he's dead; died on our honeymoon and I now own the entire company!' All her yelling and screaming faded into the background as I tried to absorb what she had just told me.

Initially I was a little saddened by the news, because I did have a strange respect for his success as an entrepreneur, and often found myself analysing what he did so that I could learn from it. I guess I wanted to know what made him tick. I also wondered how he possibly could have died during his honeymoon; perhaps the sight of Grace's hairy ass in the daylight had killed him.

But then it dawned on me that I was free of him and his tyranny and the sword that was swinging over my head had vanished. With that in mind, I turned my attention back to Grace who was still having a fit. I did my best to wait for her to finish her rant, although it felt like it was never going to end.

I honestly considered offering her a similar fate to that of her siblings, or at least shutting her down verbally, but re-evaluated it and thought it would have been the equivalent of beating a handicapped person, as she was clearly beyond the stage where any conventional means of therapy was ever going to be of assistance. On closer inspection, I realised that what set her off in the first place was the fact that I had improved what was at that stage, her business.

I can confidently say that Grace had all the qualities of a classic business owner, which is a formula that consists of tall poppy multiplied by stupidity, plus greed to the power of at least one thousand; coupled with the fact that she was an evil, gold-digging whore prima donna, who took adulation and privileged treatment as a right, and reacted to criticism with petulance. That she killed her new husband to take control of the company left no doubt in my mind.

Bearing all of that in mind, my reply to the wild woman was, 'I thoroughly appreciate what you're saying, I'm sorry for your loss and I'm grateful for the opportunity.' I went to shake her hand but she did not reciprocate and instead, stretched her long, sinewy neck and asked, 'Why should I shake your hand? You're not making me any more money.'

'Fair enough,' I replied and left.

The very next day Grace started a new company and bankrupted the old one, which made it not only easy but legal to get out of paying me for any holiday pay, wages, superannuation and any other entitlements I was owed, which again, is an enormously common practice in a legitimate business.

THE LUAU

I spent the next six years putting up with similar shit; low pay, long hours, exploitation, just to end up getting burned our burnt out and jumping from one job to another, and all the while I managed to not collect a single dollar in superannuation.

I did, however, develop a skill in setting up successful businesses for other people, then killing myself to make them rich, as I had done over a dozen times. There were both positives and negatives to doing that. The positive was that I was able to learn from my mistakes and experiment with other people's money, although the down side was I would then be discarded like used toilet paper, the second that the owners thought they were confident enough to run it on their own, and the more self-sustaining I could make it, the higher the probability that I was putting myself out of work.

I did start to ask the question, *What's wrong with me and why do I repeatedly do the same thing, all to my detriment?* Albert Einstein's theory of insanity was "doing the same thing over and over again and expecting different results". If you have no choice, it becomes a prison situation. No matter how many ways you try to dice it, if you're a prisoner, how much can you really do to change your life? Without any family or form of support whatsoever, I have to ensure that I did not fall, for the sake of my family.

My theory is that what happens to you in life is only five per cent and how you react to it, is ninety-five per cent. It was time to stop being reactive, time to be proactive.

That is when I embarked on two projects. I decided to convert my journal into this book and I constructed a business model based on the last job I had, where I started a company for a miserable example of a human being, with one desk, a pencil, and an extremely overweight and disease-ridden, illiterate telemarketer, who had by some means managed to drag the snack vending machine over to her desk. I had to let her go as she was taking too many days off for ailments I had never heard of.

Long story short, I turned that situation into a multimillion dollar a year business, and left under familiar circumstances, which translates to having been fucked over. I walked away with a sense of confidence that I was ready to do it for myself, as I had not only come up with the concept, but had also managed every aspect of the business from the ground up.

About two weeks before I was due to get stuck into building my own business, Angie threw me a surprise birthday party. She raided the contact list in my phone and invited a large number of people to a Hawaiian luau; brilliantly orchestrated as I never suspected a thing.

The party was mind-blowing. Angie had spared no expense. When I first walked into the party I could not believe my eyes; there was a pig with an apple in its mouth rotating on an open fire, tiki torches, palm trees that were made out of pineapples, Hawaiian decorations, the largest bowl of punch I had ever seen and a large crowd of people all wearing Hawaiian shirts. She also planned it so that the Hawaiian music started playing as soon as I arrived. The first thought I had, was that I was never going to be able to top that party no matter what I did. I also learned that night, that my wife could throw one hell of a celebration!

While we ate, drank and mingled with the crowd, I met an elderly man who had come along with one of my colleagues from a previous occupation. After initial introductions, we began making the proverbial small talk and then both discovered that we were setting out to start the same business at the same time and more or less in the same area. We continued our discussion and then I moved on to chat to other guests.

When the party had exhausted itself and people began to leave, I noticed that Adolf, the elderly German man was still hanging around next to the remains of the half-eaten pig, still slowly rotating above a now, low fire.

I invited him to join Angie and me and a handful of friends who were dragging their heels. Adolf informed me that he did not drink alcohol as he was a devout born-again Christian, and his faith forbids it. I went to the large ice-box and dug around until I found him a coke. As for the rest of us, we sat around with the intention of polishing off the rest of the punch, even if it was going to take all night.

Adolf told me that he believed it was no coincidence that we met that night. At that point, my brain was a little soggy from the punch, and I quietly replied, 'Nothing is a coincidence, it's all part of God's plan'. My saying that seemed to have prompted him, as the following hour or so turned into a bible study, which I didn't have a problem with but it was something I preferred to do on Sundays at church. As he was nearing the end of his religious discourse, he did a complete about turn and suggested that we go into business together, in the financial services industry! He went on to explain that he already had the licence which would have cost me time and a great deal of money to obtain, and that I would be able to contribute the skills, staff, procedures etcetera and then when on to list a lot of other things.

Although not prepared for this particular detour, I explained that I was not comfortable going into that type of arrangement as I had been badly burned so many times in the past, and went on to give him a few examples. He replied that he was revolted by what had happened to me, and that his strong religious beliefs simply would not allow him to behave in such a way. He added that in his culture there is no grey area, only black and white or right and wrong as he put it, and he was bound by his faith to only ever do the right thing.

I stopped for a moment and analysed what he said, and thought to myself, I had accumulated a life time's experience in dealing with insalubrious characters, and Adolf did not appear to bear the traits that any of the others had, plus he gave me his word as a man that he had no intention of screwing me or anyone else over for that matter. I was not in a position to make a decision, as I was pretty drunk and had Angie falling asleep on my shoulder because she too was drunk. So I told him I would sleep on it and give him a call when I had had time to think about it.

Although I didn't take him up on his offer on the spot, what he said did play on my mind, and I eventually called him after a few days and informed him that I had decided to take him up on his proposal to begin building a business together.

THE WIDOWER

Thankfully, my decision to go into business with Adolf proved a positive one, because unlike anyone I had previously dealt with, he treated me with courtesy and respect. Although his contribution to the business was nominal, I was happy to overlook that detail, as I was content to finally be able to work with a 'civilised' human being.

One of my proudest moments as a business man was when the signage went up. To see our names on a plaque behind the reception desk in lights on the outside of the building was a good feeling. Over the next few years we built the business together and quickly became renowned and well-respected within our field.

Adolf had completely earned my trust and respect, which was an arduous task in light of my past experiences. I trusted him to such a degree that I was completely comfortable giving him control over the company finances.

The business grew from strength to strength as we continued to reinvest into the business which resulted in rapid expansion. In order to achieve our targets, we agreed we would not draw more than a small wage for ourselves because the company's success was priority.

Once I found my feet as an industrialist, I went on an acquisition spree and started to form more companies, and included Adolf in everything I did, every step of the way. By that stage I was spending every waking moment of my day working, and loved every minute of it.

Having been through so much together, Adolf and I regarded each other as family; he often called me his 'brother in Christ', although we could not socialise or even speak to each other outside of regular working hours. His wife was emotionally unstable, and constantly threatened to kill herself if he was not home immediately after work or if he answered any work-related phone calls after hours or on the weekends.

That situation did become a challenge at times as I was left to deal with all the problems that arose, on my own. On the other hand, I felt terrible that there was nothing I could do to help Adolf. I had had the privilege of meeting Adolf's wife only once, as he somehow convinced her to leave the house and visit the office. The commotion that preceded her arrival was a tad over-the-top. Adolf cleaned the whole office himself and everyone was asked to dress as if we were being visited by royalty! When she arrived I felt awkward as I knew how fragile and vulnerable she was. I played it safe and mainly smiled and nodded at everything she said throughout the entire visit.

Her visit coincided with the staff lunchbreak, which meant the majority of the team was either eating, watching YouTube videos, playing video games on their computers, or just standing around talking to each other, which did not appear to upset our guest, at the time.

However, once Adolf had taken her back home and returned to work, he informed me that she was outraged when she learned we had *females* working in the office, and what made it worse is that she spotted one of the staff, who happened to be our top earner, playing video games while eating at his desk. She outwardly ordered Adolf to remove that particular member of staff from the business, in addition *to all* of the female staff. He then said we had no choice but to comply with her mandate as she had threatened to kill herself if the orders were not met!

Anyone in business would know what I mean when I say good staff is hard to find, and it had taken years to painstakingly hand-pick my team. I tried to explain to Adolf that perhaps if he clarified to his wife that the team was at lunch, and that the female staff were all married and had families who depended on them, she might have a change of heart. I also went on to explain that terminating the employment of our top earner because he was having lunch was probably not the greatest business strategy.

Adolf agreed with me but was so overwhelmed by the burden of her threats that all we could was acquiesce. I was speechless.

Out of respect and moreover my friendship with Adolf, coupled with a genuine fear for his wife's safety, I called a meeting and informed all of the staff in question that to my great dismay, I was going to have to let them go. The worst part of that meeting was not being able to give them a valid reason for what I was doing. Adolf felt so bad he kept away from the meeting. I did my most however, to support every single person in that room and assisted them all in procuring new jobs, which was somewhat easy based on my reputation and the large number of business contacts I had accrued over the years.

Adolf arrived at work late the next day and looked a mess. Before I had a chance to ask, he told me that his wife had finally gone and done it, killed herself. She had taken a small kitchen knife and used it to cut off three of her fingers on one hand, then stabbed herself in the neck several times.

He started crying, at first I didn't know what to say, or how to even start consoling him, and I think I must have been feeling his pain, because I started to feel a sharp aching in the middle of my chest.

I ordered him to go home even though he did not know what else to do. Reminding him that he had children to look after, I insisted and he left.

I didn't hear from him for a while. I was not invited or allowed to attend the funeral, as I apparently had to be a member of his 'special group', which were high-end top-shelf elite Christians and I was a mere regular Christian. Although I found it highly unusual, I respected his decision, and didn't want to intrude.

The next few months were a mammoth trial; I was still carrying the weight of what had happened in addition to the reality that I had to do the jobs of two directors. Back to back meetings, running around so much that I had hardly enough time to eat or sleep, my stress levels increased so much that I could actually start to feel them tear me apart from the inside out, though I pushed it all down and kept moving forward. I figured I had seen much worse and wasn't about to let something as trivial as work-related stress get in the way of what had to be done.

A HEAVY HEART

Adolf eventually returned to work without notice and when I saw him sitting at his desk, a flood of relief washed over me. I sat down and tried to talk to him but he seemed different; he was distant, and his face looked vacant, his eyes, empty. Certainly if I had been in his position, I know I wouldn't have handled it at all well.

His behaviour over the next few months did become increasingly irregular and eccentric. He would only eat a single piece of bread, folded in half with nothing on it, every day at the same time, washed down with water that he kept under his desk in an old milk container. He was never a big spender but that chain of events indicated trouble to me. Every now and then, sick of the bread, he would go down to the car park, alone, and take a barbeque from the back of his car and proceed to have his own private meal, next to his car. I only caught on to what he was doing when I came across it on one of the surveillance cameras. I also later found out that he would hide the surplus cooked sausages in his desk and would eat them when nobody was watching, even after they had started to produce mould. I managed to drag him away from the office a few times, and would buy him something to eat. He would inhale the food as if he were starving.

Adolf had physically returned to the office but certainly not mentally. That meant that I had to keep working my ass off in order to hold the business together, all the while having to ignore my body's warning signs, which looking at it retrospectively was probably not the best idea.

When I finally did visit a doctor and told him the symptoms, he ran a few tests only to find I was a mess; my blood pressure was too high, as was my blood sugar and I now had cholesterol, among other things.

The doctor gave me some medication that seemed to help but Angie was not satisfied that I had been tested thoroughly enough, and could not leave it alone. This meant I got dragged back to the doctor for more tests, which is my least favourite thing to do, especially when I had so much to look after at work. To my disappointment, I learned that the continual stress I was under, combined with high blood pressure and too much acid had apparently caused some serious damage to my internal organs. I was immediately booked for surgery, and all the while I was thinking that it couldn't have come at a worse time.

I was more worried about Adolf than anything else, because the poor guy had been through such a hard time with his wife's gruesome suicide, and I was worried that he was not going to be able to take the pressure of running the business on his own.

A few weeks later I went under the knife to have the damage repaired and when I left the hospital, I was given specific instructions to stay home and recover. Once home I received a call from Adolf who he told me that the business was falling apart and unless I came back quickly, he feared that there would be nothing to come back to, in the same breath he also said that I should really stay at home and rest or I would not recover. Screw that, I'd worked too hard to watch my dreams go down the drain without intervention.

The next morning I was back at the office and it was business as usual, although I did have to conceal the fact that I was in a great deal of pain, and that every so often a little blood would seep through my shirt, but I felt that the company had to come first, and moreover I did not want to let Adolf down, because he was at a point where anymore disappointment would have completely crushed him.

Over the next few weeks Adolf's conduct deteriorated further as he began to burn our staff, associates and clients and was blatantly trying to steal from everyone. When I questioned him, he muttered something about 'times being tough' and 'business is business' which did not sit well with me at all but I had bigger problems to deal with. When it was time to revisit the doctor for a review of the surgical procedure, I had apparently caused some damage by returning to work before I was supposed to, I also learned that I needed to go back in for yet some more surgery which at that stage was going to eat up the balance of our savings, and waste even more of my time.

The day before going back in to my next round of surgery I decided to sit down with Adolf and find out what was actually happening with him. I asked why it was that we were making more money than ever before but at the same time we seemed to be constantly falling behind fiscally. He did not want to respond, and told me that he was uncomfortable with that confronting question.

But after much discussion he finally told me that his church group stated to him that they could concentrate their collective powers and resurrect his wife, although they required significant contributions in order to gather the resources to make it happen.

'Oh, you should have just said so, that makes perfect sense. Are you fucking insane!' I knew then that he had completely lost his mind but also knew that it was not going to be something I could fix on the spot; consequently I figured I would leave it until after I got out of the hospital.

Learning my lesson I stayed away from the office and gave myself the appropriate time to heal, second time around. When I did return to work, I learned from Adolf that we could no longer trade as we were insolvent; also that he had somehow managed to lose the financial services' licence which allowed us to function.

After hearing that update, I felt an uncomfortable pressure in the middle of my chest. About ten minutes later I received a call from a client with whom I had dealt with back in the days of working with Grace, and he informed me that Grace told him that I had defrauded him and he would be taking legal action against me personally. He pointed out that he'd already contacted the media and even gave me the links to the stories that had been published about me on the internet. Apparently Grace also pointed out that it would have been easier to sue me and that it would have been an effortless win, as opposed to trying to take on the company. I started to feel hot and was sweating, which was anomalous because it was the middle of winter.

I told Adolf that I was not feeling well and went for a walk to get some air, which made him look uncomfortable. When I got outside I did not get very far because Angie called me and was crying. It took a while before she could pull herself together and tell me what had happened.

She finally managed to tell me that her father had called her and not only threatened our lives but the life of our son as well. I wanted to comfort her, but was unable to speak anymore because a pain started spreading through my shoulder, neck and one of my arms. I felt heavy pressure bearing down in my neck and chest.

Although I was disoriented I attempted to start walking to my car to go to Angie, but only managed to take a few steps when I saw the last person I ever expected, walk out of the new offices that were for lease across the street, and she made eye contact with me. It was Adolf's dead wife, and when she saw me looking at her, she ran back inside.

My phone started ringing again but I was too weak to answer it, the phone fell out of my hands and shattered on the ground in front of me. I felt queasy, lightheaded and short of breath.

When the reality of what had happened, finally sunk in, and I realised that Adolf and his wife were playing me from the day we met, all that we had achieved suddenly flashed before my eyes but in an entirely different context, and for the life of me I could not figure out why I was being punished, as though I had sinned beyond redemption. Anxious and uneasy, my skin felt cold and my heart began to feel irregular. I was finally overcome with a feeling of impending doom, as I collapsed in the street under the sign with my name on it.

It was as though the burden of the whole world and all of my negative experiences and betrayals had finally taken their toll and had simultaneously come crushing down on my heart. It unexpectedly occurred to me, how weak and mortal I really was.

The irony was that I had survived war, poverty, crime and more, and I was less than impressed when I realised the final curtain could come down on me because of a few phone calls and office politics.

I must have reached a pivotal point or a critical mass if you will, and my head started beating like a tribal drum as I pieced together what had happened, though I had a moment of clarity and put some perspective on everything that had ever happened up until that moment in my timeline.

THE HAND OF GOD

I had lived a life where I had to find out what my limits were and live right at the far end of them just in order to survive, all the while trying to find intelligent life on earth, or kindness in a perfect stranger, even a person who would do good just for the sake of goodness. Although my efforts were not fruitless, the ratio has been less than satisfactory.

Where most would have surrendered to defeat and a permanent cynical and jaded frame of mind, I could not and would undeniably not stop fighting for my survival. At times I considered that God had forsaken me, although that was self-pity and moreover bullshit. The truth of the matter was that God always had a plan for me, as he does for all of us, God has given me the ultimate gift, a life that has been diverse beyond belief, which has served to mould me into the man I am, not to mention the strength and resolution to fight my way through it and most importantly, a beautiful loving wife and a healthy son.

Statistically speaking, people in similar situations typically die in alleyways or motel rooms with needles hanging out of their arms, rather than persevering with one setback after another in an effort to fit back into society.

In my time I've seen some outlandish shit; I've endured the tyranny, greed and great stupidity of my fellow man on a measure of gigantic proportions. I've also had the misfortune of meeting some of the world's most tedious small-fry thinkers. I've even witnessed people write novels about how they dragged themselves up and made a life out of nothing, all the while in the same breath whining that their parents could only afford to send them on trips around the world for a few years at a time. I know my story is no more interesting and certainly not any more important than anyone else but it is a story that I feel needed to be told.

I have committed many crimes though I am not a criminal; I have stolen though I am not a thief. I have lied, though I am not a liar, well, maybe a little sometimes. All that I have done is tried to survive in a world filled with hardship. Though most would say self-preservation does not excuse the crimes that have been committed, I only saw it one way, I was either committing the crime or would end up being the victim of crime. That being said, I do not wish to glamourise the life of a criminal. I took the lemons that life handed to me and tried to make lemonade.

For anyone else out there fighting the brutal battle to survive, I understand that it's physically and emotionally exhausting but crime comes with a hefty price that nobody can see; nervous breakdowns that happen when you try to close your eyes, and nightmares that haunt you for the rest of your life. Best case scenario, you live through it, but what is left is typically dead on the inside and you're left merely going through the motions like a soulless machine.

The world continues to become an increasingly more difficult place to survive and the characters in this story were only looking after their own interest as most are programmed to do, as human beings; this results in kindness being mistaken for weakness, trust will be misconstrued as gullibility, and empathy, a sign of being soft.

Life will pound you down, put its foot on your neck and hold you to the ground if you let it. It's not about not falling down but more about getting up every time you do fall and *never* giving up. No matter how many times you get burned, trust with your whole heart, and always give without expecting anything in return, keep fighting for what you believe in, no matter the cost.

While I lay in the street looking up at the well-lit sign with my name on it, I remember sensing that something was not quite right and at the same time, I could actually feel the life drain out of my body. That's when it occurred, the light box above me started to flicker then faded to black, as I drifted off to sleep. All the pain in my body miraculously and instantly disappeared, and I was more comfortable and rested than I had ever been before. I felt reassured and somehow knew that everything would be just fine.

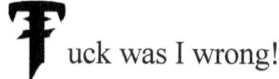uck was I wrong!

ABOUT THE AUTHOR

J.R. Rothwell is the author of the debut novel *The Devil's Grip*. His identity is cloaked for reasons that will become apparent once you have read the book. Primarily due to the fact that he is not enthusiastic about being incarcerated, moreover to safeguard the identities and reputations of the characters in *The Devil's Grip*. This debut novel is the first is the *Devil's Playground* series, and will be followed up with *Burned out Paradise*, and *Angel of a Small Death*.

Unlike the vast majority of authors out there, J.R. Rothwell does not take popular demand into consideration when writing nor what others think and will tell it how it is straight from the heart. This writing is about actual life, tangible pain, real emotion and once you read it - you will know this.

Conventional publishers advised J.R. Rothwell that *The Devil's Grip* is too dangerous and motivating which is not what they are looking for at this juncture, and that they would prefer to go with something safe. J.R. Rothwell is an avid believer that the publishers should perhaps should go and fuck themselves, as he will not adapt to mainstream demands, and if he wanted to do that he would have written a book regarding the buoyancy of turds.

www.ingramcontent.com/pod-product-compliance
Lightning Source LLC
Chambersburg PA
CBHW072003150426
43194CB00008B/985